A WILL TO

INDIGENOUS ESSAYS ON
THE POLITICS OF CULTURE,
LANGUAGE, AND IDENTITY

Indigenous Affiliations and Traditional Territories of the Contributing Authors

1. Arapaho: Northern Arapaho – Central Wyoming;
   Southern Arapaho – West Central Oklahoma
2. Blackfoot: Northern Montana and Southern Alberta Canada
3. Cherokee: Georgia, North Carolina and Northeastern Oklahoma
4. Cheyenne: Northern Cheyenne – Southeastern Montana, Central Oklahoma
5. Cree: the Cree range from Alberta Canada to Quebec

EURASIA

PACIFIC
OCEAN

AFRICA

$52.00

ID

A WILL TO SURVIVE

INDIGENOUS ESSAYS ON THE POLITICS OF CULTURE, LANGUAGE, AND IDENTITY

Edited by Stephen Greymorning

Boston   Burr Ridge, IL   Dubuque, IA   Madison, WI   New York
San Francisco   St. Louis   Bangkok   Bogotá   Caracas   Kuala Lumpur
Lisbon   London   Madrid   Mexico City   Milan   Montreal   New Delhi
Santiago   Seoul   Singapore   Sydney   Taipei   Toronto

The McGraw·Hill Companies

A WILL TO SURVIVE: INDIGENOUS ESSAYS
ON THE POLITICS OF CULTURE, LANGUAGE, AND IDENTITY

Published by McGraw-Hill, a business unit of The McGraw-Hill Companies, Inc., 1221 Avenue of the Americas, New York, NY 10020. Copyright © 2004 by The McGraw-Hill Companies, Inc. All rights reserved. No part of this publication may be reproduced or distributed in any form or by any means, or stored in a database or retrieval system, without the prior written consent of The McGraw-Hill Companies, Inc., including, but not limited to, in any network or other electronic storage or transmission, or broadcast for distance learning.

Some ancillaries, including electronic and print components, may not be available to customers outside the United States.

This book is printed on acid-free paper.

1 2 3 4 5 6 7 8 9 0 FGR/FGR 0 9 8 7 6 5 4 3

ISBN 0-07-249638-X

Publisher: *Phillip A. Butcher*
Sponsoring editor: *Kevin Witt*
Developmental editor: *Pamela Gordon*
Senior marketing manager: *Daniel M. Loch*
Project manager: *Jill Moline*
Production supervisor: *Carol A. Bielski*
Coordinator of freelance design: *Mary E. Kazak*
Art editor: *Jennifer DeVere*
Photo researcher: *Brian Pecko*
Cover design: *Mary E. Kazak*
Interior design: *Jenny El-Shamy*
Typeface: *10/12 Palatino*
Compositor: *TBH Typecast, Inc.*
Printer: *Quebecor World Fairfield, Inc.*
Cover photo: "On the Shores of Nootka" as found in Curtis, Edward S.
   The North American Indian. Cambridge, MA: University Press, 1907–30.
   © Dartmouth College Library

Library of Congress Cataloging-in-Publication Data
A will to survive : indigenous essays on the politics of culture, language, and identity /
   edited by Stephen Greymorning.
      p. cm.
   Includes bibliographical references.
   ISBN 0-07-249638-X (softcover : alk. paper)
   1. Indigenous peoples—Ethnic identity. 2. Ethnophilosophy. 3. Language and culture.
4. Language revival. I. Greymorning, Stephen.
GN380.W54 2004
306'.08—dc21

                                                                        2003046400

www.mhhe.com

DEDICATION

As we moved down that hall to the room where the collection was displayed, my heart was in my throat. I cried as I saw the collection behind 12-foot walls of plexiglass. The sacred bundles were placed the highest out of reach. I was embarrassed to watch the Elders beg the curator to touch the bundles, to take care of them, they said. Finally, he relented and the bundles came down. I cried with the old women as they talked to the spirits and called them friend. The next 20 minutes were a blur. A young member of our tribe made the personal decision to capture the pipe Blackfeet-style.

BONNIE HEAVY-RUNNER

This book is dedicated in the memory of Bonnie Heavy-Runner, and to the resilience of Indigenous peoples in their struggles, their resistance, and their will to survive.

CONTENTS

ABOUT THE EDITOR

STEPHEN GREYMORNING is an Associate Professor in the departments of Anthropology and Native American Studies at the University of Montana. He completed his doctoral degree (1992) in anthropology at the University of Oklahoma. His dissertation topic, "Indigenous Peoples and the Ethnocentrism of the Courts," was nominated for the 1995 North American Indian Prose Award. He has written many articles on language and sovereignty issues, which include: *Running the Gauntlet of an Indigenous Language Program* (1999); *The Colonization of Indigenous North America* (1999); *The Imperialism of Cultural Appropriation* (1997); *Reflections on the Arapaho Language Project*, or *When Bambi Spoke Arapaho and Other Tales of Arapaho Language Revitalization Efforts* (2001). During the 2001–2002 academic year Stephen served as the Acting Director for the University of Victoria's Indigenous Governance Programs. Stephen has served as the Executive Director of Hinono'eitiinoowu' (Arapaho Language Lodge), Ethete, Wyoming, since its inception in 1995. Stephen remains an avid competitive diver, and in 2002 he won his division at the Masters World Games in Australia. His favorite pastime is traveling about the globe with his two children, Amber and Keith, and enjoying their company.

PREFACE

The beginnings of this project first came in May 1993 when I was privileged to attend a Native American language issues conference at Hilo, Hawaii. The conference, which addressed the alarming rate that Native languages were disappearing, brought to the forefront successful programs that Indigenous peoples had implemented to turn this problem around within their home communities. It was a very exciting conference to attend. More importantly, it was very exciting to observe children and adults as second-language learners speak their ancestral language as well as English, their first language.

On one particular evening during the conference I was part of a group that talked well beyond midnight. Discussions frequently crossed back and forth between language, historical, and political issues. One individual, of Anglo-European descent and not affiliated with any program that dealt with Native language issues, was particularly interested and asked many questions. Since the majority of his questions were in areas particular to my studies, his questions were often deflected to me. The following day I was surprised when he returned to the room and extended an apology to me, stating that, had he known I had a PhD, he would have paid better attention to what was being said. Evidently not being schooled in the history of North American Indian-government relations, he found much of what had been said difficult to accept as true. He thus felt compelled to ask another who I was and whether I was qualified to speak. This lack of recognition of the value and authenticity of an Indigenous voice was something that stayed with me and was something I would again observe in one form or another years later. It propelled me along this journey to compile a book on Indigenous issues, with Indigenous peoples as its sole authors.

By 1995 I had been hired by the University of Montana, and within the second term of my hire I found further reasons to pursue this project. The event that motivated me to pull this work together stemmed from a discussion on Native issues. What was of particular interest to the people addressing me pertained to why I put so much effort into my work on Native language maintenance and restoration. At one point I commented on how near a vast majority of our languages are to slipping into extinction. The response, "What's the big deal? Cultures go extinct all the time," stunned me. I believe my retort, "You wouldn't be stating that if it was your culture that was facing a threat of extinction," had a similar impact upon the person it was directed at. I left the discussion and began further exploring the possibility of a book.

The more I investigated the topic of this book, the more I became aware of how politically charged issues on native language, culture, and identity had become, and how misinformed some scholars and the general public seemed to be about these issues. As other people's thoughts on the topic began to surface, I heard notions about American Indian culture no longer existing, outside of being used as a tool to get special services that placed them in some sort of special citizen category. What was consistently being overlooked, however, were the numerous treaties between Indigenous Nations and the United States government, in which enormous benefits were gained for America and its citizens, while usually only limited benefits, which many people perceived as special services, were gained for Indian people. I became aware of two opposing positions, one that acknowledged the existence of Indian cultures and another that claimed the existence of Indigenous peoples' cultures were the result of having been in contact with Europeans.

It was as the result of such notions that I finally extended invitations to Indigenous scholars from Africa, America, Asia, Australia, Finland, India, New Zealand, and South America. From these invitations scholars from five different countries, representing 12 different culture groups, have contributed to the present work. The underlying idea for this was that, through their writings, not only would a shared history of political subjugation emerge, but also similar manners and ways of expressing cultural relevance. The formed hypothesis was that if through these writings similar forms of cultural expressions and relevance are mirrored by Indigenous people from other countries, then this further strengthens the position that Indigenous cultures are valid and continue to survive.

Taking on a project such as this proved to be educational, frustrating, and always challenging. It proved to be an educational experience to learn how pervasive peoples' stereotypes of Indigenous peoples could truly be, and how uninformed the so-called experts could be at times. Many times I was frustrated and challenged by all of this, and sometimes I was disheartened by the creative ways publishers found to dismiss this project.

It is with sincere gratitude that I thank Mr. Mark Bass, who believed enough in the project to convince me to allow him to take it to McGraw-Hill Press; and Gregory Campbell and Thomas Foor, whose early discussions helped to motivate me to take on this task. I also want to thank Barbara Borg, College of Charleston; Kelli Costa, Franklin Pierce College; Deward Walker, University of Colorado; and Cameron Wesson, University of Illinois—Chicago for their valuable comments during the review of the manuscript; and Pamela Gordon for her patience and help with getting the manuscript ready for production. Next I would like to thank the authors who contributed their valuable Indigenous voices to this work. In particular I would like to acknowledge Bonnie Heavy-Runner, who generously gave her energy in a time of personal crisis, and Darrell Robes Kipp, who stepped in to continue her dance when she was no longer able to. In a book that extols the strength of Indigenous languages and cultures, it is with sincere appreciation that I thank Kauanoe Kamana for contributing to the book in Hawaiian, for her unwavering dedication to the Hawaiian language movement, and for the inspiration she gives to the Indigenous peoples' language movement.

The final months spent completing this book have become a blur. What I remember are numerous nights working after midnight and Gail sharing the burden of editing chapters. I could not have completed this work on schedule without the expertise of your proofreading, without your drive, or without you at my side. To you I give a Golden Feather so you will never lose your way back home. My heartfelt thanks.

Neniice'ooke'
Victoria, British Columbia, Canada,
June 29, 2002; 1:30 A.M.

INTRODUCTION

In this volume 14 Indigenous authors share their knowledge, perspectives, and experiences, helping to fill a void in the current literature on contemporary Indigenous cultures. While the number of anthologies and other literary works by Indigenous writers has steadily grown, a fair number of them include non-Indigenous perspectives. The present work represents the first time that Indigenous academics, professionals, and scholars from different countries are the exclusive authors writing about issues pertaining to their own cultures, languages, and identities. Being a compilation of only Indigenous peoples' writings gives the book a uniqueness and strength in the diversity of Indigenous perspectives that it presents. This is a marked change to the standard set in the 19th and 20th centuries when the bulk of books written about Indigenous peoples and cultures were, and to a large extent continue to be written by people who are not Indigenous.

The focus of the book is on the strength of Indigenous people's cultures, languages, and identities to survive in the 21st century. This book can be contributed to a number of motivating factors. The first of these stemmed from portrayals of many Indigenous cultures as being contrived as a type of political tool to procure special treatment. The attitude that has emerged from this perspective is of Indigenous peoples as "super" or "special" citizens receiving special treatment within their respective countries. Another factor stemmed from a movement to classify Indigenous peoples as representing ethnic groups within their ancestral countries, to be lumped together with other ethnic minority groups who are not indigenous to the country in which they live. While I believe that both perspectives are dangerous to Indigenous peoples in North America, I also believe that if this ideology takes hold, it can have serious consequences for Indigenous peoples on a global scale. One of the dangers of this is that it can serve to undermine a history of colonial and political subjugation of Indigenous people, and may also work to both dismiss and portray a history of treaty obligations as meaningless.

It should also be realized that governments, like those found in the United States and Canada, have crafted policies regarding Indigenous people in such a manner as to give those countries an ability to manipulate and, to a large degree, define who is and who is not Indigenous.[1] This is made evident in America by the U.S. Federal Acknowledgment Program, and more recently by Congressional legislation to define native Hawaiians under a political rubric that would liken them to American Indians. In Canada this can best be illustrated by the Indian Act, which historically could not only change a female Indian's identity to white, but could also change a white female's identity to Indian. Another example is the abilitiy of the government to change the tribal identity of a First Nations woman if she marries a male from another tribe. I first became aware of this when I met Marie Gladue, daughter of renowned Navajo activist Katherine Smith, whose identity was officially reclassified as a Cree Indian under Canada's Indian Act when she married a Cree man. These are examples of how persistent governments are in wielding their colonial control over the lives of many Indigenous peoples. I believe because of factors such as those already mentioned, the value of this book is clear as it presents Indigenous voices and perspectives on issues that are of great concern.

For over a century Indigenous peoples have been told, and had to listen to, who we were to be and what we were supposed to do. Having rarely been asked our thoughts or to lend our voice to the discourse, instead we are continually confronted by stereotypes that serve to enforce this dismissive practice. As editor I had to face difficult choices with editing chapters as I did not want to change the Indigenous voice of the individual authors in an effort to make it more palatable for an audience who might be expecting something different or something they are more comfortable with. In this regard, linguistic and cultural differences between the authors and the audience allow for greater insight into the issues that these authors share. To have sanitized this volume into an academic treatise would have lost the importance of the Indigenous person's unique perspective. As Arleen Adams relates in her chapter, "My father said he never liked the idea of publishers changing the story once it was told, 'they always leave out much of the most important parts of the story'."[2]

The chapters are organized in such a way as to blend language, culture, and identity—all issues of great concern to Indigenous peoples. As a result of the authors' interconnecting these topics within their chapters, it is difficult to attribute any one specific theme to any individual chapter. Nevertheless, there has been an effort to group them on a commonality of a raison d'être. However, because this is but one version of how I see the story, others may want to put a different order to how the story-chapters are delivered.

PART I:
TELLING "HIS-STORIES":
THREE INDIGENOUS PERSPECTIVES

One result of the importance placed on written history has been that people seem to have forgotten that history was once "his story," and as such it consisted of oral narratives. As Eurocentric thinking placed more and more importance on the need to record "his story," a truth was given to the exactness of the written record. In the process a different reality seems to have either been diminished or lost. This becomes clearer when recognizing that the recorded story is just one version of history and, as such, may not necessarily represent any great truth or accuracy. Something else seems also to have happened, and that was a devaluing of the truth or relevance that can come from other tellers of the story. There is one other aspect yet to tell. In many Indigenous languages phrases can carry more than one meaning, and, as is the case with telling his-stories, it carries three meanings.[3]

The first chapter, "Culture and Language: Political Realities to Keep Trick-ster at Bay," by Stephen Greymorning, discusses the political importance of language and culture. After an introduction is made, a rendering of "his-story" begins by addressing the colonization of North America through the cultural lens of a trickster tale. The story works to familiarize readers with how the independent political status of Indigenous peoples in North America was undermined and changed through political decisions, policies, and acts of gov-ernments. The background information given is important in understanding how Indigenous peoples' languages have been severely impacted by suppress-ing their cultures. The latter part of the story moves readers through a discus-sion of the uniqueness of Indigenous peoples' languages as a definer of culture and its underlying knowledge base.

In the face of a long history of political and religious subjugation, the intent of which has been to assimilate Indigenous peoples by suppressing their lan-guages and cultures, the importance of language is highlighted as a force de resistance in maintaining Indigenous peoples' distinct cultural identities. This chapter further serves to provide an important function in setting a foundation for Chapters 9 through 14 which inform the reader of the significance that lan-guage plays in Indigenous culture and identity.

Peter Irniq, commissioner of Nunavut, provides a unique insight into Inuit cultural ways in Chapter 2, "The Staying Force of Inuit Knowledge." Reading Peter's chapter is like taking a journey through the seasons of Inuit traditions of life and the land. Similar to Chapters 9 and 10, Peter recounts stories of his peo-ple that have shaped Inuit behavior and identity as they have been passed on through the generations. Through topics on hunting, naming, healing, songs, legends, and the Inuksuk, the world of the Inuit unfolds. Like the Inuksuk, whose presence proclaims we have been here and still exist on this land, Peter's writings reveal the strength and resilience of the Inuit peoples' ability not only to survive in a harsh climate but to navigate through an even harsher history of colonization and successfully emerge in control of the first Indigenous-governed territory in North America, called Nunavut—Our Land. The Nunavut treaty paved the way for capital transfer payments of $1.1 billion and placed title to lands measuring 355,842 square kilometers, roughly the eastern portion of Canada's Northwest Territories, including 35,257 square kilometers of mineral rights, in the hands of the Inuit people. This modern, comprehensive agreement is structured to guarantee Inuit people majority control over their future.

In Chapter 3, "Eualeyai: The Blood That Runs through My Veins," Larissa Behrendt relates how her grandmother was stolen as a child, as were genera-tions of other Aboriginal children, under a government policy of removal. The policy of the Aborigines Protection Board was to assimilate and save Aboriginal people regardless of the consequences to their person or cultural identity. The philosophy of this policy differs little from the philosophy of Captain Richard Henry Pratt, founding father of the American Indian boarding school: "to kill the Indian . . . and save the man," described in Chapter 5 by Ward Churchill. Larissa tells of the tragic legacies that Australian government policies have left on Indigenous Australians' lives over generations. Personalizing her own life experiences of the prejudices and stereotypes she has faced, Larissa shares a poignant and distinct perspective on life as an Aboriginal Australian woman. While Larissa's story could have been placed in Part II, it is in Part I because of its personal nature, which seemed appropriate for a beginning.

Cultural identity is a major focus of this chapter, and the author strives to educate the reader about the insidious racism that Indigenous peoples continually face. "Whenever I have achieved a goal, it has been degraded by racists who claim that it was only because someone was feeling sorry for me or the acceptance of me and my work was a token . . . All this because of the color of my skin."[4] Larissa's personal reflections give a unique voice to the struggles faced by Indigenous people globally.

PART II:
COLONIZATION AND IDENTITY

The chapters in this section examine some of the impacts that colonization has had on Indigenous peoples. Chapter 4, "Of This Red Earth," by Henrietta Mann, exposes readers to aspects of Cheyenne language, culture, and history. As with Chapter 1, Henrietta begins by using the genre of storytelling to open a door to Cheyenne ways. In this case it is through stories of Cheyenne creation and ceremony. The chapter goes on to describe how education was used as a weapon of assimilation. Under a governmental agenda of civilizing the savages, Indian children were sent to off-reservation boarding schools to distance them from their families and cultures. In these schools Indian languages were targeted with a vengeance, as were the children's spiritual and cultural beliefs. Assimilation policies were not confined to America. Such policies were actively employed in Australia, Canada, and New Zealand, as noted in the chapters by Larissa Behrendt, Peter Irniq, and Moana Jackson. Besides discussing federal assimilation policies bound in education, Chapter 4's discussion of relocation and termination policies also ties in with themes expanded on in Chapter 6.

Chapter 5, "A Question of Identity," by Ward Churchill, delves deeply into issues surrounding cultural identity and how colonization and subsequent government politics have impacted American Indians. This chapter calls for a return to the Indian way of identifying membership or citizenship, in place of the colonial bondage that has determined Indigenous peoples' identity and cultures. Ward advocates that in taking this position Indigenous peoples move towards a concrete expression of self-determination. He warns that without this important step Indigenous groups face a road that leads toward extinction.

Moana Jackson's "Colonization as Myth-Making: A Case Study in Aotearoa" (Chapter 6) focuses on the politics and processes of colonization as experienced by the Maori people of Aotearoa (New Zealand). Like Taiaiake, Moana examines the construct of colonization. Here, however, he exposes the myths that have given substance to laws used to suppress Indigenous Maori peoples. He defrocks the legal institutions and their actions in creating colonial myths used to soothe Victorian sensibilities and to enforce dispossession. Further, he states: "In each instance the myths sought to present the racist human agency of colonial greed . . . as immutable justice, as divine will, as manifest destiny, as benign civilization."[5] There was hypocrisy in this myth of a benign civilization. Moana relates that the colonizing force was so powerful that more than the physical population was shattered in its wake. The attack decimated the Indigenous soul of Maori people to the point of weakening their faith in all things, the values that had nourished it, "the language which gave meaning to its soul, the law which gave it order, and the religion which was its strength . . ."[6] ultimately affecting the belief of the Maori in themselves.

PART III:
INDIGENOUS PHILOSOPHY AND ACTIVISM

In Chapter 7, "From Sovereignty to Freedom," Taiaiake Alfred offers a very philosophical treatise on self-determination and its roots in Indigenous philosophies as the key in deconstructing the political architecture of colonial domination. Taiaiake grounds this chapter with discussions that reject the term *sovereignty* on the grounds that it is nothing more than a colonial construct and cannot be viewed as a final solution to Indian problems. While the chapter's strength lies in its discourse on the political myth of sovereignty, it concludes with a strong statement that the wisdom encoded in native languages and cultures, if heeded, can provide answers to the political entanglements of the yoke that comes with colonization.

In "She Must Be Civilized: She Paints Her Toe Nails" (Chapter 8), Sharon Venne, as an Indigenous activist, shares personal experiences gained as a consultant to the United Nations Indigenous Working Group. The chapter begins by noting that from the moment of contact Indigenous peoples have been in a war of survival, and that in spite of events that have subjected Indigenous peoples to an array of hardships, Indigenous peoples continue to survive. This chapter is informative and insightful in its exploration of political issues both at national and international levels. At its onset it asserts the international recognition of a people being Indigenous as a political identification and not a racial indicator. In spite of this, domestic legislation of individual colonizing states is consistently formed on the basis of race. Sharon does more than ask such questions as Why classify Indigenous peoples by racial identity? Why would colonizers spend so much time trying to determine who is Indigenous? or Why try to control Indigenous peoples? She lends her legal insight and experience gained at the international level to offer answers that many should find illuminating. One of the most insightful sections of this chapter is when she writes of her invitation to lecture at the Institute of Human Rights in Strasbourg and the subsequent censoring of her lectures.

PART IV:
CULTURE-WAYS OF BEING

The chapters in this section look at personal experiences and expressions that derive from being Indigenous. "The Lessons of Coyote and the Medicine Tree" (Chapter 9) by Arleen Adams, like Chapters 2, 3, 4, and 12, shares family experiences of going through the boarding school system. This chapter, in similar fashion to Larissa's chapter, also describes racial prejudices she has faced as an American Indian. For Arleen those prejudices were most strongly realized during her years as a university student. As the title suggests, the chapter places a primary focus on Coyote stories and what they, and Coyote as a culture hero, mean to the Salish people. The chapter also tells about the Ram's Horn Tree, and how development and developers are a constant threat to it and Salish sacred sites. Through these accounts, Arleen gives a personalized look into Salish peoples' history, what Salish culture has meant to her, and into her life as a Salish woman.

Chapter 10, "Mayan Ways of Knowing: Modern Mayans and the Elders," by Victor Montejo, is strongly grounded in culture, history, and traditions. Like Arleen's chapter, Victor's chapter is firmly rooted in the importance that elders and oral histories have in his people's culture. "El Q'anil: The Man of Lightning," is one such story. El Q'anil is a culture hero, and Victor relates that this story is told to every child by parents, grandparents, and Elders in order to establish a strong connection with the past. Victor states: " In this way, Mayans become rooted to the land because the landscape or sacred geography becomes the resting place or sanctuary of the ancestors."[7] This chapter calls for a returning to the teachings of the elders. It also calls for the acknowledgment of the essential role they play in maintaining and revitalizing Mayan identity and cultural ways as necessary for Mayan survival in the rapidly changing world.

Rachael Selby in "Tararua Is My Mountain" (Chapter 11) depicts the cultural revival of her people, the Maori of Aotearoa (New Zealand). Relating personal and cultural experiences of rebuilding the cultural integrity of her community, the chapter gives this book another practical component on how Indigenous peoples are surviving after the severe impacts of colonization. Rachael explains how Generation 2000, a long-term tribal development program, focused on three major streams or missions to bring about changes that would ensure a stronger and better future for her people. These three missions were the education mission, which set goals to elevate the numbers of Maori people in certain professions and to improve educational attainment in general; the Pakeha mission, with the objective of educating "non-Maori, Pakeha people, about the culture, beliefs, and values of Maori people . . ."; and the tribal mission, which sought to encourage tribal members to return to traditional homes and to learn traditional ways. Physically rebuilding and refurbishing the maraes, the ancestral meeting houses and land, has enabled the Maori people once again to conduct their cultural, social, and spiritual lives in their own distinct way. Paramount in this cultural revival has been the renewed interest in learning Maori language, which has flourished with the establishment of kohanga reo, immersion preschools.

PART V:
CULTURE AND LANGUAGE SURVIVAL

Chapter 12, "Fighting the Winds of Change: Section I," stands as a legacy to a dear friend and colleague, Bonnie Heavy-Runner. The chapter is a personal recollection of Blackfeet life and ceremony. At the time Bonnie wrote this, she was acutely aware of the crisis confronting the Blackfeet, as well as other Indigenous peoples, due to policies and practices of colonization, as discussed by other authors in previous chapters. Her heart-wrenching account of her peoples' struggle to maintain cultural balance is evident as she shared the attempted recapturing of a Blackfeet sacred item from the Glen Bow Museum in Calgary, Alberta.

> As we moved down that hall to the room where the collection was displayed, my heart was in my throat. I cried as I saw the collection behind 12-foot walls of plexiglass. The sacred bundles were placed the highest out of reach. I was embarrassed to watch the Elders beg the curator to touch the bundles, to take care of them, they said. Finally, he relented and the bundles came down. I cried with the old women as they talked to the spirits and called them friend. The next 20 minutes were a blur.
>
> A young member of our tribe made the personal decision to capture the pipe Blackfeet style. When he picked up the last star pipe and called out, no one answered, but the museum people and I wondered why. They wanted him to put it down and he refused. The room was sealed off with security, the Elders were taken by surprise; they didn't want any trouble and they began to talk to the young man. I witnessed the struggle between generations. I could see at that point that he was committed and didn't care what would happen. Finally, out of respect, with tears in his eyes, he handed the pipe to the curator and walked out. When I left the building, I could feel a thousand spirits hovering around us. I saw the young man, crying, angry, and confused because their whole belief system had crumbled in less than an hour.

Before Bonnie was able to write about the hope she saw for the future, she passed away. As a result, Section II of "Fighting the Winds of Change" addresses this aspect.

Section II, "A Culture in Renaissance," is an interview of Darrell Robes Kipp about his personal perspectives on Blackfeet culture and ceremony.

> I was very impressed and moved by her (Bonnie) ability to capture the experience of being in the Thunder Pipe Ceremony. For example, one of the things she writes about is when she had her face painted. Recently, they opened the

Thunder Pipe at the sound of the first thunder. I was present at one of the openings and one of the things that captured my imagination and captured the
moment happened after the painting of the faces. A group of about eight or
nine young women, dressed in long dresses with their hair braided and their
shawls and moccasins still on, had had their faces painted and were sitting in a
cluster on the floor near the front of the ceremony. They were very beautiful in
how relaxed and very comfortable they were. The scene, in my mind, related to
me the continuum of the various culture elements still very much present
within many tribes. Although we may worry about the demise or weakening of
cultures, we should be encouraged when we see these ceremonies today, years
after Bonnie attended, that they still hold true to the fashion of the tribe.

Section II also highlights Darrell's involvement with Nizipuhwahsin and
the role that language is beginning to play within his community, and how
some of the language-immersion students, who have become extremely good
speakers, are increasingly being asked to get up and deliver prayers at tribal
ceremonies. The discussion of his work to bring renewed hope and vitality to
the Blackfoot language gives testimony to the shift of a culture in crisis to the
birth of a cultural renaissance.

Chapter 13, "Reflections and Feelings Deriving from a Pulakaumaka within
My Heart," holds a special place because it was written by Kauanoe Kamana,
one of the leaders of the Hawaiian language revitalization movement. This
chapter is especially significant because it was first written in the Hawaiian language and then translated into English. This chapter delivers another personal
perspective on the importance of language to culture and identity. Kauanoe's
passion for her role and responsibility in the revitalization of the Hawaiian language are strongly present throughout her chapter.

So if I am asked why I became involved in the revitalization of our indigenous
language here in Hawai'i, the answer is very clear. It is my responsibility, a joyful burden that must be carried . . .

I have never ever been in doubt regarding my Hawaiian identity nor my
responsibility of carrying out the duties that need to be done. Love of God, love
of family, and love of knowledge and education are features of the worldview
of my family, and that is how I have come to be able to perceive what is real and
what is not in all activities.[8]

Chapter 14, "Hinon'eitiino'oowu' and the Work of Language Survival," by
Stephen Greymorning, tells of his personal relationship with language revitalization efforts on the Wind River Reservation in Wyoming. This chapter, like
Chapter 12 in Part V, Chapter 11 in Part IV, and Chapter 13 in Part V, is a personal account of the strategies, efforts, and personal sacrifice involved in starting a language-immersion program for children. The chapter in part is set out
like a case study giving readers insight into the detailed, almost day-to-day
inner workings involved within a language-immersion setting. The strength of
this chapter is its ability to move from the theoretical approach to an applied
model. In this way it presents a statement of Arapaho as a people with a will to
maintain a resilient culture and language. The chapter also endeavors to present

a practical model as encouragement for other Indigenous peoples involved in the work of language restoration and maintenance.

What has emerged in this book is a picture of the commonalty of shared experiences among Indigenous peoples from five different countries. In spite of perceived advancements in human rights, Indigenous peoples remain colonized within their homelands. In the face of a long history of political oppression, the struggle to maintain the integrity and uniqueness of being Indigenous continues. It is for this reason that the hope for the future remains strongly rooted in Indigenous peoples' proven resilience to survive.

NOTES

1. The word "Indian," erroneously applied by Columbus who mistakenly believed he had reached an island off the coast of India, has been used with mixed emotions by the original inhabitants of North America. In Canada, during the 70s, the application of Native, with a capital "N" was used, but also with mixed feelings. Over time, the concept of First Nations has been applied with increased acceptance. Internationally, the term "indigenous" has been applied with growing acceptance. Instead of using indigenous with a lowercase "i," I have chosen to use "Indigenous," with a capital "I," much along the same lines as Canada distinguishes between "native" when referring to place, and "Native" when referring to a particular people. It also makes sense that when indigenous is used to replace the proper noun Indian, it should maintain its lingusitic feature as a proper noun with the initial "I" uppercased.
2. Cited from "The Lessons of Coyote and the Medicine Tree," in this volume.
3. I had originally intended to leave it at that, but then decided to give the three interpretations. The first rests on the physical delivery in telling stories that may belong to one individual or many. The second refers to the physical delivery in telling different histories. The third rests on one meaning given to the word *telling,* which here would be stories or histories that reveal or impart knowledge about someone or something, and I think all three of these meanings can be applied to the stories in Section I.
4. Cited from "Eualeyai: The Blood That Runs through My Veins," in this volume.
5. Cited from Chapter 5 within this volume.
6. Ibid.
7. Cited from "Mayan Ways of Knowing: Modern Mayans and the Elders," in this volume.
8. Cited from "Reflections and Feelings Deriving from a Pulakaumaka within My Heart," in this volume.

A WILL TO SURVIVE

INDIGENOUS ESSAYS ON
THE POLITICS OF CULTURE,
LANGUAGE, AND IDENTITY

PART 1
Telling "His-Stories": Three Indigenous Perspectives

CHAPTER 1

CULTURE AND LANGUAGE: POLITICAL REALITIES TO KEEP TRICKSTER AT BAY

By Stephen Greymorning

Stephen Greymorning is an Associate Professor in the departments of Native American Studies and Anthropology at the University of Montana. During the 2001–2002 academic year, he served as the Acting Director of the Indigenous Governance Programs at the University of Victoria in British Columbia, Canada. In 1997 he taught as a visiting scholar at Southern Cross University in Australia. From 1988 to 1992, Stephen taught courses on linguistics, comparative Indian legislation, and aboriginal self-government at the University of Alberta while working on his doctoral dissertation on "Indigenous Peoples and the Ethnocentrism of the Courts." After receiving a Doctorate from the University of Oklahoma, he served as Director of the Arapaho Language and Culture Project for the Wyoming Indian Schools. While maintaining academic interests in Native sovereignty issues, his work in developing strategies toward Native language restoration continues. In this capacity Stephen serves as the Executive Director of Hinono'eitiit Hoowu' (Arapaho Language Lodge) in Wyoming. His publications include: *Running the Gauntlet of an Indigenous Language Program* (1999); *The Colonization of Indigenous North America* (1999); *The Imperialism of Cultural Appropriation* (1997); *In the Absence of Justice: Aboriginal Case Law in an Ethnocentric Court* (1997).

Introduction

For over 200 years governments in North America have enforced policies aimed at assimilating and politically dominating Indigenous North American peoples. This chapter discusses several of the political tools used throughout history by colonial powers in North America as a means of highlighting the role that language must play as a force de resistance in maintaining Indigenous peoples' distinct cultural identity against a long and continuing history of political subjugation.

In the wake of over a hundred years of political and cultural suppression, Indigenous North American cultures and resources are still under assault. An underlying focus of this chapter has been to examine how language and identity may represent the last significant political reality to anchor Native cultures against a history of government policies and practices that persist in advocating the assimilation of Native peoples into the ideological collective of the governing settler-state. Before moving into such a discussion, however, the chapter will briefly examine the legal and political subjugation Indigenous North Americans have experienced by framing an initial discussion of contact and conquest within the genre of a "Trickster" tale.

The application of a Trickster motif rests upon its widespread use within many Native American cultures. Traditionally, Trickster tales have been used to illustrate improper behavior in such a way that they served to teach what Native communities have viewed as proper behavior. Among many Native American groups, Trickster most commonly represents a character who is always getting into some type of mischief or stirring up trouble. If Trickster discovers a skill or the property of another, he always wants to claim it for himself. Whenever Trickster sees something that he likes, he is sure to conjure up some trick in order to obtain what he desires as his own. He always tends to see himself as better than those around him. Among the Arapaho, Trickster tales underwent a transformation and became Nih'oo3o' (white man) tales sometime during the early part of the 19th century. So, in effect, Trickster works well within the context of this chapter. There is one other reason for utilizing a Trickster motif. History, as recorded by those who colonize, is always told from a different perspective than the history that is remembered by those who have been colonized. Hence, the Trickster tale serves both to represent an Indigenous perspective within the tale itself and to cue the reader that an underlying interpretation and analysis has been set within the framework of an Indigenous perspective throughout the chapter.

Through the use of a Trickster motif, this chapter aspires to open up a small window for the reader to get a glimpse at another culture's "emic," or Native perspective, with regard to why it is necessary to keep Trickster at bay. To this end the chapter seeks to bring a level of understanding in relation to the role that language must ultimately play in keeping Native American culture from being totally subjugated and absorbed by a dominating culture that, in the name of development and progress, would seek to exploit all within the reach of its "Midas" touch.

When Trickster Found His Way to Turtle Island

Long ago when Trickster still lived only within the land of his people, he was very restless and wished to explore beyond the limits of his world. It had come to his attention that there existed a land known as Turtle Island far beyond the great waters, and he became desirous to discover what he could gain from this new land. When Trickster finally made it to Turtle Island, he found it to be very different from his own homeland. Trickster thought the climate harsh and unsuitable and viewed the mannerisms and lifestyles of the land's inhabitants to be crude and inferior to his own. Similarly, the people of the land also found the mannerisms of Trickster to be shocking and worth their ridicule. And so it was that they had viewed each other through the ethnocentric eyes of their own culture's values.

Now, although Trickster had always viewed himself as a clever fellow, when he first arrived, he knew nothing of the land, the people, or the environment that he had entered. As a result he found himself relying upon the land's Indigenous peoples in order to learn what resources could be harvested for food, clothing, and profit. Trickster wanted to make a home for himself and his people in this land, so, being a clever fellow, he brought seeds from his homeland to plant for his food; but his crops, like his efforts, withered in an environment to which both he and crops were foreign. For more than a century, 1497 to 1602, although many others from different Trickster clans tried to create a piece of their world within the new land, none had made a lasting impact upon the Indigenous cultures or land that in time would come to be known as North America.

Now the wants of Trickster have always been great, and he remained determined to learn the ways of the people in order to gain a stronghold upon the land. Finally, in 1603, members of a particular Trickster clan established a small settlement in the northeastern region of the land at a place that they would call Canada. Only a few years after this, members of another Trickster clan began a colony at a place they called Roanoke. Now the members of these Trickster clans were so entrenched in their own particular ways that they viewed all other people and cultures as inferior to their own. Driven by the forces of their own ethnocentrism, the two clans battled each other until, in 1759, one defeated the other and the winner claimed dominion over all the land and its people. The Trickster wars, however, had not ended. The rules that gave order to their society began to break down. Conflict and turmoil increased and eventually culminated with the Great Trickster uprising of 1776. When the dust finally settled, the land had been divided between the two clans; America in the south and Canada in the north, and from these peoples' lack of forbearance the world of Indigenous North Americas would forever be changed.

How the Course of History Was Shaped by Nih'oo30'

Historically, the focus of many of the changes enforced upon the people indigenous to North America has been to try to mold Native culture into an image of

Anglo-European culture. This is most commonly referred to as assimilation. Early on it was realized, much to the disappointment of government officials, that efforts to bring about assimilation were not having the results that had been hoped for. Instead of becoming assimilated, a number of Indigenous groups adapted elements of Anglo-European culture to fit the framework of their own particular cultures, and demonstrated advancements that at times successfully competed against Anglo-Europeans. When this occurred, political leaders in both Canada and the United States turned toward implementing legislation to bring about their desired results. When legislation did not always achieve the results sought after, the courts became the next battleground. Between the forces of legislation and the Court, governments in both Canada and the United States had acquired the necessary tools to politically subjugate Indigenous North America. The support of this claim will come with a closer look at the tools and strategies historically utilized by American, British, and Canadian governments to claim an absolute dominion over the peoples and lands of Indigenous North America.

In 1759 after a French defeat in an area near Quebec called the "Plains of Abraham," the British remained concerned over the threat of continued Indian military activity. In an attempt to quell such threats, the British issued a series of proclamations as a measure to control their own citizens.[1] The most familiar of these was the Royal Proclamation of 1763.[2] This document explicitly stated that the peace and security of Britain's North American colonies and plantations greatly depended upon the goodwill and alliance with the several Indian nations bordering the colonies. While this document has found its way into Canadian litigation, both to support and argue against the existence of Indigenous peoples' rights, most attribute a force to this document as possessing an ability to bring North America under the laws and government of Britain. When the Proclamation is placed in context with certain events and conditions that existed during the period, however, a very different impression emerges.

A momentous event that should not be overlooked when considering a potential cause and effect relationship upon the final drafting of the Proclamation occurred in the spring of 1763. During the months of May and June, warfare erupted along the frontier and a fighting force of Indigenous people, under the leadership of an Ottawa chief known as Pontiac, captured 9 of 11 British forts. With the exception of Forts Ligoner and Pitt, the Indigenous nations of the Western Confederacy were largely successful in regaining control over their traditional lands in the upper Great Lakes region.[3] From May until October, warriors of the Western Confederacy maintained an effective military posture. By the fall of 1763, Indigenous nations of the confederacy had either captured or destroyed every post west of Detroit. It was not the superiority of the British military, however, that eventually contained the Indigenous war effort, but the spread of a smallpox epidemic that finally enabled Superintendent of Indian Affairs Sir William Johnson to arrange a truce. It is worth mentioning that some believe this epidemic to have possibly resulted from the deliberate distribution of infected dress goods, such as handkerchiefs, various items of clothing, and blankets from the smallpox hospital at Fort Pitt. Sharon O'Brien noted this as

William Trent's description of a "gift" to the Delaware, 1763. "Out of regard to them [the Indians] we gave them two blankets and an (sic) Handkerchief (sic) out of the Small Pox Hospital. I hope it will have the desired effect."[4]

Historically Pontiac's resistance is given little or no credit as having any significant impact upon the final drafting of the Royal Proclamation of October 17, 1763. This oversight is a good example of how ethnocentrism has colored the writing of history to strengthen and perpetuate a myth of the superiority of Anglo-European culture during that period of European colonization.[5]

After the United States was born as a nation, America's leadership began to recognize the sovereignty and rights of various nations of Indigenous peoples through treaties. This early recognition, however, was soon followed by the U.S. government exercising its own brand of colonial control. In 1789 under Section 8 of the U.S. Constitution, the newly formed government claimed itself to possess certain powers, specifically its ability "to regulate Commerce with foreign Nations, and among the several States, and with the Indian Tribes."[6] From this clause it has been interpreted that the U.S. government possessed broad powers to regulate and manage all affairs of Indigenous North Americans. It must be noted that even though the words "Indian Tribes" appear on the same line with "foreign Nations," logic fails to explain the fact that while this clause could not endow the United States with any specific power to manage the affairs of foreign nations, it nevertheless is claimed to have endowed the American government with explicit powers to manage the affairs of Indigenous nations which, like foreign nations, had not been incorporated into the American state. Furthermore, at the time the American Constitution was adopted, the notion of managing the internal affairs of Indigenous populations was contradictory to the very spirit of the several treaties the United States had already entered into with Indigenous nations. Twenty years later, in 1809, the American Commerce and Nonintercourse Acts declared that Indian people needed protection from the practices of unscrupulous Whites. This resulted in Congress legislating the federal government with the power to manage the affairs of Indians. With these endorsements, Indigenous people from sea to sea, without their knowledge or consent, had traditional territories, property, rights, and liberties subsumed as the exclusive responsibility of the U.S. government.

Governments in both Canada and the United States have worked to create an inaccurate and myth-like image of the political subjugation they sought to exert over Indigenous North Americans. In the United States this illusion was first propagated in 1831, in the case of *Cherokee Nation* vs. *the State of Georgia*, when Supreme Court Chief Justice John Marshall claimed that the Indians were in a state of pupilage, a claim that has been used since that time to undermine any actual realization of self-determination for Indigenous Nations.[7] The case was Chief Justice Marshall's first discourse on his principle of "discovery." This also was the case where Marshall, in defining the political status of the Cherokee, stated that, though they could not be considered foreign nations, "they may, more correctly, perhaps, be denominated domestic dependent nations."[8]

In Canada, the government has at times utilized this state of tutelage concept as a means to an end—to redefine Indigenous Canadians as non-Indians.

This was accomplished through legislation that asserted that once a "Status" Indian attained a certain level of education he or she attained citizenship.[9] The catch-22 was that once Indians had become citizens of Canada, they were no longer considered to be Indians. They summarily received notice of citizenship and, by virtue of such notice, all treaty benefits were abrogated. Though Canada was much different from the U.S government in its approach and perspective, the end result was the same; a legislative Act created by an alien culture arbitrarily defining who and what is Indian, for the purpose of disempowering and controlling the lives and resources of Indigenous North Americans. In spite of the controlling force of Canadian and American governments, it is significant that in North America there still exist areas that have been occupied exclusively by Indigenous peoples for thousands of years. Counter to this fact, however, governments have taken a stance that land and resources can be taken from First Nations' peoples simply by enacting legislation to accomplish this end. It is for this reason, in part, that Indigenous peoples have undertaken efforts to empower themselves through political mediums of self-government and self-determination. Unfortunately, language has not historically been given any significant position within these efforts.

One of the first efforts aimed at self-empowerment was initiated by the Cherokee in the 1831 Supreme Court case of *The Cherokee Nation* vs. *The State of Georgia.*[10] The immediate issues and circumstances surrounding this case stemmed from Georgia's legislation of a series of Acts intended to annex Cherokee land to several counties within the state and coerce the Cherokee into emigrating out of Georgia. Georgia's governor, George Gilmer, legislated a series of acts that reportedly gave Georgia's government the last word in regulating all laws regarding Indians within the boundaries of the state. The legislation asserted Georgia's right of title to Cherokee lands, made null and void all Indian customs and laws, and declared it illegal for Indians to testify in court cases in which Anglo-Americans were involved. Governor Gilmer justified his actions on the basis of a land cession the state had made to the U.S. government in 1802. The land cession had been backed by the government's promise that as soon as the Cherokee were persuaded to give up their land peacefully, Indian title would be extinguished and the Cherokee would then be removed outside the borders of Georgia.[11] In the end Chief Justice John Marshall was able to refuse jurisdiction over this case on the basis of his opinion that the Cherokee did not constitute a foreign state within the United States. "The Court has bestowed its best attention on this question, and . . . the majority is of an opinion that an Indian tribe or nation within the United States is not a foreign state, in the sense of the constitution, and can not maintain an action in the Courts of the United States."[12]

One year later the Cherokee again pressed the Court into deliberating upon their rights as an independent sovereign people. In this case, *Worcester* v. *Georgia,* as with the previous, the governor of Georgia refused to appear.[13] Almost enigmatically, Chief Justice Marshall presented arguments that supported protecting the Cherokee from Georgia's unconstitutional acts. Repeatedly Marshall stressed that Indigenous nations were distinct independent political communities, completely separate from the states. Marshall argued that the relationship between Indian nations and the United States was that of a nation receiving the protection of a more powerful nation, not that of individuals having to abandon their national character or having to submit themselves to the laws of a superior.

Although the Supreme Court moved to protect the rights of the Cherokee, the protection of Native rights was secondary to the Court's more pressing issue of protecting the nation's federal rights against Georgia's upsurgence for state rights. This is further supported by the fact that Georgia continued to assert its unconstitutional laws over the Cherokee, and the federal government, protecting its own, forced the issue and removed the Cherokee to Oklahoma. While the Marshall cases have been credited as establishing the existence of Indigenous peoples' rights within American law, in Canada the existence of Indigenous rights was not legally pursued until the 1970s.

The existence of Indigenous North American peoples' rights in Canada is well contrasted when compared to that of America. In the United States, legal tradition regarding the rights of Indigenous peoples evolved through several court cases that ultimately led the U.S. Supreme Court, during Marshall's tenure, to elevate a theory of conquest over a principle of discovery. By Marshall's reasoning, the "discovery principle" was extended only to European nations and conferred upon them an exclusive right to determine which European nation could acquire Indian land through either purchase or conquest. With regard to conquest, Marshall claimed: "Conquest gives a title which the *courts* of the *conqueror* cannot deny, whatever the private and speculative opinion of individuals may be . . ."[14] In comparison, the emergent legal tradition of Canadian courts regarding Native people's rights and entitlement to land seems to have remained fixed upon a doctrine of discovery rights to justify dominion over the peoples indigenous to Canada. The Doctrine of Discovery, which is deeply rooted in Anglo-European beliefs in the supremacy and right of Christian-bearing cultures to subjugate and claim dominion over non-Christian cultures, sadly still continues to have a strong presence in both legal theory and the minds of American and Canadian jurists.

When comparing the extension of Anglo-European rule in Canada to that of the United States, a significant difference is immediately observed. In Canada, unlike rule in America, the subjugation of Indigenous Canadians resulted almost entirely through legislative Acts. These Acts served to self-empower British dominion on a single premise: that as a superior culture, Britain's discoveries in North America guaranteed the exercise of its rule over the land and the original occupants whom the government perceived as an inferior people. One of Canada's most shocking examples of subjugation through legislation was formulated in 1876 and called the Indian Act.[15]

Because Canada's leadership did not view Indigenous people to be high enough on an Anglo-European perceived scale of civilization, the Indian Act was passed without the knowledge or consent of the Indigenous peoples it was destined to politically subdue. As a piece of legislation the Indian Act was formulated with a specific objective—to control all aspects of Indian life, with the

explicit goal of leading the Indian toward "civilization" and eventual assimilation. The Act itself embodies 60 pages of who, what, where, and how's. It codi-
fies who an Indian is, what an Indian can and cannot do, where an Indian can
and cannot go, when that can take place, and how an Indian must act. Within
these pages can be found 38 headings that address such topics as "Definition of
an Indian," "Creation of New Bands," "Sale or Barter of Produce," "Descent
of Property and Execution of Wills," "Management of Indian Moneys," "Regulations," "Powers of the Council," "Legal Rights," "Trading with Indians," and
"Removal of Material from Reserves." Each one of these topical restrictions, as
well as others not mentioned, continues to have profound effects upon those
Indigenous North American peoples the Canadian government has defined as
Status Indians. From the time that Canadian Status Indians are born, until the
time of their death, nothing affects their lives as much as the Indian Act. It deter-
mines where they live, what education they get, how they will earn a living,
what land they will own, and who will inherit their earthly possessions when
they die.[16] Every conceivable facet of one's life—all dictated by a single piece of
legislation.[17]

One of the most profound abuses of power in North America was exhibited
by the provincial government of Alberta, Canada, in 1973. During this period
Indigenous Canadians began to press the Courts to arbitrate aboriginal rights
issues. On March 24, 1973, Chief Francois Paulette of Fort Smith, along with 15
other chiefs, attempted to file a caveat.[18] The purpose of the caveat was to protect certain lands in the Northwest Territories, for continued traditional use, by
asserting a claim of interest as an aboriginal right. While the federal government
found itself caught up in this legal battle with the Indigenous peoples of the
Northwest Territories, the provincial government of Alberta was facing the
threat of a similar situation from a band of Indians called the Lubicon Cree, who
had also filed a caveat as a legal maneuver to try to protect their traditional
lands. The provincial government maintained a strategy to delay any pending
court action, and patiently waited for the Court to make its decision on the
Paulette case. The Supreme Court ruled against Paulette and the other chiefs.
Going beyond its appointed duties, however, the Court took the liberty to send
a message to the Alberta court by declaring that its decision was due to the
nature of unpatented Crown lands in the Territories, and most importantly, had
such a case occurred in Alberta, the province would have been bound by the
caveat.[19]

Through strategic maneuvering, the Alberta provincial government was
able to delay the case long enough to allow the passage of Bill 29, which effectively changed the wording of the Alberta Land Titles Act, "to prohibit caveats
on unpatented Crown land."[20] The Land Titles Act was then retroactively applied to a point in time prior to the Lubicon Cree's attempt to register their
caveat. Never before in the history of Government-Indian relations in North
America had a government enacted retroactive legislation in order to block the
course of justice. Clearly, this action left little doubt regarding the provincial
government's ability to utilize its so-called "fiduciary" responsibility[21] as a tool
to maintain a colonial control over Indigenous people and alienate them not just

from their inherent rights, but also from rights that should normally have been granted them as "human beings."

In examining the history of the relationship between Anglo-European governments as colonizer and Indigenous peoples as colonized, an emergent pattern has shown that the colonizing governments have historically done more than merely subject Indigenous North Americans to the values, standards, and laws of its culture. In the course of extending dominion over North America, governments have tried to remold Native culture to fit an image of Anglo-European culture and have manipulated laws in order to bring about the assimilation and subjugation of Indigenous North Americans. While most people would like to believe that this is past history, in June 2000 Alaska's Senator Ted Stevens introduced legislation that sought to end tribal sovereignty for 23 tribal groups in that state. Then, during the spring of 2001, Montana's Senator Max Baucus circulated an e-mail affirming that Washington state's Republican Party had voted for a resolution supporting the abolishment of tribal governments. Such acts clearly illustrate that the threat to Indigenous sovereignty continues to reach beyond the state level. Although the Canadian government has used the Indian Act as a tool to suppress Indigenous sovereignty, the American government imposed blood quantum standards to define who is "Indian" and to limit Indigenous sovereignty. This is particularly significant because the governments of these two countries do not impose qualifying standards to define who represents eligible members of any other culture or ethnic group. Without exception these governments have claimed the exclusive power to do this for only one people: Indigenous North Americans. This is made obvious through legislation such as the Enfranchisement Act of 1869 in Canada, which "stipulated that an Indian woman who married a non-Indian male would, along with her offspring, no longer be considered Indian,"[22] and the Federal Acknowledgment Program in the United States.

In over 200 years of colonization, governments in North America have steadily worked toward the assimilation, which transmutes to eradication, of Indigenous cultures into that of mainstream American society. Today, though Indigenous people drive cars and work in a vast array of professional positions, Indigenous languages in North America remain a constant reminder and symbol of Indigenous peoples' identity. More than anything else it is due to this reality, the role languages play in shaping peoples' identity, that Indigenous people must ultimately embrace the significance of language as a political force de resistance.

The Shaping Force of Language

Prior to the birth of the United Nations, language did more than symbolize who a people were. It also played a significant role in defining nations. This is most easily made evident by looking at the names of numerous people, languages, and nations. For example, the Chinese speak Chinese and comprise the nation of China; the French speak French and comprise the nation of France; the Germans speak German and comprise the nation of Germany; the Spanish speak

Spanish and comprise the nation of Spain. But language goes far beyond this symbolic reference to a people and their nation. Language also plays a major role in shaping how a people make sense of and give meaning to the world in which they live. This is known as the linguistic relativity hypothesis, of which Edward Sapir and Benjamin Whorf were the earliest proponents. Edward Sapir noted:

> It is quite an illusion to imagine that one adjusts to reality essentially without the use of language and that language is merely an incidental means of solving specific problems of communication or reflection. The fact of the matter is that the "real world" is to a large extent built up on the language habits of the group . . . The worlds in which different societies live are distinct worlds, not merely the same world with different labels attached.[23]

In *Flutes of Fire*, Leanne Hinton gives examples of how the language habits of a group helped to shape their world with her discussion of Wintu "evidential suffixes." These suffix endings clue the listener with regard to how the speaker came by the evidence for something claimed. For instance, if something is logically deduced through a body of evidence, a suffix ending "re" is added to the appropriate verb. If something was perceived through the sense of taste or hearing, the appropriate verb would take the suffix ending "nte." If something was hearsay because it was heard from another, the speaker's claim would have to reflect a suffix ending "ke." "Thus, any statement a Wintu speaker makes must bear with it the evidence for the speaker's claim . . ."[24] Imagine how law and history would have been shaped if the English language were guided by the reality of such linguistic rules. Hinton states that many verb suffix endings exist in Wintu that do not easily find translations in English. One suffix ending is used to denote a relationship of great intimacy. Under such conditions, to state in Wintu, "My child is ill," would be translated in English as "I am ill in respect to my child." While this at first glance might seem peculiarly phrased, it is no less peculiar than an English speaker telling a friend, "I am parked not far from here," while the two walk to a car that is the actual thing that is parked close by. Other examples given reveal that a Wintu speaker could not state such phrases as "The chief ruled over the people"; "I have a brother"; "She took the baby"; and "Her dress was striped"; but instead must declare, "The chief stood with the people"; "I am brothered"; "She went with the baby"; and "She is dress striped." These examples illustrate a linguistically accepted fact that each language encodes within it a unique worldview perspective, giving speakers of different languages a culturally distinct way of perceiving and relating to the world around them. To further illustrate this, and how it is linked to a culture's identity, I will draw upon examples from three different culture groups.

The Apache of Cibecue, Arizona, express that their stories stalk their minds in such a way as to make an individual think about his or her life.

> Even if you go far away . . . to some big city, places around here keep stalking us. If you live wrong, you will hear the names and see the places in your mind. They keep on stalking you even if you go across the ocean. They make you remember how to live right, so you want to replace yourself again.[25]

Ndee dah naazííh, a place that fits this role, communicates an above-ground level where Apache men stood as lookouts to guard against surprise attacks.

One story connected to this place tells of an Apache policeman who arrested another Apache man at ndee dah naazííh for killing a white man's cow when he was off the reservation. Twice he took the man to the army fort and each time became confused in his mind and didn't report what the man with him had done. The Apache policeman finally released the man at ndee dah naazííh. The story reminds Apache what can happen if they act too much like white men. What Apache attach to this story is a time of confinement, disease, and hunger. While Apache may not consider it wrong to kill a white man's cow under these conditions, it is also viewed as improper for an Apache to act against members of their own community.

In *Wisdom Sits in Places,* Basso relates that historical tales, in addition to what they say about places, events, morals, or concepts of cultural identity, also carry a message for the person at whom they are directed. Some Apache say that these stories are like arrows causing those they hit to replace themselves: a metaphor for healing. In this regard Basso related an event in which a young girl had returned from a boarding school and attended a girl's puberty ceremony wearing pink hair rollers. A few weeks after, she showed up at a birthday party and, when her grandmother told the story of ndee dah naazííh, she took the story to heart and left. When Basso asked the grandmother if her granddaughter had become ill, she replied that she had shot her granddaughter with an arrow. Years later Basso had an opportunity to speak to the girl about the story. When he pointed to ndee dah naazííh, she replied in her own language: "I know that place. It stalks me every day."[26] Arapaho stories can have a similar effect.

In an Arapaho story, "Notkoniihii" (The Scout), U.S. army soldiers chase an Arapaho scout.

Tih yih'ooneit nuhu' beniiinenno'	When the soldiers chased him,
hoowuhceht noh he'ih bee3ih'ee	he got off and blessed
hitonih'ohi'iihi' biito'owu'.	his horse with earth.
Tihcooowuunoot hitonih'o	When he smudged his horse
nooxeihi nih'ee'ino' noh	maybe he knew it and
nihnoho'nihi'koohut nuhu' hoxtoonou.	he ran up this cliff
'Oh nuhu' beniiinenno'	But those soldiers
tihbeet noho'nihi'koohu3i',	wanted to run up,
hoowu'hou'uhuno' hoxtoonou'.	they couldn't get up the cliff.

Although this is only a small part of the story, it tells me that if you stay true to Arapaho ways, they will take care of you. In a fashion like that of Apache stories, Notkoniihii stalks me.

A different example of how language shapes one's world can be drawn from Africa. In Africa are a people called the Nuer. Historically they are a pastoral people who herd cattle. British anthropologist Evans-Pritchard states the fact that the Nuer language has hundreds of terms that relate to cattle is indicative of the economic importance of cattle to the Nuer as a pastoralist people.[27] Nuer social relationships are defined in terms of cattle so that ties of marriage past, present, and future are directly equated with the payment of cattle from one family to another. The cultural significance of cattle can be demonstrated in other ways. Ballads are composed and sung in praise of cattle. Cattle terminology is extensively used in names and titles of address. Girls, boys, women, and men have ox-names. These names were used for many different occasions: at dances, among friends; also an individual would traditionally shout out his ox-name when attacking an enemy or animal when hunting. Cattle are also given social importance, through their ability to link the living and the dead when sacrificed to ghosts of the dead, and by rendering them ceremonial significance.[28] In one such ceremony, the neck of certain bulls would be punctured. The blood would be mixed with soured milk, which the Nuer drank. Given the nature of this ceremony, one would not expect strangers from outside of Nuer culture to eagerly want to drink a mixture of soured milk and bull blood.

Another example can be drawn from the plains of North America. Among the Arapaho there is a mixture called bee'eek, which describes blood gravy. The old people who talk about the preparation of bee'eek tell how the blood of an animal, like an antelope or a buffalo, would be mixed and cooked into a kind of broth, which would then be consumed. As in the case with the Nuer, it would be unusual to expect anyone from outside of Arapaho culture to eagerly volunteer to eat bee'eek if offered. For those who declined, the question asked was, Why would one not want to taste such a dish? There is another dish called bíinee'eek. *Bíinee'eek* is a composite word that comes from *bino* for a berry also called choke cherry, and *bee'eek*, or blood gravy. While teaching at the University of Alberta in Canada, I actually put a class in the situation of volunteering to taste biinee'eek. Given the opportunity to taste this dish, out of 28 individuals, only three volunteered! Of those who didn't volunteer, the question explored was why they were reluctant to taste it.

In examining the discussion about bee'eek and bíinee'eek, some members of the class were influenced by certain words that helped to shape their perception of what bee'eek might taste like. This led some people to associate bee'eek with the taste of blood. Their perception was further reinforced by my discussion of how bee'eek was prepared, using antelope or buffalo blood,[29] which in turn was associated with the prior description of the Nuer drinking a mixture of soured milk and blood from a bull. All of this helped to create a false impression of bíinee'eek, which in its finished form is actually a very sweet mixture of berries, with no blood. These examples only touch upon the complex subtleties embedded in the transmission of language and culture. To further illustrate this, within Indigenous people's languages, as with many other languages, there are words that carry more than one meaning. In Arapaho, for instance, to instruct someone to "give it to him" you would say "biinin." This, however, also means "eat him." The phrase "ciinóhwoo" can be interpreted as "pour it," but it also means "quit dancing." If I wanted to tell someone that "I have a cold," I would say "heníiseinoo," but if the person wasn't paying attention, that phrase could be understood as "He is afraid of me." These phrases, which are only a few of many, illustrate how lacking a fully developed understanding of Arapaho could result in misinterpretations, a theme that can be found in a number of traditional narratives among other Indigenous peoples.[30] In many Indigenous peoples' languages, there are numerous words and phrases that reflect multiple meanings. If our Indigenous languages become extinct, not only will these distinct forms of words and expressions die, but also the unique way that the cultures, as expressed through languages, ascribe meaning to the world.

Our ancestors were the product of the language and culture that was transmitted to them, a language and culture that they in turn transmitted to their children. Through the intervention of a foreign people with a different set of values and a culturally different way of viewing the world, the transmission of numerous Indigenous North American languages and cultural values has been and continues to be disrupted. The resulting effect of language loss has so weakened this process of transmission that the very existence of numerous Indigenous peoples' languages and cultures is now threatened with extinction. The pace of language loss has been staggering to the point that some have estimated that, for every animal species that becomes extinct, five Indigenous peoples' languages also die. It has also been stated that if the present rate of language loss continues, the world's 6,000 languages will be reduced to a few hundred over the next 200 years.[31] To relate how this would translate to North America, in the year 1980 it was estimated that there were approximately 279 languages still spoken in North America.[32] By the year 2030 this number may be less than 60. Clearly the future survival of Indigenous languages has reached a critical point.

The threat that Indigenous North Americans face today is one of our most serious and most challenging, that of keeping our languages from becoming extinct and, by so doing, preserving the essence of our cultures. To ensure that our Indigenous languages survive, Indigenous peoples must now empower themselves to meet the challenge of this responsibility while our Elders, who stand as custodians of our languages and cultures, are still here as resources.

It has been said that Elders from among different Indian communities spoke of a time when a person from the government will go to Indian communities to determine if they meet the government's standards that define who and what is Indian. In the face of governments that have historically sought to rid themselves of their "Indian problem," and have demonstrated a pattern of arbitrarily writing legislation to meet their own ulterior motives, the warnings of our Elders resound with the message that our languages may represent the strongest political reality to keep this Trickster at bay.

NOTES

1. See Wendall Oswalt and Sharlotte Neely, *This Land Was Theirs: A Study of North American Indians*, 5th ed. (California: Mayfield Pub. Co., 1996).
2. For more information on the royal proclamation see http://www.solon. org/Constitutions/Canada/English/PreConfederation/rp_1763.html.
3. Oswalt and Neely, *This Land Was Theirs*.

4. Sharon O'Brien, *American Indian Tribal Governments* (Norman: University of Oklahoma Press, 1993), p. 47.

5. I first discussed this analysis of Pontiac's Rebellion, its containment, and its eventual impact on the drafting of the Royal Proclamation in my doctoral dissertation, "Indigenous North Americans and the Ethnocentrism of the Courts: A Cross Analysis of American Culture and Law with Canadian Culture and Law" (Oklahoma University, 1992).

6. Ralph Chandler, Richard A. Enslen, and Peter G. Renstrom, "The Constitution of the United States," *The Constitutional Law Dictionary*, vol. 2: *Governmental Powers* (Oxford: Clio Press, 1987), p. 679.

7. See *The Cherokee Nation v. The State of Georgia*, 30 US (5 Pet., 1831). Making citations to this case can be a bit tricky because the pages of the report carry a different number at the top of the page from what is noted at the bottom of the page. On the pages themself, however, are numbers that follow a left bracket and an asterisk. Quotes have thus been cited according to these reference marks.

8. Ibid. at [*17.

9. The Canadian government distinguishes between four groups of aboriginal peoples: status or treaty, nonstatus or nontreaty, Inuit, and Metis.

10. See 30 US (5 Pet., 1831).

11. See Georgia Cession, April 26, 1802, in American State Papers: Public Lands 126 (Washington: Gales and Seaton, 1832).

12. *Cherokee Nation v. The State of Georgia*, 30 US (5 Peters, 1831) at [*17. The Court was actually split: On the issue of jurisdiction four to two stood against the Cherokee; on the merits, which could not officially be addressed, four to two in favor of the Cherokee cause. Burke (1969) has also drawn attention to the fact that Marshall, although ostensibly speaking for the Court majority, was actually speaking only for himself and Justice McLean.

13. See *Worcester v. Georgia*, 31 U.S. (6 Peters, 1832). The message of Governor Wilson Lumpkin was reported in the October 29th issue of the Nile's Weekly Register (1831) at 174, column I.

14. *Johnson and Graham's Lessee v. William McIntosh*, 21 US (8 Wheaton, 1823) at 587–588 [emphasis mine]. Nine years after the Johnson decision, Marshall's thoughts regarding the principle had radically altered and his decision in *Worcester v. Georgia* was supported in part by Marshall's strongly arguing against the discovery principle. See *Worcester v. The State of Georgia*. 31 US (6 Peters, 1832).

15. Indian Acts and Amendments, 1868–1950. Treaties and Historical Research Centre, Research Branch Corporate Policy, 2nd ed. Department of Indian and Northern Affairs, Canada, 1981.

16. See *The Indian Act: The Fact, The Fears, The Future: A Nation in Transition* (Ken Murch Productions: London, Ontario: Walpole Island First Nations, 1989).

17. In June 14, 2002, minister of Indian affairs and northern development, Robert Nault, introduced the First Nations Governance Act (FNGA). This legislation is purported to provide First Nations people with tools to bring

the Indian Act under review in the interest of greater self-reliance, economic development, and quality of life for First Nations people. The legislation, however, is a point of contention among Indigenous peoples in Canada.

18. See Re Paulette's Application to file a Caveat, 6, Western Weekly Reports (1973).

19. See *Paulette, et al.* v. *The Queen,* 2, Supreme Court Records (1977).

20. John Goddard, *Last Stand of the Lubicon Cree* (Vancouver: Douglas & McIntyre, 1991), p. 51.

21. Derived from Roman law, the term refers to a person or institution acting in the capacity of a trustee. See *Black's Law Dictionary* (1991).

22. James S. Frideres, *Native People in Canada* (Scarborough: Prentice-Hall Canada, 1983), p. 23.

23. Edward Sapir, as quoted in Benjamin Whorf, *Language, Thought and Reality* (New York: MIT Press, 1956), p. 134.

24. Leanne Hinton, *Flutes of Fire: Essays on California Indian Languages* (Berkeley: University of California Press, 1994), p. 66.

25. Keith Basso, *Wisdom Sits in Places* (New Mexico: University of New Mexico Press, 2000), p. 59.

26. Ibid., p. 57.

27. For information on the Nuer, see E. E. Evans-Pritchard, *Kinship and Marriage among the Nuer* (Oxford: Clarendon Press, 1990).

28. For a more detailed discussion of this, see Leanne Hinton (1994), p. 66.

29. Over the years I have conducted this exercise in a number of different classes. Students are always reluctant to taste this blood, rich-looking mixture, most often forgetting that the gravy they like to pour over their steaks is made from the blood of a cow.

30. For an example of this, see M. Barbeau, *Huron Wyondot Traditional Narratives* (Canada: The Queen's Printer, 1960), pp. 40–44.

31. See Jared Diamond, "Speaking with a Single Tongue" in *Discover,* ed. Jared Diamond (Chicago: 1993), also W. Wayt Gibbs, "Saving Dying Languages" in Scientific American, vol. 287 (2, 2002) pp. 78–85.

32. See James J. Bauman, *A Guide to the Issues in Indian Language Retention* (Washington, DC, 1980).

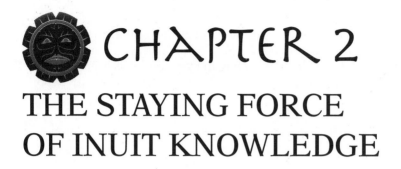

CHAPTER 2

THE STAYING FORCE
OF INUIT KNOWLEDGE

By Peter Irniq

Peter Irniq is an Inuit cultural teacher who has lived most of his life in the Kivalliq Region. Elected to the Territorial Council in 1975, Peter represented the riding of the Keewatin Region for four years. He was elected as the Minister for various Departments in the Government of the N.W.T., holding portfolios such as Social Development, Economic Development and Tourism and Natural and Cultural Affairs. He was the first Inuk to be made assistant regional director for the Department of the Executive in the Keewatin Region (1979–81). In 1992 he was made Executive Director of the Inuit Cultural Institute. In 1993 he became Director of Communications for Nunavut Tunngavik, Inc. Peter served on the Communication and Government Operations Committee and was often a spokesperson for the Commission on Nunavut in Canada and overseas. He was Assistant Director, Nunavut Heritage/Culture, Department of Education, Culture and Employment for the Government of the N.W.T., where he was responsible for developing culture and heritage programs and services to meet the needs of the new territory of Nunavut (1997–98). He became Deputy Minister of Culture, Language, Elders, and Youth (1998–99). His mandate was to be the guardian of traditional Inuit culture and language. In August 1999 Peter was seconded to the Legislative Assembly of Nunavut to set up the offices of the Official Languages, Access to Information, and Conflict of Interest Commissioners. He became Commissioner of Nunavut in April 2000.

Introduction

It is an honor that you should ask me to write a chapter about Inuit traditional knowledge. I am proud to help promote Inuit culture ways and I will tell you about the ways. I am a nomadic Inuk belonging to the Nattilikmiut (the people of the seal) and Ukkusiksalikmiun (the people from where the soap stone cooking pots can be found) ancestry, but I was born in the Aivilik (the people of the walrus) Region of Nunavut. I was taken away from home before I could fully live and understand my heritage. I am also the product of a Roman Catholic Residential School system, which is nothing new to the Aboriginal populations of the world. Assimilation was the main objective in attempting to have Inuit join the mainstream Canadian society, and they have largely succeeded!

I was kidnapped in broad daylight from my parents by a Roman Catholic priest in August 1958 so that I would go to the Turquetil Hall Residential School in Chesterfield Inlet. This is the place where I was slapped with the yardstick for speaking my language in the classroom and told "never to speak it again." Chesterfield Inlet is 250 miles south of my home, Repulse Bay. From a simple tent (12 feet by 14 feet) that slept five of us, I entered a huge three-story building for the first time in my life. Praying about 15 times a day to Jesus and reading about Dick and Jane were the orders of the day. But I did listen to what my mother and father taught me about Inuit life. I did learn about and live this life, and so I am here to tell you about it today. I have learned again to be proud of my heritage.

Inuit life, as it existed up to about 40 years ago, was a seasonal circle. We have lived this life for thousands of years. We visioned seasons. Our Inuit identity is meshed tightly with our language. We have one language with various regional dialectical differences.

Inuit are subsistence hunters and gatherers and thus have survived for many thousands of years in these difficult arctic conditions. We hunt to live and clothe ourselves. We gather vegetation, such as berries and seaweed, to supplement our diet during spring- and summertime. Since time immemorial we shared what we had with our fellow Inuit, and sharing was indeed the way. We are observers of land and waters, looking for animals and fish.

In the Circumpolar Region we are divided by international boundaries, boundaries that were not of our choosing but established by the Governments of the United States, Canada, Greenland, and the Soviet Union. The Government of Canada moved us, Canadian Inuit, into settlements in the 1960s, and much of our way of life began to disappear. Inuit became the wards of the Government of Canada. Inuit were relocated for sovereignty reasons, and social problems such as we had never before experienced began. We learned to depend on the Federal Government for social assistance.

We endured hard lives and were disciplined and committed to life. Depression was discouraged, so I laughed and smiled. I also learned that women played a much bigger role than men; not only did my mother sew all our clothes, but she was also our social worker. My father taught me how to be a successful hunter and how to sew when my clothes needed mending (especially sealskin boots) at a men's hunting camp. Today, I mend my children's clothes.

Hunting by the Circle of the Seasons

Let me begin by describing the fall activity, fishing. This activity receives the same attention as any other hunting activity, but it is the most fun thing to do. The early fall season, when it begins to freeze, is equally as exciting as the spring. This is when the puddles and small lakes begin to freeze, normally during the month of September—at least this is what it was like where I grew up in Nattiligaarjuk (Committee Bay) about 1,500 miles northwest of Winnipeg, Manitoba. Southern Canadians, Americans, and Europeans might call this place Tim-Buck-Two (Timbuktu), but this place provided food and a livelihood for my family. Seals provided much needed vitamin B, and birds and fish were our main diet; and by the summer, caribou were usually as close as one or two days' walk.

When ice formed in the lakes, we would fish for arctic char through the ice by making holes. My father, a very knowledgeable person (born perhaps in 1900 and died 1971), would direct the family to travel on foot to the good fishing spots, normally to those lakes connected by rivers to the sea. August was a good time to fish because the char had swum back upstream to spend the winter in the lakes where we would fish. Char, a delicacy to Inuit, was a welcomed diet change after our living on caribou meat for a couple of months.

For fishing tools my father carved Iqaluujat. These are small imitation fish made out of ivory tusks or caribou antlers. They are tied with a piece of thin string made out of caribou sinew and are sunk just below the ice, and the fishermen or fisherwomen jigs as they would with a regular fishhook. Iqaluujat, made to look like little fish, are called fish inviters. The difference is that they have no hook, but the fisherperson continually watches for the fish to arrive. Once the fish came to check the iqaluujaq (singular), then the fisherperson would spear the fish with a kakivaak (leister), normally made out of muskox horns, or caribou antlers when muskox horns were not available. This technique required a great deal of skill, because one had to spear the fish and know its distance from the surface of the ice to the location of the Iqaluujaq-imitation fish. Fish could come one by one or by the hundreds. When they came by the hundreds, it got confusing as to which fish to spear because they came in all sizes. The technique also required patience.

After the fish had completed their swim upstream, Inuit would then return inland, in search of caribou. Fall was a good time for caribou hunting. This was the time to obtain meat to cache for the winter months (age the meat) and skins for clothing. The hair on the caribou at this time is just right for making good clothing for the family members. It was not too thin nor too thick to sew for clothing. The caribou bulls, in particular, have plenty of fat at this time. The fat was (and still is) a good supplement for the meat we ate, but because we obviously had no electricity, we used the fat to light our tents in the evenings when the days were once again shorter. We also used the light that we had to heat our little dwellings. Not long ago I chewed a piece of fat, got rid of all the moisture and blood, made a wick out of ordinary material, then lit it. My children, who were born into the 20th century, were amazed at what I was able to do. That is how I lived in my time, a matter of 40 years ago. We also used to mix the fat with berries, and it was tasty to eat.

Caribou meat was cached to preserve it for eating during the long winter (November–March). Caching meat needed to be done properly. We would position small rocks, normally flat ones, and then pile the bigger rocks on top of each other on the meat. This prevents animals such as foxes, mice, weasels, and wolverines from "stealing the meat." Wolverines, besides being vicious, are strong and able to remove the rocks from the cached meat. By preserving meat this way, our families and dogs would have enough food to last until early spring (March). We used our dogs to pull our Qamutik (sleds); they had to be well fed in order to have sufficient strength to pull. In those days we simply could not do without them. During certain parts of the season, we came close to going hungry if no game (wildlife) was around. Even though this was a time when starvation could occur within Inuit homelands, we always strived to survive.

When the days got short in winter (December, January, and February), there was hardly any hunting activity, except for occasional caribou hunts. Being inside a small iglu (European spelling, igloo) for an extended period of time was at times lonesome and frustrating. People played games and sang traditional Inuit songs. Inuit songs were composed by hunters telling their experiences of hardships. They told about how families almost came to starvation and how lucky a hunter felt when he saw a caribou or other animal and knew he will be able to continue living.

In spring, with the arrival of longer days in March and April, it became necessary to hunt seals through the seal holes on the sea ice. This was very difficult work, because we had to wait for seals to come up while other hunters looked for seal holes with sniffing dogs, because all holes were covered with lots of snow. When the hunter caught a seal, it meant that we would have fresh meat for ourselves and for our dogs, a very welcome event. This hunt lasted for about two months. When the seal was brought home to an iglu, my mother would chip a small piece of fresh water ice (unsalted) and place it into the mouth of the seal. This was a message to all seals under the ice so that they would not be thirsty.

Another seal hunt took place in late May and during the month of June. This exercise was hunting for young adult seals that were born in March, no longer white coats but called "silver jars." Seals grow fast, and these seals were hunted through the seal holes as well and traded with the Hudson's Bay Company, a trading company that sold very essential items such as flour, biscuits, sugar, tea, and tobacco.

During the month of May, Inuit dried their caribou meat. Dried meat was also saved for the winter season. In the 1990s it was still a normal practice for Inuit to go out to their spring cabins or hunting and fishing camps and dry caribou meat. This meat had been harvested earlier in the spring for the purpose of drying.

Other important events that continue to provide Inuit with happiness are the return in the spring of the migratory birds such as geese, ducks, and other birds. At this time the snow has melted and the days become longer. This means fewer problems such as depression and loneliness exist. We used to take long walks, looking and observing. At times we would get a pleasant surprise by finding bird eggs. People smiled at each other, a sign of good friendship among fellow countrymen.

We welcomed June and July, summer, with great excitement. This was because the rivers were all flowing and the fish (arctic char) were swimming downstream again to spend time in the salt water for the next two months. These two months saw Inuit drying their fish catch. How I used to enjoy eating dried fish as a child, and I still do. Today my daughter shares my love of traditionally prepared foods.

The month of July saw the arrival of the mosquitoes! We did not have mosquito repellents in those days. My mother, for reasons unknown to me, would buy perfume and put the perfume on my head. It did not help any with the bugs, but my hair smelled good! In those days we used to burn moss to try to keep the mosquitoes away. Smoke did help to keep them away, but I always felt sorry for our poor husky dogs, which would lose the hair around their eyes and ears from being eaten by mosquitoes. Caribou lost their fat from continually having to run from the nasty little bugs. We stayed indoors a lot, but it was a nice welcome break when the stronger winds came and drove the mosquitoes away. Inuit are terrified of bugs. Each time they arrived, especially the Iguttat (bumblebees), we used to run away frightened. Whether the bugs are big or small, most of our children, even today, are extremely terrified of various bugs. Inuit named their people after various parts of the body and after animals. Iguttaq (singular for bumblebee) is a popular name. When my sister died over 16 years ago in the spring, my uncle (my father's younger brother) and his wife were fishing. He said that an "iguttaq" was flying around persistently where they were fishing. A few days later they heard that my sister had died. I knew she was dying of cancer, but the day after she died, a bumblebee came flying around near me while I was vacationing thousands of miles away in southern Canada. Perhaps this was a spiritual message. Our daughter, who is now 14 years old, is named Iguttaq after my sister.

Inuit Naming

Traditional Inuit naming is an important element of Inuit heritage. Traditional naming is over 10,000 years old as a custom of the Inuit within the Circumpolar Region. In some cases naming was planned prior to the birth of a child. Normally the Elders, the parents, or the in-laws planned the naming of an unborn child. Children were named after relatives, friends of the family, heroes, parts of the body, animals, things like wood, spirits according to our spiritual beliefs, and the stars. Every name had a purpose. For example, if a child was named after a successful individual, that child had to be as good as or better than the person he or she was named after.

Some children were named after individuals who had died, to carry on that person's life. For example, my grandfather, Ivaluqut Ipuittuq, lived in our family three times through his name: first through my older brother, who was born around 1938 and died at the age of 12 or 13; then through my adopted brother who died in 1968; and finally through my other adopted brother who, when he was born in 1969, my mother also named after my grandfather. This indicates to me that my mother not only made all the decisions to name my brothers after her father but that she dearly loved him. When I took my brother and son to Gjoa Haven a few years ago, my mother's younger sisters called Isaia their Ataata (father). Not only that, each one of my three aunts and two uncles (my mother's younger brothers) had named one of their children after my grandfather. This tells me that my grandfather was very much loved and very much respected. I believe my grandfather died in 1947. Each time my brother or my son comes to visit us, I am reminded of him and yet I only knew him from my mother's stories.

When children are named after someone, such as my grandfather, they are forever treated with respect. An Elder may request that none of the children be named after him or her for a certain period of time. Some were given additional names to protect them from bad spirits. Some were named after body parts such as Taliriktuq (one whose arm is strong); animals, as in Amaruq (wolf), Nauja (sea gull), or many others; or some were named after spirits such as Ijiraq (the caribou-like spirit). Some shamans had Ijiraq as their spirit because Ijiraq was able to provide caribou for hunters. Some were named after Nuliajuk, the half-woman, half-fish sea spirit. Nuliajuk has several other names, such as Taliivla-juuq. Mostly Nattilikmiun or Nattilik descendants named their children after Nuliajuk. As you can surmise, naming played a significant role in our Inuit culture. Naming was and still is an important aspect for Inuit heritage.

Custom adoption also continues to be a major part of Inuit life. Custom adoption is an arrangement originally made by the Elders, whereby grandparents made their decision to have their first grandchild adopted. Sometimes couples who could not have any children adopted children several times in their lives. Some parents may want to give a child away to a responsible couple. In recent years two children were given to us for adoption: one a little boy and the other a little girl. This custom is recognized by the laws of the Northwest Territories Government, and most times courts merely legalize the adoption through the legal system.

Inuksuit: Telling Stories of Inuit Place

Another very important part of Inuit culture and lifestyle are Inuksuit, rocks piled on top of each other to imitate an Inuit. They stand tall on the land and they are built to be noticed. They tell a story of where Inuit have been. Inuksuit are built by men telling generations of people about where the game is, where fishing spots are, or where Inuit used to live.

Inuit have been building Inuksuit (plural of one Inuksuk; two Inuksuuk; and *Inuksuit* refers to more than three) for thousands of years within our Inuit homelands and no doubt will build more Inuksuit in the years to come. Inuit have also marked their travels outside of their homelands with Inuksuit. Around lakes where Inuit fished, normally two or three small Inuksuit are built and point towards the lake, telling those who fish there where the good fishing spots are. My father was an experienced hunter and fisherman, and he used to build a few of them in and near Naujaat–Repulse Bay, the community where I grew up. He used to build ordinary Inuksuit mostly to mark for others where his caribou cache was or simply to indicate where we used to hunt and camp so that other Inuit hunters and their families would know that my family was there. I have many fond memories of those Inuksuit and often picture them as though they were built only a day ago.

Some Inuksuit have special names. When Inuit lived semipermanently in a hunting camp, they would build big, tall, towering Inuksuit, which our Aivilik and Nattilik tribes referred to as Sakamaktat or Sakamaksimajut. They were built to put meat on top so that animals, including our sled dogs, didn't get at the meat or eat it. Dog harnesses and caribou skins were also placed on the top of these Sakamaktat so that they, too, would not be eaten. In those days meat to eat for human consumption was always scarce, so everyone had to save food as much as possible. Dried caribou meat, for example, was placed on top of Sakamaktat.

Inuit named places using Inuksuk names as well. About eight miles to the northeast of Naujaat is a place called Inuksulik (a place that has Inuksuit). It is a place where Inuit have lived for many, many thousands of years, most likely because it is close to the seals and other marine mammals. It is also a scenic point, beautiful to arrive at and beautiful to spend several days camping at. When I was still a young man living in Naujaat, my family used to live there often, mostly for the spring sealing. Some people are named after Inuksuit. My uncle's name was Inuksuk. He was my mother's older brother. Many people in Nunavut are named after Inuksuit. It is a very famous name.

Over the course of many years while travelling through the tundra, I have built some Inuksuit. One May while travelling to Naujaat with my son, Ted, and Paul Sannertanut and his son Jobie, we built several Inuksuit along the west coast of Hudson Bay. We built these trail markers for others to see in the future. If and when they travel along the coast of Ukkusiksalik (Wager Bay), I would like them to know that someone such as myself has traveled these big lands in previous times, and I want them to know that they are not in the middle of nowhere. From there, they can figure out where to find different directions, especially leading towards Naujaat or Kangiqliniq.

One summer, while vacationing in the Lake of the Woods along Highway 17 between Kenora and slightly beyond Sioux Narrow, I noticed that someone had recently built a lot of Inuksuit. These Inuksuit were built for travelers to see and for travelers to wonder about. I also built an Inuksuk to indicate that I had traveled this highway and wished to mark my way. I admit, however, that to see Inuksuit in the south surrounded by tall trees is a little bit unusual and looks a bit out of place. Nevertheless, they promote the Inuit way of life in Inuit homelands in the Arctic.

Inuksuit tell a history about where Inuit have been. They have been there for many, many thousands of years. They are the information signs on the unmarked trail along the tundra and on top of hills and mountains. I figure some are 10,000 years old, if not more. Many are covered with lichens. That is how I am able to tell that they are very old. Traditionally, Inuksuit did not have arms or legs. I think it is because of the European influence that some people started to make Inuksuit with arms, more or less for effect.

As far as I can remember, my mother used to tell me not to knock down Inuksuit, because they were made many, many thousands of years ago. And, more importantly, she said that if I knocked down Inuksuit, my death might come sooner. Whenever I travel within my homeland, I treat the Inuksuit with respect.

Traditional Healing

In traditional times there were strong spiritual beliefs and with those beliefs good health was promoted. When I was growing up near Repulse Bay (1,300 miles north of Winnipeg, Manitoba), whenever we got sick, my mother was the one who counseled us to heal. Short-term illnesses such as headaches were perhaps something that came and would disappear in a day or less. When people had headaches, they would tie a band around their heads. Another simple medical solution was scraping a thin layer of skin from a caribou skin and placing it around a cut area, normally on your fingers. Whenever we had a major problem of diarrhea, we were told to swallow dried-up moss. This would absorb whatever was causing our stomach problems. With other problems such as boils, a mouse skin was placed on top of the affected area. Whatever was causing the problem of the boil, the mouse skin would suck out the root, the Inuk (the life of the sickness). It seemed to work each time.

Another traditional medicine cure was used when a person was drowning. After being pulled out, he was placed on his stomach and pressed down to get him to start vomiting water. The victims were sometimes placed on their back, and pressure was put on their stomach and air blown through the mouth into their lungs. Then they would start to make air bubbles. It is said that no person should wipe the air bubbles; otherwise the victim would die. In 1968 while my parents were still living a traditional life, my little brother, who was 12 years old at the time, fell in the water. He was pulled out and a similar technique was performed, but my mother was feeling both guilty and sorry for the little boy; she wiped the bubbles that were coming out of his mouth and he ended up dying.

Skin problems occurred especially during the springtime when people were spending a lot of time outdoors. Caribou fat, seal fat, or fish oil was used whenever there was a skin problem on the hands or face. Traditionally it was said that fish oil was the best treatment for skin rashes. Oils were also used as suntan lotions to protect against burns in the spring.

We also asked for help to heal from the spirits. These spirits may not have long been dead, and normally they were spirits related to us. By asking for help from the spirits, we would try to determine the cause of the problem, in this case perhaps sickness. I remember one technique used in obtaining help from the spirits called qilajuq. This technique involved either the lifting of a rock, which was most common, or the person's head or leg. I observed this technique, whereby a shaman tied a sealskin rope around a small rock, perhaps 10 inches by 12 inches; then the shaman would start to lift the rock up and down on the caribou skin. The room had to be darkened; perhaps it was easier for spirits to come.

By lifting the rock or a person's head, the shaman or anyone in the room could begin asking questions of the spirits that belonged to the shaman. "Are you the good one?" "Are you the backward one?" Then if the answer is yes, the rock would be very hard to lift, as though it were stuck on the skin. If the answer is no, then the object would be very easy to lift; after all it is only 10 inches by 12 inches, or the size of the person's head. If it is a good spirit, then it was asked why the person was so sick or, better yet, who was making him or her sick. When the cause of the sickness was known, a person who was ill seemed to start healing in the next day or two. It seemed to work.

Another way to get rid of the evil spirits was with shamanism or magical songs, called sakausiit in Inuktitut language. A shaman, normally by placing a symbol around his head or his waist, would begin to sing a magical or shamanistic song. This symbol was sort of a belt with various parts of an animal body (e.g., animal teeth or miniature carvings sewn onto it) and was placed around the shaman's head or waist. He or she would begin to sing to determine where or who the evil spirits were in the outer surroundings. Once they had figured out who the evil spirits were, they would drive them out using their own spirits. Whether this technique was used to cure the sick or to determine why there were no animals to harvest, it worked. Sometimes when a shaman was singing a song, he or she at some point would get very excited, as though someone had taken over his or her inner feelings. I sometimes observed Pentecostal or Glad Tiding churchgoers do almost the same thing, perhaps praying to a similar God.

When I was in the Repulse Bay area, I became aware of several magical songs. I used to think they only belonged to my brother-in-law, who was a shaman; but in recent years, living in Rankin Inlet, I have found out these same magical songs were sung the same way by the shamans who lived in this region. I think similar tribes were aware of the same magical songs as long as they interrelated with one another, as was the case with the Aivilikmiut or Nattilikmiut tribes or the people of Repulse Bay area and those of Pelly Bay Region, which is to the west of Repulse Bay. In many cases, these magical songs are no longer sung publicly, because they were discouraged by the Roman Catholic and Anglican missionaries when they first came here. More recent religious organizations, such as Glad Tidings and Pentecostals, certainly do not recognize the ancestral cultures such as the spiritual beliefs. Spiritual or magical songs are sung with the words "alianait, alianait" which means "joy, joy"—the same as those Christian songs such as "Joy to the World" or "Joyful, Joyful." One thing I can never understand is why Christian churches worked so hard to promote that these Inuit magical or spiritual songs were the songs of the devil, and yet they, like the Christian songs, are versed with joy. I always felt and still do that shamanism was good for the outer souls and certainly helped to keep us cured and to find animals.

Traditional Songs

I like to sing, and I sing traditional Inuit songs. When I was growing up in Nattiligaarjuk (Committee Bay), from the time that I can remember, my parents and my brother-in-law sang songs inside our dwellings, and sometimes while we were traveling by dog teams. My sister, also a good singer, did not sing as much as my parents and my brother-in-law. They were all fond of singing. Their singing made me feel that there was happiness and feelings of joy and, most of all, entertainment.

My mother, Irene Katak, sang while she was jigging for fish on the ice, whereas my father, Athanasie Angutitaq, sang early in the mornings, especially when we were in an overnighter. He also sang in our tent, or iglu, when we didn't have anything to do. Listening to him sing was pleasant and a good pastime. I remember when we hunted seal by dog team, especially in the spring, that my brother-in-law used to start singing songs when we were approaching the seals. When he started singing, the dogs would begin to run faster; and it seemed the seals would enjoy listening to the songs because they got so close. That was when one of us would jump off the qamutik and shoot the seals. Although singing seemed to make it easier to catch an animal, we didn't sing songs to others animals such as caribou and birds, for they would run away when they heard us.

There are two kinds of Inuit songs that I would like to describe. One was the hunters' song and the other was a rivalry song. Rivalry was a challenging song whereby two enemies would insult each other through their songs. I remember my father telling stories about why Inuit made such songs for each other. It is said that one individual would have had to make the first move to insult his enemy, perhaps because the other might have talked about him and started a rumor about him by telling people things like: "The other guy was a womanizer, poor hunter, etc."

Hunters' songs belonged to individuals. One should keep in mind that Inuit songs were a way of telling the other people of different things that happened to oneself. They were about love, near starvation, sadness, and success. One thing I know about being an Inuk is that we never promote ourselves as being "good" in our songs. Inuit songs can best be interpreted as almost a put-down of oneself. At the same time they are about success when everything seemed impossible. For example, there are two verses that can be translated this way from one of my father's songs: "In the land of Nivvaavik, I noticed the food (caribou) running away; how sorry I was. Aijaa, when I was in the east of Kiglavannguit, I again saw the ones with big antlers; how happy I became. Because I could not sight the one that makes a big noise (rifle), I could not catch the caribou." In telling the story, my father said that he did in fact catch the herd of 20 or so, but in his song he literally put himself down as a poor hunter.

Inuit also sang songs while in the Qalgiq (big iglu) for the drummer. I can still remember in Naujaat–Repulse Bay where the crowd gathered at the mission hall during Christmas festivities and women started to sing and the men started to drum dance one after the other. My father was one of those who danced. My mother sang for him while he beat the drum. I can still hear her sing and I still picture my father dancing with great rhythm. It excites me just thinking of them. I still attend drum dances in many parts of the Arctic. I sometimes dance and people still sing, mostly the Elders. Over the years missionaries discouraged Inuit from drum dancing because they said it was shamanistic. Inuit do not see it that way but as an entertainment and enlightenment.

These days more and more people are drum dancing again, especially the youth. I think this is the right thing to do, so I have taught my 19-year-old son and my 14-year-old daughter how to drum and dance. I think it is a good idea for our youth to drum dance but, sadly, not many of them are singing the traditional songs. I think our youth are enjoying drum dancing. However, once our Elders have disappeared, we are concerned about who is going to sing for the drum dancer.

Inuit Legends

Elders sometimes used to like to tell Inuit legends, as they still do on the local radio station and during television interviews on local TV. These legends have been passed on from generation to generation. From an early age Inuit children were taught to listen, and I used to like to listen to legends of Kiviuq, a hero in Inuit legends who is like Peter Pan or Cinderella to the Canadian and American kids.

When I was a young boy growing up in Aivilik–Repulse Bay region, I experienced and learned many things that my parents taught me relating to my culture. I learned of the myths, taboos, legends, and life within the outer world and the spiritual world. I have forgotten a lot of it, although I still hold a small portion of it and I try to tell it as closely as I can remember.

I was taught about a huge person named Amajuqjuk, who had a big pouch on his back and was able to put adults in this amauti and take them away. My father often liked to talk about seeing one, I believe in the Nattilik region, when he lived there as a young man. There was Nuliajuk, half woman and half fish, whose tail resembled the beluga tail. Nuliajuk was a sea spirit who drove seals away from under the ice. As a result hunters could not catch any more seals while hunting through their holes in the winter until Nuliajuk was driven away by a shaman. I believe the European version of this is Sedna, their sea goddess.

There was Inukpasukjuk, a giant, who left his mark in many parts of the arctic. My mother used to talk about his big footprints, and she said that when he was carrying two huge rocks on his back, which he was going to use for pillows, he went through the soft moss nearly falling and made two great big footprints. My aunts who live in Gjoa Haven say that even today you can still see these big footprints in the Itimnaarruk region (Chantery Inlet near Back River).

Other stories that I have heard include Inugaruligasukjuk (little big giant) and Inugarullikkat (tiny little people). In recent times people of Cambridge Bay talked about seeing them near their garbage dump.

Then there was Qallupilluq, a spirit feared by the Inuit of Nattilik and Aivilik. When my family and I lived in Nattiligaarjuk (50 miles west of Naujaat–Repulse Bay), and when we lived in different areas around Repulse Bay, my sister and I used to go looking for scorpion fish, little ugly fish with horns, called kanajuit in Inuktitut. We did this in the summertime, when the tide was low. Sometimes I would go with my mother, who watched over me. We used to look for these kanajuit out of enjoyment, and my father used to particularly like the kanajuq broth. He said it tasted good. I remember close encounters with Qallupilluit when I looked for scorpions with Simon Aglak, who now lives in Rankin Inlet. That was in Kuugaarjuk about 30 miles east of Naujaat–Repulse Bay. As it usually does every summer, broken pieces of ice drifted in to Kuugaarjuk. I remember there was not a lot of ice, but the two of us went down to the shore when it became low tide. We would lift the rocks in the puddles, looking for kanajuit. We each carried a pail. At one point we got quite close to a large piece of ice and, all of sudden, Qallupilluq started to pound from underneath the ice. We ran home to our tents and my mother told us not to go down to the shore again in case the Qallupilluq came after us.

An Elder, whose name is very well known to the people of Nunavut, Mariano Aupilardjuk, said this about Qallupillut: "As a child, I used to be scared of the Qallupilluq [singular of *Qallupilluluuk*; *Qallupilluit* or *Qallupillut* is three or more]. Our mother and father used to tell us not to spend too much time around the shores. This was in case Qallupilluq came after us. Qallupilluit dressed in eider duck feathers and had different sounds to them."

Aupilardjuk said that Qallupillut normally live among the old pieces of ice. I suppose that is why we used to hear them knocking around the old ice when the ice would drift back to Naujaat each summer. We used to hear them a lot in Nattiligaarjuk because Committee Bay is full of old ice that moves back and forth, especially northwest to east because of the westerly prevailing winds.

"My father used to tell me," Aupilardjuk said to me, "that if you harpoon or shoot a Qallupilluq, you turn your head away from it and make a wish for a certain sea mammal. If you wish for a walrus, whale, or another animal, then you could catch what you wished for the next day."

Conclusion

Today we have many alcohol and drug problems, causing our youth to kill themselves. We have the highest suicide rate on a per capita basis in Canada. We are trying to do something about it by involving more people. We are trying to rediscover the old values and apply them to today to ensure that our lives continue blending the best of the old and the new.

In 1993 Inuit signed a Nunavut (Our Land) Land Claims Agreement with the Government of Canada. As part of the Agreement, a new Territory known as Nunavut (Our Land) Territory was created. This Agreement now allows Inuit to be equal partners in developing and governing our homelands. It means we will receive royalties through the development of our lands from the developers themselves. Inuit today hold many political offices, especially at the Legislative Assembly (Territorial) level. We have had three Inuit Members of Parliament in Ottawa, representing us in the riding of Nunatsiaq (Beautiful Land) Riding. No doubt this will continue to be so for many years to come because the majority of the Nunavut population is Inuit.

While shaping the Government of Nunavut, we Inuit still speak our language. It has been noticed, though, that changes have taken place in our language in recent years. The dialectical differences are disappearing and the Inuktitut language is becoming one language. Our language is a living language. New words are being developed to handle modern concepts and possessions, and, as life changes, the old concepts are used less and therefore put aside. The language that was spoken when I was growing up 40 years ago is changing and evolving. Our culture as well is evolving, and it is still there.

We still continue to complete the seasonal circle, but do so by traveling with all-terrain vehicles in summertime and snowmobiles in the winter. We, of course, do not live in iglus (igloos) anymore, and I have retrofitted two houses in Rankin Inlet since moving here in 1979. We travel by air to meetings between communities and to Ottawa to find out what the Federal Government is thinking about and planning.

Modern technology allows us to know what is going on in many parts of the world. I would think that we northerners know more about what is going on in the Senate and Congress of the United States or the Parliament of Canada or the European Community than they know about us and our existence. We even do some videoconferencing to decide where and what to do next about training programs for Inuit and non-Inuit residents alike.

Yes, I am thousands of years old but 54 years in the 21st century. Even though I am unable to provide the same kind of education to my children as my parents did for me to survive on Inuit homelands, I have tried hard to teach them about living off the land and about their Inuit culture. I have taught my children how to drum and dance. I lived and caught the end of the nomadic life and watch and live in the modern space age. I long once again to live in my little corner in Nattiligaarjuk, watching my parents laugh and joke, my mother and sister drying fish and caribou meat, my brother-in-law and I walking to look for caribou. It is only a memory now, but I still laugh and joke, only on the outside now, but I will greet you and I will still smile.

I thought it appropriate to try to record the Inuit culture as much as possible and share it with others. My friend Peter Ittinuar and I were having a discussion the other day, about the knowledge of living as traditional "Eskimo" Inuk. For my part I'm glad I lived and knew this way of life. I grew up watching my father using caribou bones and antlers as tools and always wanting to live on the land and off the land, by the sea and rivers to fish. He told me about the old ways, and my mother taught me the human values: sharing of things with others and being kind to others, especially those whose parents have died. In the recent past the descendants of the Europeans always tried to interpret and fantasize about our language and culture. I want to see more Inuit involve themselves in our rich history and our culture—our way. I think in this way it will show the staying force that keeps our Inuit culture alive.

CHAPTER 3

EUALEYAI: THE BLOOD THAT RUNS THROUGH MY VEINS

By Larissa Behrendt

Larissa Behrendt is a Professor of Law and Indigenous Studies at the University of Technology, Sydney, and the Director of the Jumbunna Indigenous House of Learning. She graduated from the University of New South Wales Law School in 1992 and has since graduated from Harvard Law School with her Masters and Doctorate. She has been admitted to the Australian Capital Territory Supreme Court as a barrister of law. Larissa has worked as a practicing lawyer in the areas of Aboriginal land claims and family law and has taught at the University of New South Wales and the Australian National University Law Schools. She has also spent time working in Canada and at the United Nations with First Nations organizations. Larissa has published on property law, Indigenous rights, dispute resolution, and Aboriginal women's issues. Among a growing list of publications is her book *Aboriginal Dispute Resolution* (1995).

Introduction

My father told me that he knew he was Aboriginal without being told. He would walk down a street or into a restaurant and if there was an Aboriginal person there, their eyes would meet. Something unsaid. Something understood. Something silent. A reinforcement of his identity.

Let me tell you about the first time I traveled to the place where my ancestors lived. I am an urban Aboriginal woman. I am Eualeyai. Our land is around the land that is now called Walgett and further up to what is now the Queensland border.

My father took me to meet an elder, Granny Green. She had known my grandmother. She would call my father "Lavina Boney's boy" or "Paul Boney," using the family name of his Aboriginal family rather than his father's German name. Granny, my father, and I traveled in my father's car out to a remote property that had once been a mission. We arrived and I remember waiting in the car and looking at Granny Green's hands, so dark and withered, as my father went to the white house and asked for permission to enter a land where we were born. We drove across the property. The landscape was dry. The grass was tall. There were trees and ditches. Granny knew where everything was. She would give directions to my father, who would faithfully follow them even though it meant driving his precious new car over dry creek beds and spiky shrubs. I suspect she knew how much pride he took in his oversized car and took the long roundabout route, taking full advantage of the fact that she was the only person in the world who could order him around in this manner. When we finally stopped, we got out at what seemed like just a clump of trees. Granny began to tell us where the families had lived. My father had already been taught this. This trip was for me.

"Here," she said, pointing to branches and grass. "Here is where Lavina used to live." The landscape changed, and I could hear deep voices in a language that I did not understand. I could hear the crackle of wood and the smell of smoke. We walked around this vanished world. Eventually we came to where the end of the camp was. There was a large tree that had large branches on it. "This is where Lavina and I would play," Granny said. "This spot here— this is where she was taken from."

The heat from Walgett is oppressive, especially for a woman who is used to air conditioning. But I felt such a chill and could hear a scream. And I had this vision of Lavina, my grandmother, in a car looking out at the camp and the family and the land that she would never see again. Small brown eyes. Scared. Hurting. Terrified.

When my grandmother was taken, she was 12 years old. She was placed with a middle-class white family where she worked for two years without pay in the kitchen and laundry of a middle-class white woman—two years without any form of payment. She was 12 years old when she started working there and 14 when she finally ran away. There is no doubt in my mind that her exploitation at the hand of that family amounted to slave labor, slave labor that was encouraged, even sponsored, by the government.

Let me tell you why my grandmother was removed from her family at such a young age. It is an important part of her story. It marks the point at which the state took her from her family and controlled her life and tried to shape her identity.

In 1788, when invading Whites first stepped onto Australian soil with no intention of leaving the country again, a policy of genocide towards the Aboriginal people of Australia had begun. Aboriginal men, women, and children were slaughtered in massacres so blatant that much of the recorded history of these activities is found in letters written by perpetrators, extolling their war crimes to family members back in England. There was so little value attached to the life of an Aboriginal person that letters and journals would openly cite that the writer had been involved with the mass slaying of Aboriginal people.

By the turn of the 19th century, it was generally assumed that Aboriginal people would die out. This belief was so widely held that when the Constitution came into effect in 1901, it placed matters dealing with Aboriginals under the control of the federal government. In some isolated areas, however, Aboriginal people were placed under the care of the state. By the 1920s, as the number of Aboriginal people began to increase, the government responded by initiating an assimilation plan.

In 1909 the policy of assimilation led the New South Wales Government to pass the Aborigines Protection Act, a statute that saw its equivalent in each state within Australia. The Act provided for the establishment of the Aborigines Protection Board. The Aborigines Protection Board had power to make regulations that controlled the everyday life of Aboriginal people. The Board decided where Aboriginal people lived, when and where they worked, even what they ate.

In 1916 the powers of the Aborigines Protection Board were amended to give the Board the power to remove children from Aboriginal families and place them in the care of the state. Child neglect (proven or otherwise) did not have to be an issue to enable the Board to exercise its powers. The power of removal was used as a powerful tool for the implementation of this policy of so-called "assimilation." But the policy proved to be a form of cultural genocide, which took away children to resocialize and reculturalize them into white families, stripping them of their Aboriginal identity and culture.

It was under these powers that my grandmother was taken from her family. The Protection Board's documents stated that the reason for her removal was to "get her away from camplife." Children like my grandmother, when removed, were either placed in an institution or brought up in a white family. Most ended up in a government institution. There, girls were trained to be domestic servants and the men to be stockmen, and no child was educated over the age of 14.

The practice of the Protection Board was so widespread that not a single aboriginal family in New South Wales escaped from feeling the effects of its powers. My grandmother, like so many other children, was used as slave labor in the home of a white woman. She was denied her family. She was denied her culture. It is hard to conceive a more horrific example of the deprivation of human rights than that experienced by Indigenous children who were stolen from their families and communities.

What the government achieved by this policy was to destroy the families of Aboriginal people by removing whole generations of children. The results of this were disastrous for the Aboriginal culture because the generation to which the culture had to be passed down to had been stolen by the State. It also meant that Aboriginal people were deliberately kept in an uneducated state and therefore did not receive the skills to gain the employment that would enable them to get out of the lowest socioeconomic level of society. My father, though an excellent student at the orphanage in which he was placed, was nevertheless turned out into the streets at the age of 14.

The practices of the Aborigines Protection Board were some of the most blatant interferences with Indigenous identity in Australia. Its policies were fueled by the general public's attitudes towards the Indigenous people of the land they came to live in. The disgust with which Indigenous people were viewed was met by the paternalistic desire of the government to "save" Aboriginal people from the perceived curse of their culture. Policies designed to form and reform the identity of Aboriginal children were undertaken in humiliating ways.

Ros Bowden and Bill Bunbury, in their ABC radio program series *Being Aboriginal,* aired the following case study of an Aboriginal child institutionalized by the Aborigines Protection Board:

> Comments were made—little things, like "Oh, she'll be going walkabout soon"—stereotype comments, and I used to wonder what the hell they were talking about. I used to stand in a certain way at the kitchen sink and I didn't realise that I was standing in what is now a stereotype Aboriginal position. They'd come along and kick my knee so I'd fall and break the dishes, so I'd have to go and write another thousand lines of a bible verse—I was a great one for bible verses. But I just grew up with the feeling that being aboriginal was bad.[1]

The invasion of Australia took place just a little over 200 years ago. The last recorded massacre of Aboriginal people by a state was in the 1930s. The policy of removal of children only ended in 1969. Aboriginal people have only been classed as citizens and eligible to vote since 1967. The effects of past government policies, however, are still very much a part of Aboriginal life. Many people were not able to locate their traditional families have come from and have remained dislocated from their tribal groups. Many Protection Board documents were destroyed, making it next to impossible for Aboriginal families to locate stolen children or for children to find their way home. Grassroots organizations, like Link Up, have been created to help members of the community come to terms with the effects of the Protection Board on their lives and identities. The pain of the policy still weaves through the hearts of Aboriginal people.

The *National Report of the Royal Commission into Aboriginal Deaths in Custody* made the connection between identity and self-esteem and institutionalization. Investigations of the Royal Commission often pinpointed the time of removal from family as the beginning of the descent into a vicious cycle of depression and petty crime and feelings of low self-esteem. This is fed by a feeling of dislocation that comes from a lack of access to Aboriginal culture and heritage.

Institutionalization leaves a child socialized with a lack of love and affection. John Bowlby in *Maternal Care and Mental Health,* a report of the World Health Organization, stated that it has been

> well known since the 1950s that maternal deprivation led to inability to make more than superficial relationships; no real feeling or emotional response to situations where it is normal to respond; inaccessability, cut off from people wanting to help; lack of concentration at school, poor school performance; stealing, deceit, evasion; bed-wetting; anxiety, depression"; in the long term children who have been institutionalized had difficulty with parenting their own children.[2]

The same report found that mental illness, also a problem in the Aboriginal community, in many instances could be linked to removal from family units by the Aborigines Protection Board. These problems include substance abuse, suicide, manic depression, and high anxiety:

> The *New South Wales Aboriginal Mental Health Report* of 1991 found that the likelihood of a person's experiencing mental health problems or a mental disorder was exacerbated by a childhood history of separation from parents, neglect or institutionalization. Similarly, a study by the Victorian Aboriginal Health Service found that 54% of all respondents had a psychiatric disorder and, of these, over 50% had been separated from their parents and more than 25% had been brought up outside of their communities in foster homes or institutions.[3]

One of the most disturbing legacies of the Aborigines Protection Board is the cyclical breakdown of Aboriginal families that is now occurring. During my time as a family lawyer working for the Legal Aid Commission, the Aboriginal women I came into contact with who were in danger of losing their children to the state had almost always been removed themselves as young children. Often the child being placed in state care was the third generation to be removed from the family environment. This cyclical breakdown of the family is but one legacy of the Aborigines Protection Board. Another aspect of the fallout has been the stereotyping of Aboriginal women as bad mothers and Aboriginal men as bad fathers—a classic example of blaming the victim of a callous practice. This stereotype developed as a justification for the removal of so many Aboriginal children, completely ignoring the fact that the Protection Board removed children no matter how well looked after those children were.

Let me tell you what my grandmother means to me. I was born after she died, but I feel a connection with her. Her blood runs through my veins. I feel that she looks over me. I feel that when I walk through doors I am being carried on her shoulders. Often when I am scared, I think of her putting her arms around me. The times in my life when I have felt the strongest have been when I felt she was walking beside me. I love my grandmother. The thought of how hard her life was for her makes me angry and sad. I feel the injustice of the life she lived that was shaped by the racist policies of a Eurocentric culture. I feel anger about what happened to my grandmother. I think of her in an alien environment. I think of her alone. I think of her crying. And I think of the reality of life for my people now.

The World Around Me

My father told me of the shame he felt when he was in school. The white-washed history of Australia would be taught in the school he attended, about the way that Aborigines had tried to spear settlers and stopped explorers from forging into the frontier. He could feel all the eyes of the other children in the class burning into him and he would shrink into his seat. As a small child living in an institution, he was slowly beaten into shame.

Ever since the White people invaded Australia, Aboriginal identity has been attacked. Aboriginal people were portrayed as uncivilized, barbaric, and primitive. This negative stereotype was perpetuated to justify the invasion and dispossession of Aboriginal people. We are continually stereotyped in a negative way—as alcoholics; as unintelligent, unattractive, unsophisticated; with a propensity to steal, no capacity to be honest; as sluts and whores, bad mothers, and violent husbands. These stereotypes are used to justify the continuing oppression and poverty of Aboriginal people. The stereotype becomes a tool by which to blame the victim.

Another stereotype of Aboriginality that was created at the time was the image of the noble savage. This simple but graceful creature lived in peaceful harmony with nature and was at one with his or her surroundings. This was not the most popular stereotype, but we still encounter an ancestor of this romanticism in society today.

Early missionaries attacked Aboriginal identity. They failed to understand the culture of the Aboriginal people and the strong religious significance of land. Aboriginal people as pagan people were stereotyped as devils. Black skin was seen as unclean. Aboriginal family life was portrayed as hedonistic. Traditional values were attacked violently by missionaries who could provide havens to Aboriginal people from the violence of the frontier.

Anthropologists were similarly ethnocentric. Early anthropologists assumed patriarchy within the Aboriginal community. They therefore ignored all the sacred sites and stories of Aboriginal women. As a result, the sites of women were not protected because they were never recorded. Aboriginal women's sites are destroyed at a faster rate than those of Aboriginal men.

Negative stereotyping is prevalent in modern-day Australia. The media is a medium through which most Australians have contact with Aboriginal people. The media is selective in how it wishes to portray Aboriginal people. For example, television cameras may show a group of Aboriginal people sitting in a park and getting drunk. This gives the impression that Aboriginal people are drunkards, that they are unemployed, probably unemployable, neglect their families, and are violent. What the media does not say is that Aboriginal people drink in public because they are often not allowed to drink in the bars because the bartenders will not allow them in. Also, Aboriginal people traditionally socialize outdoors. Many are unemployed because they did not receive a proper education and are denied employment because of the color of their skin. This is a result of oppression that has included gross deprivations of human rights over two centuries.

The education system is complicit in that it does nothing to truthfully educate non-Aboriginal Australians about the violence used against Aboriginal people and their history of oppression. History books are only now being rewritten to mention the massacres of Aboriginal people. But history books still do not talk about the use of Aboriginal men, women, and children for slave labor. It is still controversial to use the word "invasion" in Australian schools. History books do not talk about how Aboriginal people have been denied land, family, expression of culture, and the right to citizenship. Non-Aboriginal people see Aboriginal people in a vacuum, not in the intricate patchworks in which they live.

When I was at school, we didn't study Aboriginal culture or history and we never spoke about contemporary Aboriginal issues. Aboriginal history was thought to be too political. I remember being reprimanded for wearing small symbols of my Aboriginality at school. I encountered a third-grade teacher who told me that "you people" never amount to anything. It is chilling to think how many Aboriginal people are disheartened and lose confidence due to the meanness and hatred that some teachers blatantly show towards Aboriginal children.

The effect of the small inherent messages that we get as children is immeasurable, but I had strong positive measures, too. I was fortunate to have parents who ensured I was proud and expressive of my Aboriginality without shame. In fact, my parents were active in trying to get the school to change its attitudes. Each year my father came to the school complaining about the lack of Aboriginal content in the curriculum. I imagine that the history department huddled together at the beginning of parent-teacher night and drew straws about who would be the one to answer all my father's questions that year. In my sixth and final year at the school, my father received a phone call from the school telling him that they would be teaching Aboriginal history that year and asking to borrow his books to prepare the classes. I remember so proudly his persistent agitation for change.

University life was not easy either. I felt very alienated. I felt that it was a place where I did not belong. There was a confidence among other students who had taken it as a given that they, like their parents, would go to a university, that they had a right to be there. They were confident about their abilities and so sure footed.

Aboriginal people, from my experience, come to study law from a very different perspective than non-Indigenous people do. I did a small private survey of people I knew studying law. Every Aboriginal person that I knew who studied law did so because of some kind of personal experience with the criminal justice system. Someone they knew died in custody, their children had been harassed by the police, or a sibling had been wrongly arrested. Not one non-Aboriginal person ever cited such personal reasons for choosing to study law. They would give answers like "My father is a lawyer"; "I'm interested in human rights"; "I want to help the poor"; "I'm the third generation to study law." Theirs was a very different background, and a very different attitude toward the law.

Let me tell you what else negative stereotyping does. Negative stereotypes injure self-image. Negative stereotypes fracture hope. They fall back heavily on us when we are denied access to services for our Aboriginality, when we are abused for our Aboriginality, when judges call us "a pest race" because of our Aboriginality.

Although it is never a mystery to Aboriginal people, non-Aboriginal people are often surprised to find out that I am Aboriginal—and even more surprised to find out that I am proud to be Aboriginal. I am accused of not being an Aboriginal person because I have light skin. If you go to a bookstore and look at the travel books on Australia, they are filled with pictures of Aboriginal people with dark skin, spears, and painted bodies. Since I do not fit that stereotype, I am constantly being told that I am not an Aborigine, at least not a real Aborigine. Urban Aboriginal people are lesser Aborigines in the eyes of White people.

It is a catch-22. They will not give me the skin-privilege of being white, but will try to deny my membership of my own race. This divide-and-conquer mentality has been used against us since invasion. This light skin that non-Aboriginal people think strips away at my identity does not make me immune from the full experience of being an Aboriginal person.

I have been called "black arse" in the schoolyard. I have been called "boong" and "coon" by university-educated people. I have to put up with White people constantly saying things to me like: "Aboriginal people are all alcoholic"; "Your dad's a welfare bum"; "You Aborigines disgust me"; "You're all savages"; "You can't be trusted." I am often referred to as "you lot."

My lighter skin does not protect me from this ugliness that White people so easily cast towards an Aboriginal person. My light skin has never stopped Aboriginal people from accepting me wholly. I have the love of my community. I have the strength of my community. I have the protection of my community. No Aboriginal person has ever questioned my Aboriginality. White people ask me what percentage of Aboriginal blood I have. In my culture we do not have notions of half-caste and quarter-caste. Those terms are only in the Whites' language. In our eyes you are either an Aboriginal person or you are not. If you see yourself as Aboriginal and are accepted by the Aboriginal community as an Aboriginal person, you are an Aboriginal person. If you describe yourself as "part Aboriginal" or of Aboriginal descent, you are considered non-Aboriginal, no matter what your skin color. We reject the notions of half-caste and quarter-caste, not only because it is a construct of White government assimilation policy, but it is a ludicrous notion in light of the Aboriginal experience. I don't get half the abuse because my mother is white. I am not given half the services that Aboriginal people are refused because my mother is white. I don't get called "half a black c— "half a n—" because my mother is white. People don't say, "You're half lazy," "You're half prone to commit crime," "You're half a black gin," because my mother is white.

I think White people sometimes can't understand why I am so proud to be a part of a race that they perceive to be uneducable, unemployable, and primitive. They can constantly make excuses for me. "But you don't act like one." "If they were all like you, we would not have any problems." "They're all alcoholics, except you"; "you're different."

I am usually the first Aboriginal person that these White people have ever met. Their white-skin privilege means that they never have to live in the poverty that we live in. They would not choose to socialize with Aboriginal people because of the stigma attached to us. But at the same time they do not understand why we don't want to be like them. I think that it is the urban Aboriginal communities that pose the greatest difficulty for non-Aboriginal people. We are often considered by outsiders to have lost our culture and to be completely integrated into non-Aboriginal life.

Let me tell you why we have a very unique culture in our city community that reflects traditional cultural values. Distinct cultural values exist today in urban Aboriginal communities, and those values reflect the traditional values of our culture and provide the fundamental differences between our culture and the non-Indigenous Australian culture. Even where traditional lifestyle has been lost, land becomes a central part of Aboriginal life. We believe it is still ours. We believe we never surrendered it. It still provides a basis for our survival. It allows economic independence and therefore autonomy and noninterference with our culture and lives. We still believe in the spiritual nature of land, and our culture remains predominantly oral. I learned from stories and lessons told to me by my parents and aunts and uncles. We still have a communal rather than an individual focus. My parents emphasized the fact that we have to do what is beneficial to the Aboriginal community before thinking about ourselves. We know that if we enrich the community and the life of the community, we help everyone, including ourselves.

We still learn to have respect for our Elders, rather than a youth-oriented culture. I spent time with older people a lot during my youth; they are very wise people who had lived through things that I will never have to live through. These people taught me to respect my Elders. There is an interesting contrast between Aboriginal and non-Aboriginal culture. When I was admitted to Harvard Law School, I was inundated with impressed non-Aboriginal people telling me how smart I was and how great I was. In my own community, while there was support and encouragement, I was still very much made to feel that this was just a small step in terms of what I would be doing for my community, and that influence within my own community would not come from my Harvard degree but from the measure of my actions when I was older. Experience is still valued much more in my community, and we still make decisions through consensus rather than authoritarian decision making. When an issue arises that is of importance to the community, people know the appropriate people to ask. There is a protocol of appropriate people to speak to and appropriate people to consult, and members of the Aboriginal community know who those people are.

The sense of community is strong, too, not just because we have the same values, but because we are so tight-knit. You can tell whom Aboriginal people are related to by their tribal groups or surnames. Often I have met Aboriginal people and we can work out that we are related through extended families. It is also our experiences that bond us as a community and distinguish us from the non-Aboriginal community. We are usually poor and dispossessed, live with the effects of the Aborigines Protection Board policies of removal, and have a different experience with the criminal justice system.

Living the Stereotypes

My father told me that you can no more sell the land than sell the sky. Our affinity with the land is like the bonding between a parent and a child. You have responsibilities and obligations to look after and care for a child. You can speak for a child. But you can't own a child.

I know that we have a very strong culture and that we walk between two cultures more than non-Aboriginal people realize. I never realized this myself until I studied overseas. I was educated in white institutions and have worked in white institutions and in law, a predominantly non-Aboriginal profession. But at the end of the day I still return home to the Aboriginal community—my Aboriginal family and friends, my Aboriginal music, art, humor, problems, issues. I realized this when I was overseas because in a predominantly white, definitely non-Aboriginal institution, there was no sense of community there at the end of the day.

Non-Aboriginal people do not understand how someone can operate in the White sphere as a student, as a teacher, and as a lawyer and not be overcome by the values of White society. There is an assumption that by operating within White society, the nontraditional society, I lose my traditional values of community, collectivism, strong sense of family, respect for Elders, cooperation, reciprocity, and cultural pride.

Let me tell you how I am stereotyped as an educated Aboriginal person. I feel that there is an assumption that to be successful in the White community you have to take on White values of individuality, competition, ambition, and materialism. There is an implied assumption that white values are superior and that I should want to adopt them.

Let me tell you how I came to study law. Learning the life story of my grandmother changed my life. The inhumanity and senselessness of her removal from her family by the government have fueled me on to make sure that Aboriginal people never have to endure such breaches of human rights again. It is a matter of making sure that our lives improve now that we are starting to address the practices of genocide used against us.

Let me tell you how people reacted to my admission to the University of New South Wales Law School. I was admitted under a Special Admissions Program. There was resentment from the people that I had been at school with. "She only got there because she is an Aborigine." No matter how well I did, once I was at the Law School, that assumption could not be budged. Ironically, some of the most resentful students dropped out after the first year. Their venom gave me the tenacity to hang on.

Let me tell you how I came to go to Harvard Law School. Someone reached out to me and gave me a word-gift of confidence. I was lucky enough to have my path cross that of a dynamic Aboriginal woman, Dr. Roberta Sykes, who mentioned that I should think about postgraduate work. Dr. Sykes was the first Aboriginal person from Australia to attend Harvard University, thus paving the way for me to be the first Aboriginal person to go to the law school. She was confident that I would get in, a confidence that I did not share. I spent my first month in Boston expecting a phone call to tell me that there had been a mistake. My year at Harvard was the first year that I lived away from my family and my people. The hardest thing about being there was the separation from the community and its values. That community love and support is something that I cannot replace.

Let me tell you how my admission to Harvard Law School was perceived. During my time at university, I used my education well. I worked at the AIDS Council of New South Wales, edited several law journals, and had my first article published. I was also teaching Aboriginal culture and history in the General Studies program at the university I was attending. But when I was admitted to Harvard, there were murmurs amongst my former classmates that I was just admitted "because I was an Aborigine." There were even rumors of letters to Harvard complaining of the admissions program because I had been admitted over other people (white people) who considered themselves more gifted than I.

Whenever I have achieved a goal, it has been degraded by racists who claim that it was only because someone was feeling sorry for me, or the acceptance of me and my work was a token—all this without any notion of what my work is about and whether it is good or not. All this because of the color of my skin, because my father is Aboriginal, because my grandmother was Aboriginal.

Let me tell you what drives me now. I feel that I have to work very hard to reconcile what happened to my grandmother. I also have to live my life to its fullest. I feel that I have to enjoy life and explore all its wonders because I feel that I have had the chances that she never had. It goes back to what I was saying about standing on the shoulders of those who went before us. I feel, as I travel through new doors that were never before opened to other Aboriginal people, that she travels with me, carrying me forward. I also feel propelled by the constant attacks on my credibility. I am not sure this bitterness is healthy; it hurts to work hard and have people be so dismissive of me because I am Aboriginal. Critique my work, not my race. Discuss my abilities, not my background.

At a dinner party I heard a man two seats down from me comment about me as if I were deaf: "She's done really well for a coon." I recounted this tale to a non-Aboriginal friend who was shocked because the person had used the word "coon." I was shocked that she didn't realize the real menace in the statement. I would have been just as insulted if the guest had said, "She's done really well for an Aborigine." It is as menacing as the seemingly innocent: "But you are far too pretty to be an Aborigine." Why is it that it is so remarkable for us to achieve? With all we have had to fight against, how could we fail? I have to admit that I secretly relish being able to confront a negative stereotype, of countering the uneducated, stupid Aboriginal that so many Australians hold out as a truism.

Let me tell you about the lingering image of the "noble savage." It has transformed into an idea that Aboriginal people, wherever they live, however they live, are spiritual beings. We are sought out for our knowledge of spirituality. We are people. We have a spiritual side—a spirituality that was as tenderly nourished as it was in any other Indigenous culture. What is disturbing about this characterization is that it characterized Aboriginal spirituality as a public commodity, not a private cultural experience. I find this characterization exploitative.

I am often faced with the argument that the positive stereotypes are better than the negative ones. I think that both are evil. I think that as a community we will lose ourselves if we fall into imagining ourselves through the romanticized eyes of our colonizers. All stereotypes confine the world in which we live. Stereotypes confine the parameters through which the individual can live. Stereotypes, negative or positive, make it difficult to walk the lines between the two cultures. I can do it only because my Elders support and guide me. I am learning the tools that White men and White women have used against my community so that we can fight back. I do that to learn to empower my community.

I do not want to adopt the whiteness of the dominant culture. I want to preserve my Aboriginality. White people do not understand the difference. Our interaction with them is not to become like them, but to become stronger against the kinds of things that eradicate cultures and identity. We are happy to be who we are and we are fighting to protect that identity: to allow our community to exist and to allow our culture to continue to live.

A Wish for the Future

My father told me that people are different. If you place a coin on the street and watch the way passersby react to it, you will see this. Someone will see it but not think it is worth picking up. Someone will bend over slowly to pick it up. Someone else will grab the coin quickly and run before they are spotted. All have different reactions. All are people but with different reactions. We are all just individuals and we react to our environment differently.

Let me tell you what my hopes for the future are. Australia prides itself on supposedly being a multicultural society, so quickly ignoring its consistent deprivation of the human rights of Indigenous people and ignoring its appallingly racist anti-Asian past institutionalized by the repugnant White Australia Policy. Australia needs to come to terms with this history. Truth will help Australia come to terms with the stereotypes they have about Aboriginal Australians. Only then will the dominant culture stop imposing its concepts of identity on the Indigenous community.

Conclusion

As a nation we need to aspire to become a nation where the institutions and policies are conducive to creating a space for the development of the identity of all the members of the community. Under such an aspiration there will finally be respect for Indigenous culture and identity. Respect—this was what was missing in the relationship between my grandmother and the white people who controlled her life. If we approach our relationship with each other with respect for our humanity, we will take the first step towards creating a climate of tolerance and acceptance.

These are high hopes. The realities are sobering. The reality is that very few people listen when they hear the words "Let me tell you . . ."

NOTES

1. Ros Bowden and Bill Bunbury, ABC Radio Program Series: *Being Aboriginal: Comments, Observations, and Stories from Aboriginal Australians* (1990).
2. Cited in *Telling Our Story: A Report by the Aboriginal Legal Service of Western Australia (Inc) on the Removal of Children from Their Families in Western Australia,* July 1995, p. 33.
3. Ibid.

PART II

Colonization and Identity

CHAPTER 4

OF THIS RED EARTH

By Henrietta Mann

Henrietta **Mann** is enrolled with the Cheyenne-Arapaho Tribes of Oklahoma and has a Ph.D. in American Studies from the University of New Mexico. She is the first person to occupy The Endowed Chair in Native American Studies at Montana State University—Bozeman. She has taught at The University of Montana, Missoula; Haskell Indian Nations University; Harvard University Graduate School of Education; and the University of California, Berkley. She has also served as the national coordinator of the American Indian Religious Freedom Act Coalition for the Association of American Indian Affairs. In 1991, *Rolling Stone* magazine named Henrietta one of the 10 leading professors in the nation. She has been an interviewee and consultant for several television and movie productions, including *In the White Man's Image* and *Last of the Dogmen*. Henrietta has lectured throughout the United States and in Mexico, Canada, Germany, Italy, and New Zealand.

Introduction

Ma'heo'o, the great Creator of All That Is, made four substances with which to create the Cheyenne world: sinew, sweet grass, buffalo fat, and red earth paint. "The red earth paint," *Ma'heo'o* said: "will be the beginning of the substances that make earth." From the mud and dirt of this red earth, he made human beings with their four limbs, and he called the winds from the four directions to come and give them breath. *Ma'heo'o,* the Grandfather of All That Is, has absolute love for his children made of this red earth who are known as the Cheyenne and who constitute but one group of the many culturally diverse Indigenous peoples of this land.

The inclusive Cheyenne term for the first peoples of this land is *xamaa-vo'-estaneo'o. Xamaa* means "indigenous, aboriginal, natural" and *vo'estaneo'o* is the plural form of *vo'estane,* which means a person.[1] Together, *xamaa-vo'estaneo'o* means indigenous, aboriginal, and/or natural people, the name by which the Cheyenne refer to those made of this red earth. In addition to generic names for themselves like the Cheyenne *xamaa-vo'estaneo'o,* the First Nations also have specific tribal names for themselves.

The Italian navigator Christopher Columbus, assuming he had reached the East Indies of Asia and not realizing how far off course he was, called the people he encountered on the shores of this "Turtle Island" *los indios,* the Indians. This fact of history had dramatic effects upon the Indigenous nations of the Americas, one of which was the acceptance of "American Indians" as the permanent misnomer for the citizens of these first nations. This is an important distinction because over the past five centuries the use of the term *American Indians* has served to denigrate the cultural integrity of Indigenous peoples and to deny them their respective identities and cultures given to them by the Creator.

Columbus' mistake has had severe consequences for Indigenous peoples because those that came here never attempted to correct the error of geography. It also compounded attitudes of European supremacy in that they were blatantly disrespectful by not even attempting to ascertain who these people really were. This has historical significance because it set the tone for the ensuing relationship with Indigenous peoples, which must be acknowledged in its historical context. Today, millions of Indigenous peoples of the Western Hemisphere are asserting their basic human right as distinct nations with unique cultures to be who and what they are. They also share a common heritage as the red children of their mother, the earth. It is no coincidence that they inherited her sacred red color of life and happiness.

The "Hearted-Alike People"

Long ago in everyday life, the Cheyenne always painted their faces and bodies with red earth paint. Acknowledging this custom in their name for them, the Dakota called them *Shaiyena.*[2] Thus, in the anglicizing process the Dakota word *Shaiyena* became Cheyenne. The Cheyenne know themselves, however, as *Tse-tsehese-stahase,* which translates closely into English as the people who are alike or have "like-hearts" or more descriptively as the "hearted-alike people."

Among the "hearted-alike people," members of the spiritual community may use red earth paint on nonceremonial occasions. In their sun dance prayer for all life, dancers use pale red earth to paint their faces and bodies. It is symbolic of their sacred relationship with the earth from whom they are made, to whom they belong, with whom they live in respectful reciprocity, and to whom they return in death. They are not only of this red earth, but they are the keeper people of the earth as well.

Being an earth keeper is a spiritual responsibility of all Indigenous peoples, the Cheyenne included. They have never forgotten this as they walk the medicine wheel of earth and make the four sacred stops that mark their paths of life from infancy to youth to adulthood and to old age. They are mindful of their sacred obligations to their spiritual mother the earth and renew her life-giving power through their ceremonies. Such is the role of each generation as they walk their time on earth.

The Cheyenne divide their time on earth into four periods of history: "(1) The ancient time, when they were happy, but were decimated by a terrible disease, [and] were left as orphans; (2) the time of the dogs, when these animals were used as beasts of burden; (3) the time of the buffalo; (4) the time of the horse, which is recent history."[3] Their tribal history is an odyssey from the far north in Canada to the northern plains of Montana and the southern plains of Oklahoma.

It also is a pilgrimage from their sacred mountains to their beloved homelands. In these places of great spiritual knowledge *Ma'heo'o* taught their two prophets and sent them out with the two most holy of Cheyenne medicine bundles, which form the basis of their deeply rooted spiritual life and identity as a people. The two ceremonies that accompany these medicine objects are the means through which the earth and all things on, in, above, and below it are renewed. In these ceremonies, the earth is the altar from which they sent up their prayers to *Ma'heo'o*, and out to the four spirit powers who live at the four sacred directions of the world.

Cheyenne ways are timeless. They are very, very old and contain much traditional wisdom and knowledge. Simultaneously, they are exceptionally contemporary and provide the strength of values and cultural direction that allow one to cope with the unknown and ordinary stresses of living. Resilience and the unchanging spiritual core of tribal traditions have assured their survival as a people.

Colonization and the Clash of Cultures

The Cheyenne have had to cope with externally imposed pressures from strangers who not only wanted their lands but who brought diseases such as whooping cough, measles, smallpox, and cholera with them. Diseases such as these resulted in tragic and rapid population decline. The trauma was further compounded by the federal Indian policies of treaty-making, creation of reservations, allotment, and continual reorganization, which all contributed to the mass dislocation of the people justified as "Manifest Destiny."[4]

The general Indian affairs policies created under the guise of Manifest Destiny were also reflected in the government's Indian education policy. Provisions for the education of Indian children were incorporated into many of the last treaties negotiated with the various Indian nations. As an example, Article 7 of the Medicine Lodge Treaty of 1867 provided for the compulsory education of Cheyenne and Arapaho children: "In order to insure the civilization of the tribes entering into this treaty, the necessity of education is admitted, especially by such of them as are or may be settled on said agricultural reservation, and they therefore pledge themselves to compel their children, male and female, between the ages of six and sixteen years, to attend school."[5] Tribal leadership reaffirmed their belief in the necessity of education, and the government saw education as a means to "civilize," and civilization meant change that was to begin with the children.

Education as a Weapon of Assimilation

In 1871 the reservation policy replaced treaty-making. As a result schools were established on reservations which were called Indian Industrial Training Schools or Manual Labor Schools. Under his 1869 peace policy, President Ulysses S. Grant, in an unprecedented action, delegated the nomination of Indian agents to the various Christian denominations. Consequently, the schools had a three-prong assimilation approach, which was to educate Indians on reservations, "civilize" them, and make them into Christian converts through religious instruction.

America's hunger for land led to yet another change in policy called allotment, the result of the passage in 1887 of the General Allotment Act, also referred to as the Dawes Severalty Act. The purpose of this legislation was to further break up the Indian land base, and the educational counterpart was aimed at breaking down the community, culture, and identity of the Indian child. This was to be accomplished with the establishment of off-reservation boarding schools located near urban areas. The first of these was the Carlisle Indian Industrial Training School in Pennsylvania. When Carlisle opened its doors in 1879, the Cheyenne were among the first group of students to be enrolled. It was there that the task of de-Indianizing Indian children began with a vengeance and Indigenous languages bore the frontal assault.

Education, Christianity, and civilization were synonymous, and Carlisle served as the model for the other 24 off-reservation schools that were established by the turn of the century. Some of them were located in places far removed from family and reservations, such as Genoa, Nebraska; Lawrence, Kansas; Salem, Oregon; and Riverside, California. Basically they were parochial schools, operated with federal funds, in which strict military discipline was imposed.

Richard Henry Pratt, a West Point graduate who established Carlisle, strongly influenced the militaristic orientation of these schools. They created a generation of marginal individuals whose cultural foundations were weakened by the relentless attack mounted against them by the church working with the government. It is a monumental tribute to the spirit of Indigenous peoples in the United States that they not only survived the assaults upon cultural identity in off-reservation boarding schools, but they survived other equally devastating policies of cultural genocide as well.

Assimilating a New Deal

The federal government shifted from the allotment policy to reorganization with the passage of the Indian Reorganization Act (IRA) in 1934. Called the Indian "New Deal," its first provision called for a termination of the allotment process. Its primary purpose, however, was for tribes to establish elective tribal councils by adopting constitutions and by-laws that had been formulated by the federal government. While basically providing for a degree of tribal self-government, in actuality, all tribal council actions were subject to the approval of the Secretary of the Interior or his designated agent, which was the Bureau of Indian Affairs (BIA). These new forms of tribal governments supplanted traditional governing bodies and created tension between traditional leaders and so-called "progressives."

This new direction of Indian policy toward local governance also resulted in local education initiatives by involving the states in the education of Indian children. This was formalized by the passage of the 1934 Johnson-O'Malley Act (JOM), which was a companion piece of legislation to IRA. JOM authorized the Secretary of the Interior to contract with the various states for the education of Indian children and authorized federal funding to local school districts in which Indian children were enrolled.

JOM was intended to supplement local funds and was targeted toward meeting the educational needs of Indian children, which meant their "cultural" needs. Unfortunately, in some instances, JOM funds disappeared into schools' general operating budgets and Indian children realized few benefits. State public schools continued the historical practice of assimilation and, like their federal predecessors, failed to incorporate culturally relevant content into their curricula. Furthermore, teaching personnel were not trained to teach culturally diverse students, and they continued to damage the identity of Indian students, which oftentimes resulted in low self-esteem.

It was as though the distinct cultures of Indigenous peoples did not exist or matter in the minds of the majority of White educators who taught Indian children. If these Indigenous cultures did exist to the educators, they were dismissed as being caught in a time warp with no contemporary validity except as museum relics or objects of curiosity. It was difficult for American Indians to be viewed as human beings, much less to acknowledge that they had miraculously managed to carry their respective tribal identities and cultures with them into the twentieth century.

In the mindset of the federal government, Indians could not remain Indians; they had to change and education was the vehicle through which this could be accomplished. Consequently, in the early 1950s the BIA designed adult vocational training programs, which were based in urban areas, such as

San Francisco, Los Angeles, Minneapolis, and Dallas. They uprooted Indians, sent them to the cities, trained them, and found them employment. They called it relocation.

The Indian Relocation Program demonstrates the harsh reality of the government's anti-Indian attitude, in which relocation was viewed as just another vehicle for assimilation. It was intended to place Indians in the urban melting pots of the country and lose them there. It was another way of separating individuals and entire families from their communities and cultural environment in much the same way that children had been sent to off-reservation federal boarding schools. The only difference was that it was adults this time and not children, but the goal was the same, which was to dilute tribal identity and erode Indian cultures.

The person responsible for this policy was Dillon S. Myer, who became Commissioner of Indian Affairs in 1950. Mr. Myer had a philosophy and experience he obviously took with him to the BIA. He had been a former director of the Japanese War Relocation Authority, under which Japanese Americans were placed in concentration camps after the bombing of Pearl Harbor. His experience in uprooting and relocating people was immediately implemented into Indian policy.

A Policy of Termination

This policy nightmare was accompanied by termination, another equally appalling policy aimed at Indians. House Concurrent Resolution 108 provided the legislative basis for termination and was a way to "free" Indians from federal supervision and integrate them once and for all into mainstream America. This was contrary to the legal standing of treaties as the supreme law of the land, and to the trust relationship existing between the United States of America and the various Indigenous nations. Nonetheless, some termination bills were passed by Congress resulting in the termination of most of the smaller tribes in California, the Klamaths of Oregon, the Menominees of Wisconsin, and others. Their status as federally recognized tribes was withdrawn, as was their status as Indians. It is still a basic issue of identity from the government's perspective: that the government holds the right to recognize you as an Indian, or not recognize you as Indian. The reality is that termination affected the identity of entire nations of peoples. It was but one more form of assimilation that was forced upon Indigenous nations by Dillon S. Myer, an aggressive terminationist, and the Congress of the United States of America.

National Tragedy—National Challenge:
A Policy of Self-Determination Begins

One can ask the question, When will it stop or change? Indian policy began to shift in the 1960s with President John F. Kennedy but more specifically with President Lyndon B. Johnson. In March 1968 President Johnson delivered his special message to Congress on Indians, entitled "The Forgotten American." The most significant of his remarks was his repudiation of termination and commitment to a policy of Indian self-determination.

The Indian self-determination policy resulted in Indian involvement at differing federal programmatic levels. One example, within education and called Project TRIBE (Tribal Responsibility in Better Education), created local advisory school boards for federal schools. Their role was to review the school budget, formulate solutions, and make recommendations on school matters, which was actually a milestone in Indian education.

A multiyear "investigation into the problems of education for American Indians" was released in 1969, and the conclusions were a major indictment of the federal government's failure to live up to its responsibility to Indian children.[6] The report, *Indian Education: A National Tragedy—A National Challenge*, which was also called the Kennedy Report for its chairman Edward M. Kennedy, stated:

> We are shocked at what we discovered . . . For there is so much to do—wrongs to right, omissions to fill, untruths to correct . . . We have developed page after page of statistics. These cold figures mark a stain on our national conscience, a stain which has spread slowly for hundreds of years. They tell a story, to be sure. But they cannot tell the whole story. They cannot, for example, tell of the despair, the frustration, the hopelessness, the poignancy, of children who want to learn but are not taught; of adults who try to read but have no one to teach them; of families which want to stay together but are forced apart . . . We have concluded that our national policies for educating American Indians are a failure of major proportions.[7]

This report is significant because it presents government officials making unequivocal statements about their government and the poor quality of education it has condoned or provided for the Indian children involved in the study and for the generations that preceded them. Wrongs, omissions, untruths, despair, frustration, and hopelessness are sharp words, but they are inadequate in describing centuries of cultural oppression and the attempted annihilation of Indigenous peoples and their cherished ways of life. It must be remembered that education targeted the most vulnerable group of all. The federal government aggressively promoted education as the vehicle for change, and the Kennedy Report documents its failure.

The Kennedy Report was highly critical of BIA schools, but it did not exempt public schools, mission schools and private schools from its criticism concerning assimilation. The report states:

> From the first contact with the Indian, the school and the classroom have been a primary tool of assimilation. Education was the means whereby we emancipated the Indian child from his home, his parents, his extended family, and his cultural heritage. It was in effect an attempt to wash the "savage habits" and "tribal ethic" out of a child's mind and substitute a white middle-class value system in its place.[8]

The report was direct about the assimilation by education goals of schools. The report made 60 recommendations for legislative, policy, administrative, and programmatic changes, but few have been implemented. Of them, the most significant was the passage of the Indian Education Act (Title IV of Public Law 92-318, Educational Amendments of 1972). It authorized federal funding for local educational agencies, special programs and projects, and Indian adult education programs. It also established an Office of Indian Education in the U.S. Department of Education, a position of deputy commissioner of education, and a National Advisory Council on Indian Education. Other provisions included teacher training and fellowships in prescribed fields of study. Most important, however, was the mandated involvement of Indian people in the planning, design, implementation, and evaluation of programs and projects, which gave them more control over the education of their children.[9]

Federal emphasis upon Indian participation resulted in the passage of Public Law 93-638 in 1975, which was called the Indian Self-Determination and Educational Assistance Act. It granted authority to the Secretary of the Interior and the Secretary of Health, Education, and Welfare to contract with any tribe that so desired the operation of any programs or services their agencies provided, which also could be retroceded to the government at the tribes' discretion.[10] This legislation afforded tribes the opportunity and funding to enter into 638 contracts with the government to operate their own programs. Some tribes elected to contract with the BIA for the operation of their own schools, which has resulted in more culturally congruent curricula and innovative educational programs designed to maintain tribal culture and strengthen identity.

For the Welfare of Our Children and Religion

The Congress also enacted other legislation that has reaffirmed the commitment to Indian self-determination and cultural integrity. One was the Indian Child Welfare Act of 1978, which gave authority to Tribal Courts to decide Indian child adoption and placement matters. Preference was given first to a child's family or extended family, next to other tribal members, and then to other Indian tribal people. It removed Indian child guardianship matters from state courts with the intent of curtailing the number of adoptions of Indian children by non-Indians. It was also a commitment to the value of family or Indian extended family, which can provide the cultural teachings critical to a child's sense of identity.

It is impossible for Indigenous North American peoples to think of life as anything but Indian, and their spirituality is the core that maintains them. Consequently, because of infringements upon their spiritual beliefs and practices, the American Indian Religious Freedom Act (Public Law 95-341, S.J. Res. 102) was adopted as a joint resolution by the Congress on August 11, 1978. Indians celebrated its passage and looked upon it as an affirmation of culture and identity.

Referred to as AIRFA, the legislation was brief and comprised of two basic sections of which the first stated:

Henceforth it shall be the policy of the United States to protect and preserve for American Indians their inherent right of freedom to believe, express, and exercise the traditional religions of the American Indian, Eskimo, Aleut, and Native Hawaiians, including but not limited to access to sites, use and possession of sacred objects, and the freedom to worship through ceremonials and traditional rites.[11]

In section two, federal agencies, in consultation with traditional spiritual leaders, were to assess their policies and identify any barriers to the exercise of American Indian religious freedom and recommend any corrective legislative action that the president was to report to Congress.[12]

Federal agencies evaluated their policies, and 10 on-site hearings were held with tribal leaders and ceremonial people. The Task Force Report was completed in August 1979, and it documented 522 infringements on Indian religious freedom. It was a tragic commentary about a country's treatment of its Indigenous peoples of allowing even one violation of First Amendment rights, much less 522 of them. The violations of religious freedom ranged from the use of eagle feathers to desecration of and/or accessibility to Indian sacred sites, and a host of others in between. The report clearly demonstrated the need for AIRFA, the necessity for administrative changes in federal policy, and passage of legislative remedies.

Erosion of American Indian religious protection continued in the decade following the passage of AIRFA, which proved in court case after court case that it was not enforceable. There was no more guarantee for the possession of eagle feathers than there had been when Cheyennes and Arapahos were arrested for violating the 1976 Bald Eagle Protection Act. Members of the Native American Church who use peyote as a sacrament were being subjected to their usual religious persecution. Indian inmates in penal institutions were not afforded access to their medicine people in the same way that other prisoners had access to their ministers and priests. Indian sacred sites were being developed for tourism and recreation purposes and being exploited for the natural resources they contained, such as oil, gas, geothermal energy, timber, and uranium.

Then, in 1988 the United States Supreme Court ruled in the case of *Lyng* v. *Northwest Indian Cemetery Protective Association* that the U.S. Forest Service could manage its property as it chose, even though it would destroy the religions of the Karok, Yurok, and Tolowa Indians of northern California. The Forest Service's own expert witness concluded that the Gasquet-Orleans (G-O) Road would destroy the tribes' religion, a world renewal center, but it nonetheless did not trigger the protection of the Free Exercise Clause of the First Amendment. This ruling alarmed the Indigenous community because it eroded their First Amendment protection under the United States Constitution, and their best strategy was to amend AIRFA, which a few sympathetic members of Congress have attempted several times.

In 1990 the U.S. Supreme Court continued its erosion of Indians' First Amendment rights by ruling in *Employment Division, Department of Human Resources of Oregon* v. *Smith, et al.* that Oregon's prohibition of the sacramental use of peyote was constitutionally permissible. The ruling sent shock waves throughout the country's religious community and three years later resulted in Congress passing into law the Religious Freedom Restoration Act (Public Law 103-141, November 16, 1993). This law, however, did not go far enough in protecting the use of peyote and other Indian religious practices, and Indians continued to push for amendments to AIRFA.

Finally, on October 6, 1994, President Clinton signed into law Title II of the Native American Free Exercise of Religion Act, which makes the traditional use and possession of peyote by Indians lawful. An estimated 250,000 to300,000 Indians use peyote, which some have traced back 10,000 years to the Aztecs, making it one of the oldest practiced religions in the Western Hemisphere.

This Act (Public Law 103-344) amended the American Indian Religious Freedom Act, but only as it pertains to protecting the traditional use of peyote. Three other areas of religious concerns have yet to be legislatively protected, which are: (1) prisoners' religious rights, (2) religious use of eagles and other animals and plants, and (3) protection of sacred sites. Many people are uninformed or ill informed about American Indian spiritual ways, including prison officials. Some people do not understand the importance of eagle feathers, animals' parts, and plants in Indian ceremonies. Probably the least understood, however, is Indigenous peoples' spiritual relationship to the land where their churches, cathedrals, tabernacles, and temples are natural formations on a sacred landscape.

Indigenous people have places in their homelands that are just as sacred as Jerusalem, the Wailing Wall, and others. In fact, this country honored the sacredness of place for others during the Persian Gulf War, but it has not done this for American Indians. Jerry Flute, Director of the Association on American Indian Affairs, stated in Congressional testimony that:

> During the recent Desert Storm campaign, General Powell and General Schwarzkopf made a decision not to bomb religious sites in Iraq. In the midst of war with a ruthless enemy, the United States nonetheless recognized that there are certain spiritual values which transcend all disputes between governments and peoples and that it was essential that these values be recognized, respected and protected. Yet in this country, the same recognition, respect and protection is not provided to the religious sites of Native Americans, nor to our religious practices. What the United States so clearly sees when it looks overseas, it cannot see in its own backyard.[13]

There are 70 to 100 known sites considered sacred to Indigenous peoples in this country. For the Cheyenne, their natural church and the most sacred of all places on earth is Bear Butte, now a South Dakota State Park, which has already been desecrated. It has a parking area, observation platforms, hiking trails, and a visitors' center, all of which detract from the sacredness of the place. Despite this, Cheyennes still go to Bear Butte to pray, to fast, to make their offerings, to seek direction for their hearts, and to renew their identities as the "hearted-alike people." They go there to collect their sacred paints and other items that are necessary to their ceremonies, because they cannot obtain them anywhere else. It is still the spiritual center of their universe.

The Old Red Paint of Life

Ma'heo'o, the Creator of All That Is, planted the "hearted-alike people" in the womb of their mother, the earth, and after a time he called them to come to live on the earth's surface to walk a Road of Life. He called two good men each to come to a sacred mountain where he and all the sacred powers of the world taught them the sacred ways of the medicine bundles, which they brought to the hearted-alike people to sustain them in war and peace.

These two men, the Cheyenne Prophets, told the people of the aggressive strangers that would come to them from the east, who would bring sickness and change, and who would place many obstacles on their Road of Life. It has happened as they said and generations of Cheyenne children have been subjected to civilization, education, and Christianity, but amazingly they have survived. The strangers, indeed, brought many changes to this Indian earth in the form of land hunger, assimilation, education, religion, expropriation and exploitation, government policy, and laws.

Throughout all this, the Grandfather Sacred Above and the Grandmother Sacred Below have blessed their grandchildren with great medicine knowledge and vitality of spirit that keeps them prayerful minded and humble as they walk through time on the road that follows the sun always into the sunlight. It is the road of light, love, respect, and happiness. The Cheyenne have certain responsibilities in walking this road, and the most important is to maintain the sacredness of their lives and to respect the sacredness of all life that is. They must continue to honor themselves and celebrate the strength and tenacity of their cultural ways that have withstood centuries of continual genocidal assault. They must be peaceful warriors in order to maintain the sacredness of earth. They must paint their faces and bodies with the old red paint of life and remember that they are the beautiful and beloved *xamaa-vo'estaneo'o*, Indigenous children of this red earth.

NOTES

1. Rev. Rodolphe Petter, *English-Cheyenne Dictionary* (Kettle Falls, WA, 1913–15), pp. 581–582.
2. *English-Cheyenne Dictionary* (Lame Deer, MT: The Language Research Department of the Northern Cheyenne Title VII ESEA Bilingual Education Program, 1976), p. 19.
3. Petter, p. 229.
4. The term was first used to imply divine sanctioning of territorial expansion. The term gained popularity after appearing in an 1845 issue of the *United States Magazine and Democratic Review*.
5. *Treaties & Agreements of the Indian Tribes of the Southwest: Including Western Oklahoma* (Washington, DC: The Institute for the Development of Indian Law, n.d.), p. 90.

6. U.S. Congress, Senate Committee on Labor and Public Welfare, Special Subcommittee on Indian Education, *Indian Education: A National Tragedy— A National Challenge,* S. Res. 80, 91st Cong., 1st Sess., 1969, pp. i, ix.

7. Ibid., p. xi.

8. Ibid., p. 9.

9. U.S. Department of Health, Education, and Welfare, *The Indian Education Act of 1972,* prepared by the National Advisory Council on Indian Education (Washington, DC, n.d.), p. 5.

10. *Indian Self-Determination and Education Assistance Act,* Public Law 93-638, 93rd Cong., Jan. 4, 1975.

11. Christopher Vecsey, ed., *Handbook of American Indian Religious Freedom* (New York: The Crossroad Publishing Company, 1991), p. 138.

12. Ibid.

13. Jerry Flute, Testimony before the Senate Select Committee on Indian Affairs, American Indian Religious Freedom Act Oversight Hearing—Portland, Oregon, March 7, 1992, in *Indian Affairs,* Number 125, Winter/Spring 1992, p. 5.

CHAPTER 5
A QUESTION OF IDENTITY

By Ward Churchill

 **Ward Churchill** (Cherokee) is professor of American Indian Studies and Chair of the Department of Ethnic Studies at the University of Colorado—Boulder. He is one of the most outspoken Native American activists. In his lectures and numerous published works, he explores the themes of genocide in the Americas, historical and legal (re)interpretation of conquest and colonization, literary and cinematic criticism, and indigenist alternatives to the status quo. He is also a past national spokesperson for the Leonard Peltier Defense Committee. Among his numerous books are *Fantasies of the Master Race* (1992, 1999), *Struggle for the Land* (1993, 1999), *A Little Matter of Genocide* (1997), and *Acts of Rebellion* (2002).

Introduction

Among the most vexing and divisive issues afflicting Native North America at the dawn of the twenty-first century are the questions of who has a legitimate right to say he or she is American Indian, and by what criteria or whose definition this may or may not be true. Such queries and the answers to them hold an obvious and deeply important bearing, not only upon the personal sense of identity inhering in millions of individuals scattered throughout the continent but in terms of the degree to which some form of genuine self-determination can be exercised by the more than 400 nations indigenous to it in coming years. Conversely, they represent an accurate gauge of the extent to which the sovereignty of North America's Native peoples has been historically eroded or usurped by the continent's two preeminently colonial settler-states, the United States and Canada, and a preview of how the remainder stands to be eradicated altogether in the not-so-distant future.

Defining for itself the composition of its membership or citizenry in whatever terms and in accordance with whatever standards it freely chooses is, of course, the very bedrock expression of self-determination by any nation or people. The ability to maintain this prerogative is thus a vital measure of its sovereign standing.[1] By the same token, intervention in or preemption of this plainly internal function by any external entity may be taken as signifying a blatant abridgment of a nation's right to self-determination and a corresponding diminishment of its sovereignty. For that very reason, under conditions of colonialism, where one nation is subordinated directly to the political, economic, or strategic interests of another, and most especially in the kind of internal colonial systems prevailing in North America, where the colonizing powers have virtually subsumed the territoriality of the colonized within their own claimed geographies, such domination may be seen as a structural imperative.

Things cannot be put so straightforwardly in practice, however, since as early as 1960 colonialism in all forms has been flatly prohibited by international law.[2] In these circumstances, the kinds of subterfuge designed to create false appearances are an essential aspect of maintaining and perfecting the modes of colonial order. Hence, it is necessary for the colonizer not merely to preempt the sovereignty of the colonized, but to co-opt it, inculcating a comprador consciousness among some segment of the colonized population in which the forms of domination imposed by colonialism will be advocated as a self-determining expression of will emanating from the colonized themselves.[3]

At this point, with the codes of colonial domination embraced by many native people as comprising their own traditions, and articulation of the latter often perceived as a contravention of Indigenous sovereignty, the colonized become for all practical intents and purposes self-colonizing. In this most advanced and refined iteration of imperial order, confusion accomplishes much more cheaply, quietly, and efficiently what physical force was once required to obtain. Meaningful resistance, never mind decolonization, among those so thoroughly indoctrinated and deluded as to accept and enforce the terms of their own subjugation in the name of liberation is, on its face, quite impossible. Yet resistance and decolonization are not simply rights, but obligations under international law and most other recent philosophical and moral schemas of justice.[4]

The situation presents a dilemma of the first magnitude. Resolving it, and thereby actualizing the potential for a coherent and constructive Indigenous response to the realties that now confront us, and those that will confront our future generations, requires a systematic unraveling of the web of mystification through which North America's Native peoples have been bound ever more tightly into the carefully crafted mechanisms of our oppression and eventual negation. The purpose of this chapter is to make a contribution in this regard by sorting out that which traditionally has been part of the "Indian way" of identifying membership or citizens of our polities from that which has not, and to sketch out the mechanisms through which the latter has supplanted the former. From the resulting vantage point, it should prove possible to ascertain with some clarity the methods that must be reasserted if we are ever to truly throw off the yoke of colonial bondage, and those which must be rejected as perpetuating and perfecting the colonial structure.

The Traditional Way

There is not, and has never been, much of a genetic or hereditary distinction to be drawn between Indigenous peoples in the Americas. In part, this devolves upon the probability that the great proliferation of culturally distinct entities evident in the hemisphere by the time the European invasions commenced around 1500 had all evolved from three—or perhaps four—discernible "gene stocks," figures correlating rather well to the evident number of root linguistic variants.[5] More to the point, native peoples have for the most part always maintained relatively high degrees of sociocultural inclusiveness and consequent reproductive interactivity or interbreeding among one another.

Since time immemorial, Cheyennes (or their precursors) have intermarried with Arapahoes, Ojibways with Crees, Cayugas with Ononadagas, Yaquis with Turamaras, Choctaws with Chickasaws, and so on, ad infinitum. In such instances, depending on whether the cultures in question were matrilineal or patrilineal, either the male or female spouse would become a part of the other's society, as would their offspring. Genealogy rather than genetics was the core component of societal composition, although procedures for incorporation of individuals and sometimes whole groups by adoption, naturalization, or occasional merger were similarly well established and practiced with varying degrees of scale and frequency by most peoples, either periodically or continuously.

As non-Indians began to appear in substantial numbers across the hemisphere, literally thousands of "White Indians"—mostly English and French, but Swedes, Scots, Irish, Dutch, and others as well—who, dis-eased with aspects of their own cultures, had either married into, been adopted by, or petitioned for naturalization as member citizens of Indigenous nations.[6] By then, the phenomenon had become pronounced enough that it had long since precipitated a crisis among the Puritans of Plymouth Colony and figured in their waging of a war of extermination against the Pequots in 1637.[7]

The attraction of "going native" remained so strong, and the willingness of Indigenous peoples to accept Europeans into their societies so apparent, that it prevailed even among those captured in Indian and White warfare.[8] During the 1770s, George Croghan and Guy Johnson, both acknowledged authorities on the native peoples of the mid-Atlantic region, estimated that the great bulk of the several hundred English prisoners of all ages and both genders taken by the Indians had been adopted by them rather than being put to death.[9] At about the same time, Benjamin Franklin lamented that:

> [W]hen white persons of either sex have been taken prisoners young by the Indians, and lived a while among them, tho' ransomed by their Friends, and treated with all imaginable tenderness to prevail with them to stay among the English, yet in a Short time they become disgusted with our manner of life, and the care and pains that are necessary to support it, and take the first good Opportunity of escaping again into the Woods, from thence there is no reclaiming them.[10]

The literature of the period is literally filled with similar observations. Colonel Henry Bouquet, who headed a 1764 expedition to take charge of "captives" returned under terms of a treaty with England by the Shawnees, Miamis, and other peoples of the Ohio River Valley, issued orders that "they are to be closely watched and well Secured [as] most of them, particularly those who have been a long time among the Indians, will take the first Opportunity to run away."[11] The Reverend William Smith, chaplain and chronicler of Bouquet's foray, noted that most younger Whites seemed to view their "liberators" as captors and "parted from the savages with tears."[12]

Some, like 14-year-old John McCullough, managed to escape Bouquet's column and quickly reunited himself with his native family.[13]

> Although most of the returned captives did not try to escape, the emotional torment caused by the separation from their adopted families deeply impressed the colonists. The Indians "delivered up their beloved captives with the utmost reluctance; shed torrents of tears over them, recommending them to the care and protection of the commanding officer." One young woman "cryed and roared when asked to come and begged to Stay a little longer." "Some, who could not make their escape, clung to their savage acquaintance at parting, and continued many days in bitter lamentations, even refusing sustenance." Children "cried as if they would die when they were presented to us." With only small exaggeration an observer . . . could report that "every captive left the Indians with regret."[14]

Many Indians reciprocated by refusing to surrender those they had married, adopted, or otherwise accepted—especially children—under any but the most coercive circumstances.[15] In cases where there was no viable alternative, the record is replete with examples of adoptive native parents regularly visiting and otherwise maintaining familial relations with such children for the remainder of their own lives. Of course, children born of a union between Indian and non-Indian were almost invariably never relinquished at all (not the least because Whites, not Indians, tended to frown upon such "mixed-blood" offspring and thus made little or no effort to claim them).[16]

By 1830 at the latest, the notion of defining "Indianness" in terms of "race" had been rendered patently absurd. It has been reliably estimated that somewhere between one-third and one-half of all Native peoples still residing east of the Mississippi River were at that point genetically intermixed not only with one another, but with "Negroid and Caucasoid racial stock" as well. This is a genetic and demographic pattern that would spread rapidly westward over then next half-century.[17] There is little if any indication, moreover, that most Indigenous societies tended to view this increasing admixture as untoward or peculiar, much less threatening, in and of itself (this is as opposed to their often bitter resistance to the cultural, political, and material encroachments of Euro-American "civilization").

The Racial Dimension of Divide and Rule

It is instructive that while U.S. policy makers professed to embrace racism on both scientific and philosophical grounds, standpoints implying at least minimal consistency in application, they advanced its principles in a "pragmatic" fashion, which was both transparently self-serving and utterly contradictory. Since Blacks were considered to be property, yielding value not only in their labor, but also as commodities that could be bought and sold, it was profitable to breed them in ever larger numbers. To this end, an elaborate system of "quantifying" their racial admixture was devised—classifications such as "maroon," "quadroon," and "octoroon"—by which to assess their relative worth.[18] The overriding premise, however, was the "one-drop rule": A person with any amount of "Negroid blood" could be considered Black for purposes of law, even if computation of their "quantum" revealed them to be 127/128 White.[19]

Native people, by contrast, legally were understood to own property, mainly land and minerals within that land, coveted by Whites.[20] It followed then, and still does, that any and all manner of reductions in the number of Indians at large in North America corresponded directly to diminishment of the cloud surrounding the dominant society's claims of clear title to and jurisdictional rights over its purported landbase.[21] Hence, any racial admixture at all, especially with blacks, often was deemed sufficient to warrant individuals, and sometimes groups, being legally classified as a non-Indians, regardless of their actual standing in Indigenous society.[22] On this basis, most noticeably in the South, but elsewhere as well, the Indigenous societies themselves were proclaimed to be "extinct," their entire membership being simply redefined as belonging to such catch-all categories of presumed racial inferiority as "mulatto" or "colored."

While the intermingling of Natives with "Blacks" was invariably cast in a negative light, the mixing of Indian with "White stock" came to be viewed more favorably. As Thomas Jefferson, America's "most admired . . . slaveholding philosopher of freedom," observed in 1803, a calculated policy of subsuming native genetics within a much larger White gene pool might serve as an alternative to outright extermination as an answer to what he termed the "Indian Question."[23] "In truth, the ultimate point of rest and happiness for them is to let our settlements and theirs meet and blend together, to intermix, and become one people. Incorporating themselves with us as citizens of the United States, this is what the natural progress of things will, of course, bring on, and it will be better to promote than retard it."[24]

Completely oblivious to the reality of North America's abundant indigenous agriculture, and to the fact that "Whites" had learned to cultivate corn and other crops from Indians rather than the other way round, President Thomas Jefferson actually urged a delegation of Munsee, Lenni Lenape, and Mohican leaders to adopt a "farming way of life" when they visited him in 1808. "You will become one people with us," he went on to tell the astonished Indians. "Your blood will mix with ours, and will spread with ours across this great land."[25]

The sentiments underlying Jefferson's "humanitarian" strategy were framed less pleasantly, but with remarkable clarity, by J. C. Nott, a racial theorist whose views were endorsed by Samuel Morton and other prominent scientists of the day. With reference to the idea that at least five southern "tribes"—the Cherokee, Choctaw, Chickasaw, Creek, and Seminole—had been "civilized" in their own right before forcibly being evicted from their homelands during the 1830's,[26] he offered the following observation:

> It has been falsely asserted that the *Choctaw* and *Cherokee* Indians have made great progress in civilization. I assert positively, after the most ample investigation of the facts, that the pure-blooded Indians are everywhere unchanged in their habits. Many white persons, settling among the above tribes, have intermarried with them; and all such trumpeted progress exists among these whites and their mixed breeds alone. The pure-blooded savage still skulks untamed through the forest, or gallops athwart the prairie. Can any one call the name of a single pure Indian of the *Barbarous* tribes who—except in death, like a wild cat—has done anything worthy of remembrance (emphasis original)?[27]

It followed, according to the noted phrenologist, Charles Caldwell, that the "only efficient scheme to civilize the Indians is to *cross the breed*. Attempt any other and you [will have no alternative] but to *extinguish the race* (emphasis original)."[28] Such views, posing the alternative of genetic and cultural absorption to literal "extirpation," were embraced avidly by no less than Lewis Henry Morgan, the "founding giant" of American anthropology. Indeed, Morgan was of the expressed opinion that the former option was preferable to the latter mainly because a blending of minute quantities of Indian "blood" into that of the White "mainstream" would serve to "toughen our race" even while it "painlessly" eradicated the Indigenous population as such.[29]

All told, by 1860 or shortly thereafter, Euro-American academics had forged the full range of conceptual tools necessary for their government to use the traditionally inclusive structures of Native societies in a manner that would facilitate their rapid division, fragmentation, and, so it was thought at the time, ultimate dissipation en toto. Slowly but steadily, a national consensus was emerging to the effect that this represented the most appropriate solution to what by then had been transfigured into the "Indian Problem" within the popular discourse.[30] What remained necessary was for these tools to be applied systematically, through the implementation of a comprehensive and coherent policy (or set of policies). To this end, experimentation had long since begun.

The Impositions of United States Policy

Probably the first concerted effort on the part of U.S. officialdom to use the incorporation of whites and their mixed-blood offspring as a wedge with which to pry Indigenous societies apart began in the late 1700s, when Moravian missionaries were asked to serve as de facto federal emissaries to the Cherokee Nation.[31] Imbued with the mystical notion that White "Aryan" genetics correlated to such "innate" endowments as intellect and moral capacity, which in their minds corresponded with the potential to adopt "civilized" (Christian) outlooks and values, the Moravians and, after 1803, their Presbyterian colleagues "went out of their way to befriend" mixed-bloods rather than "pure" Indians while pursuing their goals of obtaining religious converts cum political allies.[32]

Predictably, this racial bias translated into a privileging of mixed-bloods in both political and material terms, regardless of their rank within the Cherokee polity and irrespective of whether they desired such "benefits." Such a situation was quite reasonably resented by other Cherokees, most especially those whose authority was undermined or supplanted by such external manipulation. The result, obviously intended by the United States, was the opening of deep cleavages among Cherokees that greatly weakened them in military as well as political and cultural terms, circumstances which amplified considerably the decisive advantages the United States already enjoyed in its drive to dispossess them of their property. Meanwhile, similar initiatives had been undertaken vis-à-vis the Creeks, Choctaws, Chickasaws, and others.[33]

Although the United States refrained from attempting such maneuvers during the first 30 years of treaty-making with Indigenous nations, an interval roughly corresponding to the period in which the young Republic, a veritable revolutionary outlaw state, desperately required the legitimation that could be bestowed via Native recognition of its sovereign status as Indigenous sovereignty having already been recognized through treaties with the European powers, special provisions pertaining to mixed-bloods entered its formal diplomacy with Indians beginning with a 1817 Treaty with the Wyandots and several other peoples of the Ohio and Pennsylvania region.[34] Thereafter, the performance was repeated in compact after compact, at least 53 times by 1868.

In only few instances, such as the 1847 Treaty with the Chippewa of the Mississippi and Lake Superior in which it is recognized by the United States that "half or mixed bloods of the Chippewas residing with them [should simply] be considered Chippewas," is there acknowledgment of the right of Indigenous nations to naturalize citizens as they saw fit.[35] In the great bulk of cases, such treaty provisions are plainly designed to accomplish the opposite effect, distinguishing those of mixed ancestry from the rest of their people almost always by unilaterally privileging them in a material fashion. Usually, this followed upon the model established in the above-mentioned 1817 treaty, the Eighth Article of which provided that, while the Indians themselves would hold certain lands in common, those "connected with said Indians, by blood or adoption" would receive individual tracts averaging 640 acres each.[36]

There were several variations on the theme. In one, exemplified by the 1818 Treaty with the Miami, chiefs as well as mixed-bloods and intermarried "Whites" were assigned individual parcels, one-to-six sections each in this case, while the rest of the people were assigned a tract in common; hence, not only were mixed-bloods figuratively elevated to the same standing as chiefs by external fiat, but the Miamis' actual leaders implicitly were linked to them rather than to their people as a whole.[37] On other occasions, as in the 1855 Treaty with the Winnebago, missionaries were substituted for chiefs.[38] Even in cases like the 1861 Treaty with the Cheyenne and Arapaho, where full-bloods and mixed-bloods were nominally treated the same, regardless of social rank—that is, everyone was allotted a parcel and/or monetary award—mixed-bloods often were singled out to receive larger quantities.[39]

In a number of instances, as with the 1857 Treaty with the Pawnee, provisions were designed explicitly to induce an outright physical separation of mixed-bloods from their people, a practice that was particularly odious in instances such as that addressed in the 1865 Treaty with the Osage in which "breeds" were the only group allowed (or coerced) to remain within a traditional homeland from which the rest of their nation was removed.[40] In the 1831 Treaty with the Shawnee, the notion of blood quantum was first applied in a formal way to determine who would—or, more importantly, who would not be recognized by the United States as a "real" Indian.[41] Moreover, racism aside, the treaties often employed a virulent sexist bias, tracing descent, acknowledging authority, and bestowing land titles along decidedly patriarchal lines even (or especially) in contexts where female property ownership, political leadership, and matrilineality were the Indigenous norms. This was a means of subverting the integrity of Native culture, undermining their sociopolitical cohesion, and confusing or negating their procedures for identifying member/citizens.[42]

In 1871, sensing that the capacity of most Indigenous nations to offer effective military resistance was nearing an end, Congress suspended further treaty-making with Indians.[43] There then followed a decade of reorganization during which the government shifted from what had been primarily a policy of physically subjugating Native peoples to an emphasis upon assimilating what remained of them, both geographically and demographically.[44] While there were a number of aspects to this transition, notably, the extension of U.S. criminal jurisdiction over reserved Native territories via the Seven Major Crimes Act of 1885,[45] its hallmark was passage of the 1887 General Allotment Act, a measure expressly intended to dissolve the collective relationship to land that was the fundament of traditional cultures by imposing the allegedly superior Anglo-Saxon system of individuated property ownership.[46]

The main ingredient of the Act was that each Indian, recognized as such by the United States, would be assigned an individually deeded parcel of land within existing reservation areas. These varied in size, depending on whether the Indian was a child (40 acres), unmarried adult (80 acres), or head of a family (160 acres). Once each Indian had received his or her personal allotment, becoming a U.S. citizen in the process, the law prescribed that the balance of each reservation be declared "surplus" and opened up to homesteading by non-Indians, corporate usage, or placed in some form of perpetual federal trust status: that is, designation as national parks and forests, military installations, or for other federal government purposes. In this manner, some 100 million of the approximately 150 million acres of land still retained by Indigenous nations for their own exclusive use and occupancy at the outset passed to Whites by 1934.[47]

The bedrock upon which the allotment process was built was the compilation of formal rolls listing those belonging to each Native people, reservation by reservation. While the Act itself posited no specific criteria by which this would be accomplished, responsibility for completing the task was ultimately vested in the individual federal agents assigned to preside over the reservations. Endowed as they were with staunchly racialist perspectives, and fully aware that whatever definitional constraints might be applied in determining the overall number of Indians would translate directly into an increased availability of property to their own society, it was predictable that these men would rely heavily upon the sort of blood quantum standards already evident in treaty language.[48]

In practice, it was typically required that a potential enrollee/allottee be able to demonstrate that she or he possessed "not less than one-half degree of blood" in the particular group in which he or she wished to be enrolled (intertribal pedigrees were seldom accepted, even for ostensible full-bloods, and the overall standard was almost never allowed to slip below quarter-blood).[49] The upshot was that anywhere from a third to two-thirds of all those who might otherwise have been eligible to receive allotments were denied not only land, but federal recognition, as being member/citizens of their nations.[50] In total, government functionaries admitted to the existence of only 237,196 Native people within U.S. borders by the late 1890s, of whom only a small percentage were less than half-blood members of specific groups.[51]

To ice the cake of racialist reconfiguration of Indian identity, the Act provided that those enrolled as full-bloods would, under the legal presumption that they were genetically incompetent to manage their own affairs, be issued "trust patents" for their allotments, to be "administered in their behalf by the Secretary of the Interior or his delegate" (the latter term meaning the local Indian agent) for a quarter-century.[52] Mixed-bloods, by virtue of their white genetics, were deemed to be competent for such purposes and therefore issued patents in fee simple. This, along with other blatantly preferential treatment bestowed as a matter of policy upon those of mixed ancestry, drove the final wedges into many once harmonious Indigenous societies. In the more extreme instances, such as that of the Kaws in Kansas, the full-bloods' visceral response was to repudiate mixed-bloods altogether, demanding their elimination from the tribal roll and seeking to expel them as a body from their society.[53]

By the turn of the century, then, virtually every Indigenous nation within the United States had, by way of an unrelenting substitution of federal definitions for their own, been stripped of the ability to determine for themselves in any meaningful way the internal composition of their constituencies. The manner in which this had been accomplished, moreover, ensured that rifts even among those still recognized by the government as being Indians were of a nature that would all but guarantee eventual dissolution of Native societies, at least in the sense they had traditionally understood themselves. Allotment and the broader assimilation policy of which it was part had truly proven themselves to be, in the words of Indian Commissioner Francis E. Leupp, "a mighty pulverizing engine for breaking up the tribal mass."[54]

Internalization

The breakup and diminishment of the reservation landbase were not the only factors leading to confident predictions that there would be no Indians culturally recognizable as such in the United States by some point around 1935.[55] Beginning in the 1860s, there had been an increasing emphasis on "educating" Native youth on the ways of the dominant society, a trend that was rapidly consolidated in the 1880s as a concomitant to allotment and other assimilationist techniques. While there were several options available, such as reservation-based day-schools—all of them less expensive and more humane— the mode selected for delivery of such instruction was primarily that of off-reservation boarding schools located in places as remote as possible from Native communities.[56]

The model for what became an entire system was the Carlisle Indian School, established in Pennsylvania in 1875 by Captain Richard Henry Pratt, a man whose main qualification for the task seems to have been that he had earlier served as warden of a military prison at Fort Marion, Florida.[57] Following Pratt's stated objective of "killing the Indian" in each student, Carlisle and other facilities such as Chilocco, Albuquerque, Phoenix, Haskell, and Riverside (by 1902 there were two dozen of them) systematically "deculturated" their pupils.[58] Children brought to the schools as young as age six were denied most or all direct contact with their families and societies for years on end. They were shorn of their hair and required to dress in the manner of Euro-America, forbidden to speak their languages or practice their religions, prevented from learning their own histories or being in any other way socialized among their own people.[59]

Simultaneously, all students were subjected to a grueling regimen of indoctrination in Christian morality—mainly the "virtues" of private property, sexual repression, and patriarchy—proper English and arithmetic, officially approved versions of history, civics, and natural science—the latter devoted mostly to inculcating prevailing notions of racial hierarchy.[60] To instill the "work ethic"— that is, to prepare students for the lot assigned their racial group once they had been absorbed by Euro-America—they also were required to spend half of each day during the school year engaged in industrial vocational training, a label for uncompensated manual labor. During the summers, most of the older boys were "jobbed out" at very low wages to work on White-owned farms or at local businesses. The girls were assigned to White households as domestics and the like.[61]

Individual Indigenous families and, often, whole societies resisted the process. In 1891 and again in 1893, Congress authorized the use of police, troops, and other forcible means to compel the transfer of children from reservation to boarding school and to keep them there once they had arrived.[62] Hence, despite the best efforts of their Elders, and not infrequently of the students themselves, a total of 21,568 Indigenous children—about a third of the targeted age group— were confined in the schools in 1900.[63] As of the late 1920s, the system had been diversified and expanded to the point that upwards of 80 percent of each successive generation of Native youth was being comprehensively "acculturated" in a more-or-less uniform fashion.[64]

By 1924, assimilation had progressed to the point that a "clean-up bill" was passed through which the responsibilities, though not necessarily all the rights, of U.S. citizenship were imposed upon all Indians who had not already been naturalized under the Allotment Act or other federal initiatives.[65] Although it appeared as though this might represent the culminating statutory ingredient necessary to allow for the final absorption of Native America, fate intervened in a most unexpected fashion to avert this result (formally, if not in terms of more practical cultural, political, and economic realities). This, rather ironically, took the form of resources: The mostly barren tracts of land left to Indians after allotment—thought to be worthless by 19th century policy makers—had by the late 1920s been revealed as some of the more mineral-rich territories in the world.[66]

Loath to see these newfound assets thrown into the public domain (many had strategic value, real or potential), the more forward-looking federal economic planners quickly perceived the utility of retaining them in trust, where they might be exploited at controlled rates by preferred corporations for designated purposes and in the most profitable fashion imaginable. This resulted in 1925 with a recommendation by a committee of 100 officially selected academic experts and business leaders that allotment and the more draconian objectives of assimilation policy be immediately abandoned in favor of preserving the reservations in some permanently subordinated capacity and inaugurating a policy of carefully calibrated economic development therein.[67]

This, in turn, led to passage of the 1934 Indian Reorganization Act (IRA), through which what remained of traditional Native governments were for the most part supplanted by federally designed "tribal councils" meant to serve as the medium for long-term administration of the newly conceived internal colonial domain.[68] Although the IRA was imposed behind the democratic facade of reservation-by-reservation referenda, the record reveals that Bureau of Indian Affairs (BIA) field representatives obtained favorable results by presenting skewed or patently false information to voters in a number of instances, flatly rigging the results in others.[69] While democratic appearances were reinforced by the fact that the government of each reorganized reservation functioned on the basis of its own "tribal constitution," the reality is that these "founding" documents were essentially boilerplate contraptions resembling corporate charters hammered out on an assembly-line basis by Bureau personnel.[70]

Nowhere is this more obvious than in the language of the IRA constitutions pertaining to criteria of tribal membership. Although there are certain variations between instruments, most simply aped the then-prevailing federal quantum standard of quarter-blood minimum, while all of them, regardless of the degree of blood required, advanced genetics as the linchpin of identity.[71] That there was no noteworthy resistance among Native supporters of the IRA to this conspicuous usurpation of Indigenous tradition is unsurprising, given that they were all but invariably drawn from the ranks of those indoctrinated in the boarding schools to see themselves in racial rather than national, political, or cultural terms.[72]

With the embrace of the IRA constitutions by what were projected as solid majorities on most reservations, Euro-American definitions of and constraints upon Indian identity were formally as well as psychologically and intellectually internalized by Native America. From there on, the government could increasingly rely upon Indians themselves to enforce its race codes for it. Indeed, whenever the existence of the latter has been made a point of contention, Washington has been able to lay the onus of responsibility directly at the feet of the IRA governments it not only conceived and installed, but which remain utterly and perpetually dependent upon federal patronage for their base funding and whatever limited authority they might wield.[73] They, in turn, defend such negation of Indigenous sovereignty in the name of maintaining it.[74] A more perfect shell game is impossible to imagine.

Enter the Purity Police

The reconfiguration and structural assimilation of the mechanisms of Indigenous governance (by the early 1990s, IRA-style councils were being openly referred to as a third level of the federal government itself) were facilitated and reinforced, not only by the increasingly pervasive indoctrination of Native students via the educational system, but also by the lingering effects of allotment.[75] Foremost in this respect was the "heirship problem" created by the fact that the reservation landbase had been reduced to a size corresponding to the number of Indians recognized by the Bureau of Indian Affairs as existing during the 1890s, with no provision made for a population rebound of any sort.[76] As the matter was politely explained in 1994:

> Upon the death of the original allottees the allotments, or portions of them, have descended to heirs or devisees. As these heirs in turn have died, their holdings have been subdivided among their heirs or devisees, and so on through the years. As a result, about half of the allotted Indian lands are in heirship status. The authors of the original legislation failed to anticipate the problems that would be caused by the partitioning of an individual's land following

his death. Thousands of the allotments in an heirship status are subject to so many undivided interests that they can be utilized only with great difficulty by their Indian owners . . . Undivided interests in a single allotment can often be expressed by fractions with a common denominator of 1,000,000 or more [by this point].[77]

In other words, there was no reserved land available to accommodate the 50 percent increase over the turn-of-the-century number of recognized Indians recorded in the 1950 U.S. Census.[78] Rather than remediating the problem by transferring some portion of the lands unlawfully stripped away from Native people back to its rightful owners, the government launched a massive and sustained program to relocate the Native "population surplus" from the land altogether, dispersing them for the most part in major urban areas. At the same time, as an incentive for them to leave, funding for on-reservation programming of all sorts was sliced to the bone and sometimes deeper. One result is that, while well over 90 percent of federally recognized Indians lived on the reservations in 1900, fewer than 45 percent do so today.[79]

Another federal cost-cutting measure, beginning in the mid-1950s, was to simply "terminate" recognition of entire nations whose reservations were found to be devoid of minerals, or who were deemed to be too small and insignificant to warrant the expenditures necessary to administer them.[80] A total of 103 peoples, ranging from large groups like the Menominee in Wisconsin and Klamath in Oregon to the tiny Mission Bands of Southern California, were unilaterally dissolved, their remaining lands absorbed into the U.S. territorial corpus and their population effectively declared to be non-Indians, before the process ran its course in the early 1960s.[81] Only a handful, including the Menominee but not the Klamath, were ever reinstated.[82]

Predictably, rather than seeking to combat such trends, federally installed and supported tribal councils amplified them. In the face of declining federal appropriations to Indian affairs, they, by and large, set out to reduce the number of Indians eligible to draw against them. Arguing that the fewer people entitled to receive benefits such as health care and commodity foodstuffs, or to receive per capita payments against mineral extraction, water diversions, and past land transfers, the larger the share for those who remained, the councils were able to peddle their bill of goods to many—though by no means all—of their increasingly impoverished reservation constituents. In short order, the IRA constitutions on many reservations were amended or rewritten to reflect higher blood quantum requirements for tribal enrollment.[83] In a number of instances, reservation residency was required as well, a stipulation that excluded the children of relocatees regardless of their documentable "degree of Indian blood."[84]

The council heads, through a federally funded lobbying organization dubbed the National Tribal Chairmen's Association (NTCA), launched an aggressive campaign to recast the definition of *Indian* in the public consciousness, and which, they made it clear, by law, as being only those "enrolled in a federally recognized tribe."[85] Redefined as *non-Indians* in this perverse scenario was everyone from terminated peoples like the Klamaths to the unenrolled traditionals still living on and about many reservations, from nations like the Abenakis of Vermont, who had never consented to a treaty with the United States and were thus formally unrecognized, to the NTCA members' own nieces and nephews residing in cities.[86] Also sacrificed in the proposed ethnic purge were thousands of hapless children, orphaned and otherwise, whom federal welfare agencies had caused to be adopted by non-Indian families.[87]

The government declined to adopt the NTCA's simplistic nomenclature of "Indianness." Instead, it conjured up a proliferation of what by now amount to at least 80 different and often conflicting definitions of its own, each of them conforming to some particular bureaucratic or policy agenda, most sporting a larger or smaller claque of Indian subscribers queued up to defend it under the presumption they would somehow or another benefit by their endorsement. Under such conditions, it is possible to challenge the legitimacy of virtually any-one identifying himself or herself as Indian on one or several grounds (often having little or nothing to do with genuine concerns about identity per se).[88] The result has been a steadily rising tide of infighting between and among Native peoples over the past 40 years.[89]

The Way Ahead

The internalization of Euro-America's conception of race by Native peoples, the virulence with which it is now being manifested in all too many sectors of the Indigenous community, and the ubiquity of the confusion and divisiveness this has generated among Indians and their potential supporters represent a culmi-nation of federal policy initiatives originating nearly 200 years ago. To all appearances, Native North America has been rendered effectively self-coloniz-ing and, if present attitudes persist, it stands to become self-liquidating as well. The tale is told in the demographic data pertaining to those who are federally recognized.

> During the twentieth century population recovery of American Indians there has been an increasing mixture between them and non-Indian peoples. Data concerning this may be obtained from the 1910 and 1930 U.S. censuses of Amer-ican Indians . . . [In 1910] 56.5 percent of American Indians enumerated in the United States were full-blood—150,053 out of 265,682—with the blood quan-tum of 8.4 percent (22,207) not reported . . . In the U.S. census of 1930, however, 46.3 percent—153,933 out of 332,397—were enumerated as full-bloods and 42.4 percent (141,101) were enumerated as mixed-bloods, with the degree of Indian blood of 11.2 percent (37,363) not reported. Thus, whereas the American Indian population size increased by slightly over 66,000 from 1910 to 1930, the number of full-blood American Indians increased by only 4,000; most of the increase was among mixed-blood Indians.[90]

Such trends have not only continued but accelerated. The number of sup-posed full-bloods has thus dropped to almost nothing among populous peoples like the Minnesota and Wisconsin Chippewa. Full-bloods now represent only 5 percent of the whole, while the proportion and composition of mixed-bloods has climbed dramatically.[91] At present rates of intermarriage, the segment of the federally recognized Native population evidencing less than one-quarter degree blood quantum, presently less than 4 percent, will have climbed to 59 percent or more by 2080.[92] To tighten or even adhere to quantum requirements in the face of such realities is to engage in a sort of autogenocide by definitional and statistical extermination.[93] As historian Patricia Nelson Limerick has observed in this connection:

> Set the blood quantum at one-quarter, hold to it as a rigid definition of Indians, let intermarriage proceed as it [has] for centuries, and eventually Indians will be defined out of existence. When that happens, the federal government will be freed of its persistent "Indian problem."[94]

Cognizant of this, some smaller peoples like the Umatillas in Oregon have already undertaken to preserve racial cant while offsetting the consequent prospect of definitional self-extinguishment by proposing revision of their constitutions to require that future enrollees demonstrate some degree of blood, no matter how minute, in addition to "at least one-quarter degree of blood . . . in another federally recognized tribe or tribes."[95] Left conspicuously unexplained in such convoluted formulations is exactly how being a quarter-blood Lakota or Mohawk supposedly makes a person one bit more Umatilla than does being a quarter-blood Irish, Ibo, or Han. In the converse, no explanation is offered as to why a person genealogically connected to the group would be less Umatilla in orientation, absent some sort generic Indian genetic structure, than a person who had it.

The implications of this become most striking when it is considered in juxtaposition to the actual rather than federally recognized size of the present Indigenous population of the United States and the potential power deriving from its scale. Jack Forbes, perhaps the closest examiner of the issue, has noted that since 1969:

> the Bureau of the Census, conspiring with the Office of Management and Budget and political special interests, has [deliberately obfuscated] the "racial" character of the U.S. population and, as part of the process, has "lost" some six to eight million persons of Native American ancestry and appearance with a scientifically useless "Hispanic/Spanish" category. In addition, [seven million or more] persons of mixed African and Native American ancestry remain uncounted as such because of the way census questions were asked and the answers tallied.[96]

Forbes estimates that, even using standard blood quantum criteria, the actual Native population of the lower 48 in 1980 was well over 15 million rather than the 1.4 million officially admitted by the Census Bureau.[97] Employing traditional Indigenous methods of identifying population rather than racial criteria per se would have resulted in an even higher count still. As of 1990 when the official count reached nearly two million, inclusion of these most rapidly growing sectors of the Native population results in an aggregate of as many as 30 million persons overall.[98] The ability to wield political and economic clout inherent to the latter tally, as opposed to the former—which comes to less than 0.5 percent of the overall U.S. population—is self-evident.

Fortunately, there is at least one concrete example of how things might be taken in the direction of realizing this potential. The Cherokee Nation of Oklahoma (CNO) in its 1975 constitution took the unprecedented step, still unparalleled by other 20th-century Indigenous governments, of completely dispensing with blood quantum requirements in its enrollment procedures and resuming its reliance upon a more traditional genealogical mode of determining citizenship.[99] This had the effect of increasing the number of persons formally identified as Cherokees from fewer than 10,000 during the late 1950s to slightly over 232,000 by 1980 (and about 300,000 today).[100] On this basis, the Cherokees, whose reservation was dissolved pursuant to the 1898 Curtis Act, have been able to assert what amounts to a split jurisdiction over their former territory.[101] Moreover, while much has been made by assorted race mongers about how this course of action was "diluting" whatever was left of "real" Cherokee culture and society, the precise opposite result was obtained in practice.

> The Oklahoma Cherokee, without a reservation landbase, have been able to survive tribally by an inclusive definition of what it is to be Cherokee. Their definition allowed relatively large numbers of people with Cherokee lineage but relatively small amounts of Cherokee blood into the tribe. This allowed the tribe to reestablish itself after virtual "dissolution" and to achieve political power in Oklahoma. The tribe, in turn, has protected a smaller group of fullblood, more traditional Cherokee from American non-Indian ways of life.[102]

Plainly, in and of itself, the CNO initiative has neither ended the internecine bickering over identity that has precluded anything resembling unity among Native people, much less established the basis upon which to free even the Cherokees from internal colonial domination by the United States. It does, however, represent a substantial stride in the right direction. If the model it embodies is ultimately seized and acted upon by a broadening spectrum of Indigenous nations in the years ahead, the tools required for liberating Native North America may at long last be forged. In the alternative, should the currently predominating racialist perspectives associated with the IRA regimes prevail, the road to extinction can be traversed rather quickly.

NOTES

1. For discussion see Andres Rigo Sureda, *The Evolution of the Right to Self-Determination* (Leyden: A. W. Sythoff, 1973); Aureliu Cristescu, *The Right to Self-Determination: Historical and Current Developments on the Basis of United Nations Instruments* (UN Document E/CN.4/Sub.2/404/Rev.1 (1981); Michla Pomerance, *Self-Determination in Law and Practice* (The Hague: Marinus Nijhoff, 1982).

2. See Declaration on the Granting of Independence to Colonial Countries and Peoples (U.N.G.A. Res. 1514(XV), 15 U.N. GOAR, Supp. (No. 16) 66, U.N. Doc. A/4684 (1961), adopted by the United Nations General Assembly, Dec. 14, 1960). The right of all peoples to self-determination, as well the procedures and structures by which a rapid, orderly, and universal process of

decolonization was/is to occur, was enunciated as a matter of international law in the Charter of the United Nations (59 Stat. 1031, T.S. No. 993, 3 Bevans 1153, 1976 Y.B.U.N. 1043, Oct. 24, 1945). Both texts are included in Burns H. Weston, Richard A. Falk, and Anthony D'Amato, eds., *Basic Documents in International Law and World Order* (St. Paul: West Publishing, 1990), pp. 16–32, 343–344.

3. See Albert Memmi, *The Colonizer and the Colonized* (Boston: Beacon Press, 1965), p. 89; Memmi develops the idea further in his *Dominated Man* (Boston: Beacon Press, 1969). A superb analysis of the manner in which such results are achieved is provided in Martin Carnoy's *Education as Cultural Imperialism* (New York: David McKay, 1975).

4. A good overview is provided in Richard Falk, *Human Rights and State Sovereignty* (New York: Holmes & Meier, 1981).

5. The three groupings are designated by linguists and geneticists alike as being "Amerind," "Na-Dene," and "Eskimo-Aleut"; see Joseph H. Greenberg, *Language in the Americas* (Stanford: Stanford University Press, 1988). Of the trio, Amerind is by far the oldest and most extensive, demonstrating a continuous presence in the hemisphere for at least 40,000 years—and perhaps 70,000 years or longer—and encompassing most of the area from central Canada to Tierra del Fuego; L. S. Cressman, *Prehistory of the Far West: Homes of Vanquished Peoples* (Salt Lake City: University of Utah Press, 1977); Richard Wolkomir, "New Finds Could Rewrite the Start of American History," *Smithsonian* 21, no. 12 (1991), pp. 130–132, 134–144. The current argument that there may have been a fourth stock is well made in Theodore Schurr, et al., "Amerindian Mitochondrial DNAs Have Rare Asian Mutations at High Frequencies, Suggesting They Derived from Four Primary Maternal Lineages," *American Journal of Human Genetics* 46, no. 3 (1990), pp. 613–623; also see Satoshi Harai, et al., "Peopling of the Americas: Founded by Four Major Lineages of Mitochondrial DNA," *Molecular Biology of Evolution* 10, no. 1 (1993), pp. 23–47.

6. See, for example, James Axtell, "The White Indians of Colonial America," in *The European and the Indian: Essays in the Ethnohistory of North America* (New York: Oxford University Press, 1981), pp. 168–206.

7. Richard Drinnon, *Facing West: The Metaphysics of Indian-Hating and Empire-Building*, 2nd ed. (New York: Schocken, 1990), pp. 3–34.

8. See generally, J. Norman Heard, *White into Red: A Study of the Assimilation of White Persons Captured by the Indians* (Meyuchen: Scarecrow Press, 1973). Also see Richard Drinnon, *White Savage: The Case of John Dunn Hunter* (New York: Schocken Books, 1972).

9. William Robertson, "The Opinions of George Croghan on the American Indian," *Pennsylvania Magazine of History and Biography* 71 (1947), p. 157; Milton W. Hamilton, "Guy Johnson's Opinions on the American Indians," *Pennsylvania Magazine of History and Biography* 77 (1953), p. 322.

10. See Benjamin Franklin's letter to Peter Collinson, dated May 9, 1753, in Leonard W. Larabee, et al., eds., *The Papers of Benjamin Franklin,* vol. 4 (New Haven: Yale University Press, 1959), pp. 481–482.

11. Sylvester K. Stevens and Donald H. Kent, ed., *The Papers of Col. Henry Bouquet*, vol. 17. (Harrisburg: Pennsylvania State Historical Society, 1940–43), p. 38.

12. William Smith, DD, *Historical Account of Colonel Bouquet's Expedition against the Ohio Indians, 1764* (Philadelphia, 1765), p. 80. Also see William S. Ewing, "Indian Captives Released by Colonel Bouquet," *Western Pennsylvania Historical Magazine* 39, no. 3 (1956), pp. 187–203.

13. See "A Narrative of the Captivity of John McCullough, Esq.," in *A Selection, of Some of the Most Interesting Narratives, of Outrages, Committed by the Indians, in Their Wars, with the White People, 2 vols.* Archibald Loudon, ed. Vol. 1 (Carlisle, 1808–11), pp. 326–327.

14. Axtell, *The European and the Indian: Essays in the Ethnohistory of North America*, p. 177. He is quoting from Smith's *Historical Account of Colonel Bouquet's Expedition against the Ohio Indians, 1764*, p. 80. *Bouquet's Expedition*, 390–391; "Provincial Correspondence: 1750 to 1765," p. 500; Frederick Post, "Relation of Frederick Post of Conversation with Indians, 1760," *Pennsylvania Archives*, no. 3 (1853).

15. See William Walton, *The Captivity and Sufferings of Benjamin Gilbert and His Family, 1780–83.* (Philadelphia, 1784), pp. 103, 107.

16. This tendency is remarked upon by Brewton Berry in the first chapter of his *Almost White: A Study of Certain Racial Hybrids in the Eastern United States* (New York: Macmillan, 1963).

17. Jack D. Forbes, *Africans and Native Americans: The Language of Race and the Evolution of Red-Black Peoples*, 2nd ed. (Urbana: University of Illinois Press, 1993), pp. 249–264. At least one credible analyst has gone further, asserting that the "available evidence indicates that the ethnic mixture between Indians and Negroes is of vastly greater proportions than has hitherto been realized . . . The American Negro population of today is a composite of African, White and Indian elements"; see M. F. Ashley Montagu, "Origins of the American Negro," *Psychiatry* 7 (1944), pp. 163–174.

18. The system appears to have been adapted from the more comprehensive set of categories developed by the Spanish and Portuguese for use in Central and South America. The Latino schema, unlike its North American derivative, included classifications for Black/Indian, Indian/White, and Black/White/Indian admixtures; see, for example, Magnus Mörner, *Race Mixture in the History of Latin America* (Boston: Little, Brown, 1967), p. 58; Nicolás Sánchez-Alboronoz, *The Population of Latin America: A History* (Berkeley: University of California Press, 1974), pp. 129–130.

19. For one of the better elaborations and analyses, see John Codman Hurd, *The Law of Freedom and Bondage in the United States* (New York: Negro Universities Press, 1968).

20. Perhaps the greatest conundrum confronting U.S. jurists during the early days of the republic was the fact that aboriginal peoples were clearly vested with property rights vis-à-vis their territories under the Doctrine of Discovery and other prominent elements of international law; Robert A.

Williams Jr., *The American Indian in Western Legal Thought: The Discourses of Conquest* (New York: Oxford University Press, 1990).

21. The premise was/is two-fold. First, under the principle that "vacant land" (*territorium rez nullius*) could be claimed outright by whoever was willing to occupy and develop it, the United States incurred a clear and official interest in pretending that, not only were there not large numbers of Native peoples present in North America by the late eighteenth century, but there never had been (this is a theme still pursued with a vengeance by America's academic apologists and other professional liars). Second, by progressively defining an ever-increasing proportion of even admitted Indigenous populations out of existence on racial grounds, federal policy makers could conveniently negate much—or sometimes all—of their residual property interests (this, too, is an ongoing theme). It should be noted that the process by no means devolved upon such factual/definitional manipulations in any exclusive sense. Outright physical eradication of numerous native peoples, either partially or completely, was also an integral aspect; for a more detailed and comprehensive examination of these issues, see my *A Little Matter of Genocide: Holocaust and Denial in the Americas* (San Francisco: City Lights, 1997). Also see the relevant sections of Russell Thornton's *American Indian Holocaust and Survival: A Population History Since 1492* (Norman: University of Oklahoma Press, 1987), and David E. Stannard's *American Holocaust: Columbus and the Conquest of the New World* (New York: Oxford University Press, 1992).

22. See, for example, Chapters 7 and 8 in Forbes, *Africans and Native Americans*. Also see Edward B. Reuter, *Race Mixture: Studies in Intermarriage and Miscegenation* (New York: McGraw-Hill, 1931).

23. The characterization of Jefferson accrues from Stannard, *American Holocaust: Columbus and the Conquest of the New World,* p. 120.

24. Quoted in Julie Schimmel, "Inventing the Indian," in *The West as America: Reinterpreting Images of the Frontier, 1820–1920.* William H. Truettner, ed. (Washington, DC: Smithsonian Institution Press, 1991), p. 174. On unintendedly genocidal implications of Jefferson's perspective, see Bernard W. Sheehan, *Seeds of Extinction: Jeffersonian Philanthropy and the American Indian* (Chapel Hill: University of North Carolina Press, 1973).

25. Quoted in Reginald Horsman, *Race and Manifest Destiny: The Origins of Racial Anglo-Saxonism* (Cambridge: Harvard University Press, 1981), p. 108. On the nature, extent, and quality of native agriculture (which greatly surpassed that of Europe on all counts), see Jack Weatherford, *Indian Givers: How the Indians of the Americas Transformed the World* (New York: Fawcett Columbine, 1988).

26. The notion that Indians might be "redeemed" through acculturation to "civilized" ways dates back at least as far as the arguments put forth in their regard by Bartolomé de Las Casas at Valladolid in 1550; see Lewis Hanke, *Aristotle and the Indians: A Study in Race Prejudice in the Modern World* (Chicago: Henry Regnery, 1959); also Lewis Hanke, *All Mankind Is One: A*

Study in the Disputation Between Bartolomé de Las Casas and Juan Ginés de Sepúlveda on the Intellectual and Religious Capacity of American Indians (DeKalb: Northern Illinois University Press, 1974). In the United States, a somewhat derivative argument—that apparent racial distinctions were "environmentally induced," and that Indians (and Blacks) were thus as fully human as Whites—was advanced by Samuel Stanhope Smith in his *Essay on the Causes of Variety of Complexion and Figure in the Human Species,* reprint of 1810 enlargement of 1787 original (Cambridge: Harvard University Press, 1965). The idea that the "Five Civilized Tribes" might be exemplary of the resultant native potential was expounded by Secretary of War Henry Knox, among others, as early as 1792; see: Reginald Horsman, *Expansion and American Indian Policy, 1783–1812* (East Lansing: Michigan State University Press, 1967), pp. 54–65. On the problematic aspects of using the term "tribes" to describe Indigenous nations, see "Naming Our Destiny: Toward a Language of American Indian Liberation," in *Struggle for the Land: Indigenous Resistance to Genocide, Ecocide, and Expropriation in Contemporary North America* (Monroe: Common Courage Press, 1994), pp. 291–357.

27. Quoted in Robert F. Berkhofer, Jr., *The White Man's Indian: Images of the American Indian from Columbus to the Present* (New York: Vintage, 1978), pp. 58–59. Unsurprisingly, Nott, along with his subsequent collaborator and coauthor George R. Gliddon, ended up being a staunch advocate of racial wars of extermination in a manner that clearly prefigured Hitler:

> Nations and races, like individuals, have an especial destiny: some to rule, and others to be ruled . . . No two distinctly marked races can dwell together on equal terms. Some races, moreover, seem destined to live and prosper for a time, until the destroying race comes, which is to exterminate and supplant them . . . [H]uman progress has arisen mainly from the war of the races. All the great impulses which have been given to it from time to time have been the results of conquests and colonizations.

Quoted from: J. C. Nott and George R. Gliddon, *Types of Mankind, or Ethical Researches, Based upon the Ancient Monuments, Paintings, Sculptures, and Crania of Races, and upon their Natural, Geographical, Philosophical, and Biblical History* (Philadelphia: Lippencott, Grambo, 1854), pp. 77, 79. For an example of Morton's encouragement of Nott's research, see his letter in "Nott's 'Caucasion and Negro Races," in *Southern Quarterly Review* 8 (July), p. 160.

28. Quoted in R. W. Haskins, *History and Progress of Phrenology* (Buffalo: n.p., 1839), pp. 110–111. Like Nott and Gliddon, Caldwell would become an open advocate of physical genocide. "Civilization," he opined, "is destined to exterminate [Indians], in common with wild animals"; see Charles Caldwell, *Thoughts on the Original Unity of the Human Race* (New York: Harper Bros., 1830), p. 151. Varying analyses, all cogent, will be found in Roy Harvey Pearce, *The Savages of America: A Study of the Indian and the Idea of Civilization,* 2nd ed. (Baltimore: Johns Hopkins University Press, 1965); Richard Slotkin, *Regeneration Through Violence: The Mythology of the American Frontier, 1600–1860* (Middletown: Wesleyan University Press, 1973); Brian Dippie,

The Vanishing American: White Attitudes and American Indian Policy (Middletown: Wesleyan University Press, 1982), especially Chapter 2.

29. Quoted in Robert E. Beider, *Science Encounters the Indian, 1820–1880: The Early Years of American Ethnology* (Norman: University of Oklahoma Press, 1986), p. 220. Morgan has generally been cast as a "progressive," given that Karl Marx and Freidrich Engels were heavily influenced by his *League of the Ho-de-no-sau-nee or Iroquois* (New York: Dodd, Meade, 1851) when preparing their book *The Origins of the Family, Private Property and the State* (1884), included in *Marx and Engels: Selected Writings,* vol. 3 (Moscow: Foreign Language Publishers, 1973). *Origins,* in turn, has been highly touted by (white) socialist-feminists, then and now; see, for example, Sheila Rowbotham, *Women, Resistance and Revolution: A History of Women and Revolution in the Modern World* (New York: Pantheon, 1972).

30. For a good overview of this evolution, see Francis Paul Prucha, *Americanizing the American Indian: Writings of the "Friends of the Indian," 1800–1900* (Lincoln: University of Nebraska Press, 1973). Also see George D. Harmon, *Sixty Years of Indian Affairs: Political, Economic, and Diplomatic, 1789–1850* (Chapel Hill: University of North Carolina Press, 1941).

31. The Moravians, who were the first missionaries to be admitted by the Cherokees, had begun their efforts to establish a foothold in that people at least as early as 1735. They were unsuccessful until, having received federal backing four years earlier, they were able to arrange a formal meeting with the Cherokee National Council in 1799. The first mission in Cherokee country opened a year later; see Edmund Schwarz, *History of the Moravian Missions among the Southern Indian Tribes of the United States* (Bethlehem: Times Publishing, 1923). Also see Eugene C. Routh, "Early Missionaries to the Cherokees," *Chronicles of Oklahoma* 15, no. 4 (1937), pp. 449–465; Henry T. Malone, "The Early Nineteenth Century Missionaries in the Cherokee Country," *Tennessee Historical Quarterly* 10 (1951), pp. 127–139. On broader federal policy during this seminal period, see Francis Paul Prucha, *American Indian Policy in the Formative Years: The Trade and intercourse Acts, 1790–1834* (Cambridge: Harvard University Press, 1962).

32. William G. McLoughlin, *Cherokees and Missionaries, 1789–1839* (New Haven: Yale University Press, 1984), p. 26. It is reliably estimated that about a quarter of all Cherokees were mixed-bloods by 1825, although the missionary practice of seeking them out led to gross overestimations of their numbers. As early as 1805 federal agent Return J. Meigs reported that "the numbers of the real Indians and those of Mixed blood are nearly equal"; see National Archives, Microfilm Record Group M-208.

33. See, for example, Berkhofer, *Salvation and the Savage;* R. Pierce Beaver, *Church, State, and the American Indian: Two and a Half Centuries of Partnership in Missions Between Protestant Churches and the Government* (St. Louis: Concordia, 1966); Henry W. Bowden, *American Indians and Christian Missions* (Chicago: University of Chicago Press, 1981). The Lower Creeks exhibited by far the sharpest response, their recalcitrant faction—called Red Sticks

(Baton Rouge)—going to war in 1814 in an all-out attempt to drive the missionaries, white settlers, and anyone aligned with them out of their territory; Joel W. Martin, *Sacred Revolt: The Muskogees' Struggle for a New World*
(Boston: Beacon Press, 1991).

34. See 7 Stat. 160; proc. Jan. 4, 1819; text in Kappler, *Indian Treaties, 1778–1885*,
pp. 145–152. The other Indigenous peoples were the Senecas, Lenni Lenapes
(Delawares), Shawnees, Potawatomies, Ottawas, and Chippewas. For expli-
cation of the point that early U.S. treaty-making with Indians was motivated by the need to obtain native recognition, see Vine Deloria, Jr.,
"Self-Determination and the Concept of Sovereignty," in *Economic Development in American Indian Reservations,* Roxanne Dunbar Ortiz and Larry
Emerson, ed. (Albuquerque: Native American Studies Center, University
of New Mexico, 1979), pp. 22–28. On the background of European treaty-
making with indigenous nations, see Dorothy V. Jones, *License for Empire:
Colonialism by Treaty in Early Colonial America* (Chicago: University of
Chicago Press, 1982).

35. 9 Stat. 904, proc. Apr. 3, 1848; Kappler, *Indian Treaties, 1778–1885,* pp. 567–
568. Other examples include 1866 treaties with the Seminoles (14 Stat. 755,
proclaimed Aug. 16, 1866); see Kappler, *Indian Treaties, 1778–1885,* pp.
910–915; Choctaw and Chickasaw (14 Stat. 769, proc. July 10, 1866) in Kappler, *Indian Treaties, 1778–1885,* pp. 918–931; Creeks (14 Stat. 785, proc. Aug.
11, 1866) in Kappler, *Indian Treaties, 1778–1885,* pp. 931–937; and Cherokee
(14 Stat. 799, proc. Aug. 11, 1866) in Kappler, *Indian Treaties, 1778–1885,* pp.
942–950. The second article of both the Seminole, Creek, and Cherokee
treaties provides that Blacks living among the Indians, whether full- or
mixed-blood "shall have and enjoy all the rights of native citizens." Articles
26 and 28 of the Choctaw/Chickasaw treaty acknowledged that "all persons
who have become citizens by adoption or intermarriage of either of said
nations, or who may hereinafter become such" would be accorded the right
of any other Choctaw or Chickasaw, and that every "white person who,
having married a Choctaw or Chickasaw, resides in the said Choctaw or
Chickasaw Nation[s], or who has been adopted by the legislative authorities, shall be subject to the laws of the Choctaw and Chickasaw Nations
according to his [or her] domicile, and to prosecution and trial before their
tribunals, and to punishment according to their laws in all respects as
though he was a native Choctaw or Chickasaw." A variation enunciated in
the seventh article of the Cherokee treaty, repeated in various other instruments in which "consolidation of tribes" was effected, is that "other Indians" might be considered as naturalized Cherokees.

36. 7 Stat. 160, in Kappler, *Indian Treaties, 1778–1885.* Related examples include
the 1819 Treaty with the Chippewa (7 Stat. 203, proc. Mar. 25, 1820) in which
three mixed-bloods named Riley are singled out to receive 640 acre tracts;
the 1824 Treaty with the Quapaw (7 Stat. 232, proc. Feb. 19, 1825), Article 7
of which names mixed-bloods to receive their own parcels. See Kappler,
Indian Treaties, 1778–1885, pp. 210–11; the 1826 Treaty with the Chippewa
(7 Stat. 290, proc. Feb. 7, 1827), Article 4 of which lists half-breeds assigned

individual parcels. See Kappler, *Indian Treaties, 1778–1885*, pp. 268–273; the 1829 Treaty with the Winnebago (7 Stat. 323, proc. Jan. 2, 1830), Article V of which lists mixed-bloods to receive individuals parcels; see Kappler, *Indian Treaties, 1778–1885*, pp. 300–303; the 1830 Treaty with the Choctaw (7 Stat. 233, proc. Feb. 24, 1830), which, by a separate appended article (7 Stat. 340), sets out a long list of White men and mixed-bloods to receive personal tracts; refer to Kappler, *Indian Treaties, 1778–1885*, pp. 310–309; the 1831 Treaty with the Ottawa (7 Stat. 359, proc. Apr. 6, 1832), Article XIV of which sets aside land specifically for half-blood Ottoways Hiram Theobault and William McNabb; see Kappler, *Indian Treaties, 1778–1885*, pp. 335–339; the 1842 Treaty with the Wyandot (11 Stat. 581, proc. Oct. 5, 1842), Article 4 of which allots parcels to specific individuals deemed "Wyandotts by blood or adoption"; see Kappler, *Indian Treaties, 1778–1885*, pp. 534–537; the 1863 Treaty with the Red Lake and Pembina Bands of Chippewa (13 Stat. 667, proc. Mar. 1, 1864; Ibid., pp. 853–855, Article 8 of which specifies that each "male half-breed or mixed blood who is related by blood to said Chippewas" will receive an individual 160 acre parcel; see again Kappler, *Indian Treaties, 1778–1885*, pp. 853–855; the 1865 Treaty with the Cheyenne and Arapaho (14 Stat. 704, proc. Feb. 2, 1867), Article 5 of which posits a whole list of mixed-bloods drawn from the Bent, Guerrier, and other families to receive 640 acres each. See Kappler, *Indian Treaties, 1778–1885*, pp. 887–891.

37. 7 Stat. 189, proc. Jan. 15, 1819; see Kappler, *Indian Treaties, 1778–1885*, pp. 171–174. Another example is the 1826 Treaty with the Potawatomi (7 Stat. 295, proc. Feb. 7, 1827), Article 6 of which sets out a long list of mixed-bloods and intermarried Whites to receive parcels along with designated chiefs. See Kappler, *Indian Treaties, 1778–1885*, pp. 273–277.

38. 10 Stat. 1172, proc. Mar. 3, 1855; see Kappler, *Indian Treaties, 1778–1885*, pp. 690–693. Another example is the 1855 Treaty with the Chippewa (10 Stat. 1165, proc. Mar. 3, 1855), Article 6 of which specifies that mixed-bloods and named missionaries will each receive 80-acre parcels. See Kappler, *Indian Treaties, 1778–1885*, pp. 685–689.

39. Article 2 provides that each Indian will be assigned an individual 40-acre plot, while a "P.S.," added by the Senate post hoc, provides that two mixed-bloods, George Bent and Jack Smith, would be allotted 640 acres apiece (12 Stat. 1163, proc. Dec. 5, 1861). See Kappler, *Indian Treaties, 1778–1885*, pp. 807–811. A comparable example is found in the 1859 Treaty with the Sauk and Fox (15 Stat. 467, proc. July 9, 1860), Article 2 of which specifies that Indians would be assigned 80-acre plots while, under Article 10, mixed-bloods and women married to Whites were allotted parcels of 320 acres each. See Kappler, *Indian Treaties, 1778–1885*, pp. 796–799. In the 1848 Treaty with the Menominee (9 Stat. 952, proc. Jan. 23, 1849) Article 4 provides that $30,000 will be paid to chiefs; $40,000 to mixed-bloods. See again Kappler, *Indian Treaties, 1778–1885*, pp. 572–574.

40. Under Article 9, individually titled parcels are set aside for mixed-bloods wishing to live apart from their people (11 Stat. 729, proc. Mar. 31, 1858). See Kappler, *Indian Treaties, 1778–1885*, pp. 764–767. Other examples include

the 1819 Treaty with the Cherokee (7 Stat. 195, proc. Mar. 10, 1819), Article 3 of which sets out a list of mixed-bloods to receive individually titled parcels separate from their nation; Kappler, *Indian Treaties, 1778–1885*, pp. 177–181; the 1830 Treaty with the Sauk and Fox (7 Stat. 328, proc. Feb. 24, 1831), Articles IX and X of which establish separate reservations for mixed-bloods; Kappler, *Indian Treaties, 1778–1885*, pp. 305–310; and the 1858 Treaty with the Ponca (12 Stat. 997, proc. Mar. 8, 1859), Article 3 of which provides that individually titled parcels would be allotted to mixed-bloods wishing to live apart from their people. Refer to Kappler, *Indian Treaties, 1778–1885*, pp. 772–775. In the 1832 Treaty with the Sauk and Fox (7 Stat. 374, proc. Feb. 13, 1833), Article V reserves for Antoine LeClair, "interpreter and part-Indian," two sections of land in an area forcibly ceded by his people. Refer to Kappler, *Indian Treaties, 1778–1885*, pp. 349–351. Similarly, in the 1832 Treaty with the Potawatomi (7 Stat. 378, proc. Jan. 21, 1833), Article II sets aside tracts for persons of Indian descent within an area ceded by the Indians themselves; Kappler, *Indian Treaties, 1778–1885*, pp. 353–555.

41. Article XIII sets aside 640 acres for Joseph Parks, described as being of "one-quarter blood"; 7 Stat. 355, proc. Apr. 6, 1832. See Kappler, *Indian Treaties, 1778–1885*, pp. 331–344.

42. See, for example, the 1863 Treaty with the Red Lake and Pembina Bands of Chippewa (note 46, below). The combination of racism and sexism on the part of U.S. treaty commissioners led to some rather bizarre outcomes, as when, under Article 5 of the 1818 Treaty with the Chickasaw (7 Stat. 192, proc. Jan. 7, 1819) in Kappler, *Indian Treaties, 1778–1885*, pp. 174–175, a mixed-blood named John McCleish was awarded property "in consequence of his having married a white woman," thereby confounding the typically deep Euroamerican male aversion to native men mating with "their" females. In any event, the extraordinarily disruptive effects of the United States's imposing patriarchal (Christian) forms on traditionally matrilineal and gender-balanced native societies is well documented; see Rennard Strickland, *Fire and Spirits* (Norman: University of Oklahoma Press, 1975).

43. This was accomplished by attachment of a rider to the annual *Appropriations Act* (Ch. 120, 16 Stat. 544, 566, now codified as 25 U. S. C. 71). It should be noted that, while canceling the government's prerogative to enter into new treaties, the rider provided that "nothing contained herein shall be construed to invalidate or impair the obligation of any treaty heretofore made with any such Indian tribe or nation."

44. The crux of this somewhat confused—and confusing—reordering of priorities can be located in the Grant administration; Elsie M. Rushmore, *The Indian Policy during Grant's Administration* (New York: Marion Press, 1914). More broadly, see Henry E. Fritz, *The Movement for Indian Assimilation, 1860–1890* (Philadelphia: University of Pennsylvania Press, 1963); Frederick A. Hoxie, *A Final Promise: The Campaign to Assimilate the Indians, 1880–1920* (Lincoln: University of Nebraska Press, 1984).

45. Refer to Ch. 341, 24 Stat. 362, 385, now codified at 18 U. S. C. 1153. The crimes at issue in this wholly unilateral U.S. assertion of jurisdiction of

other nations were murder, manslaughter, rape, assault with intent to kill, arson, and burglary. For background, see Sidney L. Harring, *Crow Dog's Case: American Indian Sovereignty, Tribal Law, and United States Law in the Nineteenth Century* (Cambridge: Cambridge University Press, 1994), pp. 100–141.

46. See Ch. 119, 24 Stat. 388, now codified as amended at 25 U. S. C. 331 et seq., also known as the *Dawes Act* or *Dawes Severalty Act,* in honor of Massachusetts Senator Henry L. Dawes, its prime sponsor and supposed "Friend of the Indian"; D. S. Otis, *The Dawes Act and the Allotment of Indian Land* (Norman: University of Oklahoma Press, 1973); Wilcomb E. Washburn, *Assault on Tribalism: The General Allotment Law (Dawes Act) of 1887* (Philadelphia: J. B. Lippincott, 1975). On the "Friends," who were by this point organized as the "Indian Rights Association," see Prucha, *Americanizing the American Indian;* William T. Hagan, *The Indian Rights Association: The Herbert Welsh Years, 1882–1904* (Tucson: University of Arizona Press, 1985); Vine Deloria, Jr., "The Indian Rights Association: An Appraisal," in *The Aggressions of Civilization: Federal Indian Policy Since the 1880s,* Sandra L. Cadwalder and Vine Deloria, Jr., ed. (Philadelphia: Temple University Press, 1984), pp. 3–18. Concerning the explicit intent of Dawes and others of his group to undermine and destroy any autochthonous sense of identity among Native people, see Wilbert H. Ahern, "Assimilationist Racism: The Case of the 'Friends of the Indian,'" *Journal of Ethnic Studies* 4, no. 2 (1976), pp. 23–32; Alexandra Harmon, "When Is an Indian Not an Indian? The 'Friends of the Indian' and the Problems of Indian Identity," *Journal of Ethnic Studies* 18, no. 2 (1990), pp. 95–123.

47. Orphaned children received the same 80-acre allotment as an unmarried adult; Kirk Kickingbird and Karen Ducheneaux, *One Hundred Million Acres* (New York: Macmillan, 1973); Janet A. McDonnell, *The Dispossession of the American Indian, 1887–1934* (Bloomington: Indian University Press, 1991).

48. In actuality, this had always been the case. While blood quantum was seldom mentioned directly in treaty language—"half-breed" being a standard American colloquialism by which to describe persons of obvious Indian/White admixture, regardless of actual proportion—U.S. treaty commissioners and Indian agents habitually employed a quarter-blood minimum standard in compiling their lists of "mixed-bloods" scheduled to receive land titles, monetary awards, and so forth. Persons of less than one-quarter Indian blood were thus formally construed as being "non-Indian," even though they were often considered full members of Native societies and discriminated against as "non-whites" by Euro-Americans; for analogues, see Naomi Zack, *Race and Mixed Race* (Philadelphia: Temple University Press, 1993).

49. The problem was compounded by the fact that, at least among some native peoples, the strongest remaining elements of traditionalism declined to participate in the process at all. Among the Oklahoma Cherokees, for example, a sizable faction of full-bloods refused to enroll on the entirely appropriate bases that they neither desired to become citizens of the United States nor

were willing to concede the prerogative of defining or recording who was/was not Cherokee to a foreign government. The result of this dynamic, in simplest terms, was that many of the most self-consciously Native people left in the United States by 1890 were never officially recognized as such by the federal government, while the more acculturated were, almost by definition, enrolled. This clear bias in identification procedures has resulted in a marked and lingering accommodationist skew in "Indian" political perspectives. For a good emic examination of how these dynamics played out among the Cherokees, see Emmett Starr, *A History of the Cherokee Indians* (Oklahoma City: Warden, 1922).

50. Conversation with Jack D. Forbes, April 1993 (notes on file). Plainly, if the higher end of this estimated range is correct, there would have been precious little reservation land available for the United States to declare "surplus."

51. U.S. Bureau of the Census, "Table 2: Indian Population by Divisions and States, 1890–1930," *Fifteenth Census of the United States, 1930: The Indian Population of the United States and Alaska* (Washington, DC: U.S. Government Printing Office, 1937), p. 3. It should be noted that this is all that officially remained of an aggregate Indigenous population that numbered perhaps 15 million people in 1500, an approximate 97.5 percent reduction. Instructively, the latter figure corresponds perfectly with the 2.5 percent of its original landholdings this population was officially estimated to still retain by 1890; see U.S. Bureau of the Census, *Report on Indians Taxed and Indians Not Taxed in the United States (except Alaska) at the Eleventh U.S. Census: 1890* (Washington, DC: U.S. Government Printing Office, 1894). On the size of the pre-invasion Native population, see Thornton, *American Indian Holocaust and Survival.* Also see Henry F. Dobyns, "Estimating Aboriginal American Population: An Appraisal of Techniques with a New Hemispheric Estimate," *Current Anthropology* 7 (1966), pp. 395–449; *Their Numbers Become Thinned: Native American Population Dynamics in Eastern North America* (Knoxville: University of Tennessee Press, 1983).

52. This enabled the agents to exercise near dictatorial powers over their hapless "wards," a matter that quickly resulted in the checkerboarding—that is, the long-term leasing of any usable land to non-Indian ranching and agricultural interests at discount rates, leaving only the most unproductive acreage under the most nominal Native control—of many reservations; Refer to Vine Deloria, Jr., and Clifford M. Lytle, *American Indians, American Justice* (Austin: University of Texas Press, 1983), p. 10.

53. For a close study of the process among the Kaws, see William E. Unrau, *Mixed Bloods and Tribal Dissolution: Charles Curtis and the Quest for Indian Identity* (Lawrence: University Press of Kansas, 1989).

54. Francis E. Leupp, *The Indian and His Problem* (New York: Scribner's, 1910), p. 93.

55. Turn-of-the-century literature is replete with such references. See, for example, B. O. Flower's "An Interesting Representative of a Vanishing Race," *The Arena* 16 (July 1896), pp. 240–250; Simon Pokagon, "The Future of the Red

Man," *Forum* August (1897), pp. 698–708; William R. Draper, "The Last of the Red Race," *Cosmopolitan* 33, no. 3 (January 1902), pp. 244–246; E. S. Curtis, "Vanishing Indian Types: The Tribes of the Northwest Plains," *Scribner's Magazine* (June 1906), pp. 657–671; James Mooney, "The Passing of the Indian," *Proceedings of the Second Pan American Scientific Congress, Sec. 1: Anthropology* (Washington, DC: Smithsonian Institution, 1909–1910); Ales Hrdlicka, "The Vanishing Indian," *Science* 46, no. 1185 (1917), pp. 266–267; J. L. Hill, *The Passing of the Indian and the Buffalo* (Long Beach: n.p., 1917); John Collier, "The Vanquished Indian," *Nation* 126, no. 3262 (January 11, 1928), pp. 38–41.

56. Both reservation-based boarding schools and several varieties of missionary or BIA-run day schools offered lower attendant cost and avoided the isolation of students from familial and sociocultural input. Isolation was thus a goal for which the government was willing to pay a certain premium; on funding, see David Wallace Adams, *Education for Extinction: American Indians and the Boarding School Experience, 1875–1928* (Lawrence: University Press of Kansas, 1995), pp. 26–27. On the Christian day schools, see Francis Paul Prucha, *The Churches and the Indian Schools, 1888–1912* (Lincoln: University of Nebraska Press, 1979).

57. Fort Marion was the location to which many of the strongest Native fighters of the Plains and Southwest Indian Wars—Cheyenne Dog Soldiers, Geronimo's Chiricahuas, and others—were sent to be broken after laying down their arms; Frederick J. Stefon, "Richard Henry Pratt and His Indians," *Journal of Ethnic Studies* 15, no. 2 (1987), pp. 86–112. On the establishment of Carlisle, see Louis Morton, "How the Indians Came to Carlisle," *Pennsylvania History* 29, no. 1 (1962), pp. 53–73. For Richard Henry Pratt's own view of things, see his "American Indians, Chained and Unchained: Being an Account of How the Carlisle Indian School Was Born and Grew in the First 25 Years," *Red Man* (June 1914), pp. 393–411.

58. Pratt's view that the role of education was to "kill the Indian in him and save the man"—a play upon General Phil Sheridan's famous 1871 pronouncement that "the only good Indian is a dead one"—was first publicly articulated in a speech entitled "The Advantage of Mingling Indians with Whites," delivered to the 1892 National Conference on Charities and Corrections. It is most famously repeated in his autobiographical *Battlefield and Classroom: Four Decades with the American Indian, 1867–1904*, reprint of 1905 original (New Haven: Yale University Press, 1964). Studies of some of the other boarding schools mentioned include Lillie G. McKinney, "History of the Albuquerque Indian School," *New Mexico Historical Review* 20, no. 2 (1945), pp. 109–138; Robert A. Trennert, *The Phoenix Indian School: Forced Assimilation in Arizona, 1891–1935* (Norman: University of Oklahoma Press, 1988); K. Tsainina Lomawaima, *They Called It Prairie Light: The Story of the Chilocco Indian School* (Lincoln: University of Nebraska Press, 1994).

59. See, generally, Adams, *Education for Extinction;* Sally J. McBride, *Ethnic Identity and the Boarding School Experience of West-Central Oklahoma American Indians* (Washington, DC: University Press of America, 1983); David

Wallace Adams, "From Bullets to Boarding Schools: The Educational Assault on the American Indian Identity," in *The American Indian Experience: A Profile: 1524 to the Present*, Philip Weeks, ed. (Arlington Heights: Forum Press, 1988), pp. 218–239; Michael C. Coleman, *American Indian Children at School, 1850–1930* (Jackson: University Press of Mississippi, 1993). Official confirmation of even the more extreme characterizations of the process will be found in U.S. Bureau of Indian Affairs, *Rules for the Indian School Service* (Washington, DC: U.S. Government Printing Office, various editions, 1890–98, inclusive).

60. As Commissioner of Indian Affairs, Thomas Jefferson Morgan put it in 1890: "The general purpose of the Government is preparation of Indian youth for assimilation into the national life by such a course of training as will prepare them for the duties and privileges of American citizenship"; refer to: *Annual Report of the Commissioner of Indian Affairs, 1890* (Washington, DC: U.S. Government Printing Office, 1890), cxlvi. To this end, the "Indian student would have to study American history and in the process come to internalize the national myths that were central to it, including the idea that the westward sweep of the American empire, that is to say the dispossession of Indian land, was clearly justifiable"; Adams, *Education for Extinction*, p. 24. Moreover,

> Indians needed to be individualized. In many ways, the issue of individualization went to the very heart of the Indian question. In the [Eurocentric] mind, Indians were savages mainly because tribal life placed a higher value on tribal community than on individual interests. Never was this more true than in the economic realm. Tribal society had somehow gotten matters all wrong: rather than operating on the progressive principle that the whole of society stood to benefit when the individual's acquisitive instincts were given their full play, tribal life was rooted in the idea that community welfare depended upon the individual curbing material desires. Whereas a Protestant American measured an individual's worth by his capacity to accumulate wealth, an Indian did so by what he [or she] gave away . . . It was not simply that [Christian whites] wished to snatch Indians' souls from a hellish fate; their commitment to Christianization was also rooted in the assumption that civilization, as the highest stage of [human] social evolution, was erected upon a firm foundation of Christian morality.

Quoted from ibid., 22–3. Not only was all this incessantly drummed into students in the classroom setting, but they were invariably required to join in extracurricular celebrations of salient events in the history of their own peoples' demise; Estelle Reel, *Course of Study for the Indian Schools of the United States: Industrial and Literary* (Washington, DC: Bureau of Indian Affairs, 1901).

61. In 1892 Indian Commissioner Morgan announced that "the whole underlying structure of the industrial school . . . is that intelligent, systematic labor by both men and women lies at the basis of civilization, and that if Indians are ever to be lifted to a higher plane it must be through the training

of boys and girls alike to the performance of whatever manual labor may be essential for their welfare"; quoted from: *Annual Report of the Indian Commissioner* (Washington, DC: U.S. Government Printing Office, 1892), p. 617. The work experiences—performing stoop labor in Colorado's beet fields, for instance—were called "outings." For a good overview of the exploitation of males, see Robert A. Trennert, "From Carlisle to Phoenix: The Rise and Fall of the Indian Outing System, 1878–1930," *Pacific Historical Review* 52, no. 3 (1983), pp. 267–291. On more feminine applications, see Trennert's "Victorian Morality and the Supervision of Indian Women Working in Phoenix, 1906–1930," *Journal of Social History* 22, no. 1 (1988), pp. 113–128. For official articulation, see Reel, *Course of Study for the Indian Schools of the United States: Industrial and Literary.*

62. The first measure, effected on March 3, 1891, authorized the Commissioner of Indian Affairs to "make and enforce by proper means such rules and regulations as will secure the attendance of Indian children of suitable age . . . at schools established and maintained for their benefit"; *The Statutes at Large of the United States of America,* vol. 26, p. 1014. The second specifically authorized the commissioner to "withhold rations, clothing and other annuities from Indian parents or guardians who refuse or neglect to send and keep their children . . . in school"; see again, *The Statutes at Large of the United States of America,* vol. 27, p. 637. For implementation of both laws, see Office of Indian Affairs Circular No. 130, Jan. 15, 1906. It should be noted—and emphatically so—that this forced transfer of children was nothing so innocuous as a misguided policy. Such a course of governmental action is delineated as one of five categories of genocidal state conduct under Article II of the 1948 Convention on Prevention and Punishment of the Crime of Genocide; see Ian Brownlie, ed., *Basic Documents on Human Rights,* 3rd ed. (Oxford: Clarendon Press, 1992), pp. 31–35. This may be one reason why the United States, alone among major nation-states, declined to ratify the Genocide Convention for 40 years after its promulgation as international law; refer to Lawrence J. LeBlanc, *The United States and the Genocide Convention* (Durham: Duke University Press, 1991).

63. Lawrence F. Schmeickebeir, *The Office of Indian Affairs* (Baltimore: Johns Hopkins University Press, 1927), p. 216. It was estimated in the April 6, 1912, issue of *Native American* that there were some 70,000 indigenous children in the overall pool.

64. See Evelyn C. Adams, *American Indian Education: Government Schools and Economic Progress* (New York: King's Crown Press, 1946).

65. See The Indian Citizenship Act of 1924 (ch. 233, 43 Stat. 25). Aside from the Allotment Act, other measures that had already conveyed citizenship upon selected groups of Indians was the Omnibus Bill of 1910 (which authorized the establishment of competency commissions to preside over the process) and a BIA policy announced by Indian commissioner Cato Sells in 1917 pertaining to those who volunteered for military service; refer to Michael T. Smith, "The History of Indian Citizenship," *Great Plains Journal* 10, no. 1

(1970–1971), pp. 25–35; Gary C. Stein, "The Indian Citizenship Act of 1924," *New Mexico Historical Review* 4, no. 3 (1972), pp. 257–274.

66. In aggregate, the reservations contain about two-thirds of U.S. domestic uranium reserves, a quarter of the readily accessible low-sulfur coal, as much as a fifth of the oil and natural gas, as well as substantial deposits of copper, bauxite, molybdenum, zeolite, gold, and much else; see: Ronald L. Trosper, "Appendix I: Indian Minerals," in *American Indian Policy Review Commission, Task Force 7 Final Report: Reservation Resource Development and Protection* (Washington, DC: U.S. Government Printing Office, 1977); Bureau of Indian Affairs, *Indian Lands Map: Oil, Gas, and Minerals on Indian Reservations* (Washington, DC: U.S. Government Printing Office, 1978).

67. Lewis Meriam, et al., *The Indian Problem: Resolution of the Committee of One Hundred by the Secretary of the Interior and Review of the Indian Problem* (Washington, DC: U.S. Government Printing Office, 1925); *The Problem of Indian Administration* (Baltimore: Johns Hopkins University Press, 1928).

68. See Ch. 576, 48 Stat. 948, now codified at 25 U.S.C. pp. 461-279; also known as the *Wheeler-Howard Act* after its main congressional sponsors, Senator Burton K. Wheeler and Representative Edgar Howard, although its major proponent was actually Indian Commissioner John Collier. There are a number of good studies of the IRA and its passage, among them Graham D. Taylor's *The New Deal and American Indian Tribalism: The Administration of the Indian Reorganization Act, 1934–1945* (Lincoln: University of Nebraska Press, 1980). Also see Kenneth R. Philp, *Assault on Assimilation: John Collier's Crusade for Indian Reform, 1920–1954* (Tucson: University of Arizona Press, 1977); Vine Deloria, Jr., and Clifford M. Lytle, *The Nations Within: The Past and Future of American Indian Sovereignty* (New York: Pantheon, 1984).

69. On disinformation and suppression of dissenting views, see Rupert Costo, et al., "Federal Indian Policy, 1933–1945," in *Indian Self-Rule: First-Hand Accounts of Indian-White Relations from Roosevelt to Reagan.* Kenneth R. Philp, ed. (Salt Lake City: Howe Bros., 1986), pp. 47–69. For what may be the most extreme example of rigging the outcome of a referendum, see Charles Lummis, *Bullying the Hopi* (Prescott: Prescott College Press, 1968). Also see Thomas Biolosi, *Organizing the Lakota: The Political Economy of the New Deal on the Pine Ridge and Rosebud Reservations* (Tucson: University of Arizona Press, 1992).

70. Of the 164 indigenous nations suffering reorganization, 92 were provided with such constitutions—effectively converting them into something more nearly approximating business entities than national polities—while 72 ended up with corporate charters, pure and simple; see Kenneth R. Philp, "The Indian Reorganization Act Fifty Years Later," in *Indian Self-Rule*, Kenneth Philp, ed. (Salt Lake City: Howe Bros., 1986), pp. 14–29.

71. For analysis of three such constitutions, see Thornton, *American Indian Holocaust and Survival*, pp. 190–200.

72. At Hopi, for example, only about 15 percent of the voting age population had been processed through the schools. It was precisely the same 15 per-

cent who turned out to vote for reorganization, while the remaining 85 percent, followers of the traditional Kikmongwe leadership, declined to participate in any way at all; see Oliver LaFarge, *Running Narrative of the
Organization of the Hopi Tribe of Indians* (unpublished manuscript contained
in the LaFarge Collection, University of Texas at Austin).

73. In what may be the best-known instance, the problem of blood quantum
was raised by the 1972 Trail of Broken Treaties delegation to Washington in
point 11 of its 20-Point Program for reforming federal/Indian relations,
demanding that the use of such criteria be abandoned. The Nixon administration responded that this would be "contrary to the position taken by the
members of tribes in their referendums adopting constitutions setting forth
their membership requirements" under the IRA. Taking up the issue with
federal authorities is inappropriate and misguided, the administration concluded, since the Indians' "argument is really with the tribes who prescribe
their membership pursuant to constitutions and by-laws that have been
adopted"; refer to ed., B. I. A., *I'm Not Your Indian Any More: The Trail of Broken Treaties*, 3rd ed. (Mohawk Nation via Rooseveltown: Akwesasne Notes,
1976), p. 76. For background, see Jack D. Forbes, *Native Americans and Nixon:
Presidential Politics and Minority Self-Determination* (Los Angeles: UCLA
American Indian Studies Center, 1981); Vine Deloria, Jr., *Behind the Trail of
Broken Treaties: An Indian Declaration of Independence*, 2nd ed. (Austin: University of Texas Press, 1984).

74. Witness the performance of the National Council of Tribal Chairmen
(NTCA), a federally subsidized association of presiding heads of IRA coun-
cils, whose officials defended the government by publicly attacking Trail of
Broken Treaties participants as "irresponsible" and "unrepresentative of
Indian interests," "renegades" who "possessed no constituency among
Indians" and threatened "tribal sovereignty" by standing up for Indigenous
rights; see ed., B.I.A., *I'm Not Your Indian Any More*, pp. 31–32. It is worth
noting that Webster Two Hawk, then president of the IRA council on the
Rosebud Sioux Reservation, head of the NTCA, and the many who made
these statements to the media—equivalent as they were to denunciations of
the partisan resistance by Vichy French leader Pierre Laval during the occupation of France by Germany during World War II—was himself shortly
voted out of office by his people. They replaced him with Robert Burnette, a
major Trail organizer; refer to Robert Burnette with John Koster, *The Road to
Wounded Knee* (New York: Bantam, 1974). On the analogy, see Geoffrey
Warner, *Pierre Laval and the Eclipse of France* (London: Macmillan, 1968); H.
R. Kedward, *Resistance in Vichy France: A Study of Ideas and Motivations* (New
York: Oxford University Press, 1978).

75. For articulation of the "third level" concept, see U.S. Senate, Select Committee on Indian Affairs, *Final Report and Legislative Recommendations: A
Report of the Special Committee on Investigations* (Washington, DC: 101st
Cong., 2nd Sess., U.S. Government Printing Office, 1989). This is essentially
the same subterfuge attempted by the French in placing administration of
its Algerian colony under the Home Department rather than its Colonial

Office during the 1950s; Joseph Kraft, *The Struggle for Algeria* (Garden City: Doubleday, 1961).

76. For early analyses of the issue, see Ward Shepard, "Land Problems of an Expanding Indian Population" and Allan G. Harper, "Salvaging the Wreckage of Indian Land Allotment," in *The Changing Indian,* Oliver LaFarge, ed. (Norman: University of Oklahoma Press, 1943), pp. 72–83, 84–102.

77. Wilcomb Washburn, *Red Man's Land, White Man's Law,* 2nd ed. (Norman: University of Oklahoma Press, 1994), pp. 150–151. The analysis here is overly charitable, given that mere "oversights" in legislation are corrected by subsequent amendment. That the government was fully aware of the implications of the heirship problem by the late 1950s—and probably much earlier—is abundantly evidenced in its own documents; see U.S. House of Representatives, Committee on Insular Affairs, *Indian Heirship Land Study* (Washington, DC: 86th Cong., 2nd Sess., U. S. Government Printing Office, 1966). To date, nothing effective has been done to alter the impacts.

78. There were 343,410 "official" Indians in the United States in 1950, up from less than a quarter-million 50 years earlier; U.S. Bureau of the Census, "Part 1: United States Summary," *Census of 1950, Vol. 2: Characteristics of the Population* (Washington, DC: U.S. Government Printing Office, 1953).

79. Thornton, *American Indian Holocaust and Survival,* p. 227; U.S. Bureau of the Census, *1990 Census of the Population, Preliminary Report* (Washington, DC: U.S. Government Printing Office, 1991).

80. Termination occurred pursuant to House Concurrent Resolution 108, effected on August 1, 1953. The complete text appears in Part II of Edward H. Spicer's *A Short History of the Indians of the United States* (New York: Van Nostrand Rinehold, 1969). Dillon S. Myer, the man who had presided over the mass internment of Japanese Americans during World War II, was appointed Commissioner of Indian Affairs for the specific purpose of overseeing the process of tribal dissolution; see Richard Drinnon, *Keeper of Concentration Camps: Dillon S. Myer and American Racism* (Berkeley: University of California Press, 1987).

81. Refer to Fixico, *Termination and Relocation: Federal Indian Policy, 1945–1960;* also see Larry W. Burt, *Tribalism in Crisis: Federal Indian Policy, 1953–1961* (Albuquerque: University of New Mexico Press, 1982).

82. On the struggle of the Menominee, see Nicholas Peroff, *Menominee DRUMS: Tribal Termination and Restoration, 1954–1974* (Norman: University of Oklahoma Press, 1982). Principal leader of this successful effort was a young woman named Ada Deer, a performance that established her political reputation and led, eventually, to her appointment as Commissioner of Indian Affairs under the Clinton administration. Ironically, she has used this powerful position to champion the termination of other Indigenous peoples.

83. The poverty is very real, albeit induced by intentional federal default on its treaty and other obligations to Native people rather than by virtue of there being "too many Indian impersonators freeloading off of the system," as one recently put it. The poorest county in the United States throughout the

1950s and 1960s was Shannon County, on the Pine Ridge Sioux Reservation, in South Dakota, where unemployment ran into the 90th percentile and per capita income averaged $1,200 per year into the early 1970s (things have not improved a lot since); see Cheryl McCall, "Life at Pine Ridge Bleak," *Colorado Daily*, May 16, 1975. Overall, Indians remain by far the poorest population aggregate in North America, with all the dire effects this implies (average male life expectancy on the reservations is still well under 50 years); U.S. Department of Health and Human Services, Public Health Service, *Chart Series Book* (Washington, DC: U.S. Government Printing Office, 1988).

84. In the 1935 Constitution and Bylaws of the Confederated Salish and Kootenai Tribes of the Flathead Reservation, for example, enrollment criteria were delineated as consisting of all "persons of Indian blood whose names appear on the rolls of the Confederated Tribes [initially established at the time of the Dawes Commission] as of January 1, 1935." This was amended in 1960 to require that, to enroll, one must "possess one-quarter (1/4) degree or more blood of the Salish or Kootenai Tribes or both, of the Flathead Indian Reservation, Montana"; refer to Thornton, *American Indian Holocaust and Survival*, pp. 197–198.

85. The NTCA is now called the National Tribal Chairman's Fund. Its lobbying offensive during the mid-to-late 1960s is covered by Robert Burnette in his book *The Tortured Americans* (Engelwood Cliffs: Prentice-Hall, 1971).

86. At a meeting with members of the Abenaki National Council in 1991, it was explained to me that, in their view, the question of federal recognition put things exactly backwards. "The question is not whether we are recognized by the federal government," as one elder put it, "but whether we recognize *it*. After all, we Abenakis, not the United States or the State of Vermont, were the first people here. Unless they can show us a treaty in which our ancestors recognized their right to land which unquestionably belonged to the Abenaki—which they can't—then it's still our land by law. Our law, their law, international law, it all comes out the same on this point."

87. Many of these children—almost none of whom were enrolled—were subjected to blind adoptions; that is, they were denied by judicial decree, usually at the request of the adoptive family, all knowledge concerning the identity of their natural parents, much less the nature of their Indigenous heritage; see: Tillie Blackbear Walker, "American Indian Children: Foster Care and Adoption," in U.S. Department of Education, Office of Educational Research and Development, National Institute of Education, *Conference on Educational and Occupational Needs of American Indian Women, October 1976* (Washington, DC: U.S. Government Printing Office, 1980).

88. My own experience in this regard may be indicative. In 1991, having attracted a certain notoriety as a codirector of the Colorado AIM chapter, I suddenly found my Native identity being questioned. A "real" Indian would make public the names of his/her Indigenous relatives upon demand, it was asserted (although the question of why the right to privacy of

my own relatives—or those of any other Native person—should be inherently less than other people's was never explained). After a time, I was convinced by my uncle to publish this information in the local paper. At that point, the point of "concern" among my critics suddenly switched from genealogical issues to the question of whether I was recognized as a Native by the local Indians (within which I had lived and worked as an Indian for 20 years, and by which I had been repeatedly elected to my AIM position). When this query provoked an outpouring of letters to the editor in the affirmative, the criteria were changed again—this time to demanding "proof" that I was "enrolled in a federally recognized tribe" (this was couched in terms of the "sovereignty of the tribes" to determine who is/is not Indian). When it was established that I am, in fact, an enrolled member of the United Keetoowah Band of Cherokees, the Band itself was assailed as being "questionable," despite the fact that it is federally recognized. It should be noted that the primary vehicles for this concerted campaign of character assassination were *Indian Country Today* and *News from Indian Country*, both of which enthusiastically embrace the IRA mode of reservation governance, while I am rather obviously one of its harsher critics. As to the reinforcement of sovereignty argument, the very idea that a self-appointed gaggle of Lakotas and Chippewas might presume to decide for Cherokees who is or is not Cherokee speaks for itself. It should be noted that the one Keetoowah in the mix, Shelly Davis, was actually fired by *News from Indian Country* because she insisted that (a) I actually am Keetoowah, and (b) that the paper had no right to distort Band rules to make it appear that I am an honorary member, as it continues to do.

89. For an altogether poignant and insightful examination of the impacts of this Fanonesque reality on all-too-many native people, see Patricia Penn Hilden, *When Nickels Were Indians: An Urban Mixed-Blood Story* (Washington, DC: Smithsonian Institution Press, 1995).

90. Thornton, *American Indian Holocaust and Survival*, pp. 174–175.

91. Lenore Stiffarm and Phil Lane, Jr., "The Demography of Native North America: A Question of American Indian Survival," in *The State of Native America: Genocide, Colonization, and Resistance*, M. Annette Jaimes, ed. (Boston: South End Press, 1992), p. 45.

92. U.S. Congress, Office of Technology Assessment, Indian Health Care (Washington, DC: U.S. Government Printing Office, 1986), p. 78.

93. Some tribal councils have increased quantum requirements to one-half; see Thornton, *American Indian Holocaust and Survival*, p. 190. On the concept of "autogenocide," coined to describe Khmer Rouge policies in Cambodia during the mid-to-late 1970s, see Michael Vickery, *Cambodia, 1975–1982* (Boston: South End Press, 1984).

94. Patricia Nelson Limerick, *The Legacy of Conquest: The Unbroken Past of the American West* (New York: W. W. Norton, 1987), p. 338.

95. During the early 1990s, the Umatilla tribal council commissioned University of Colorado anthropologist Deward E. Walker to conduct a study of

what would happen if it simply adhered to its present quarter-blood Umatilla requirements for enrollment. The prognosis was that, given the present rate of "outmarriage," there would be virtually no one enrollable as a Umatilla by some point around 2050. It was then that discussion of constitutional revisions began in earnest; discussion with Deward E. Walker, April 1997 (notes on file).

96. Jack D. Forbes, "Undercounting Native Americans: The 1980 Census and the Manipulation of Racial Identity in the United States," *Wicazo Sa Review* VI, no. 1 (1990), p. 23. The Census Bureau itself inadvertently confirms the thrust of the argument, explaining that it construes that the racial category "White" is to include "all persons reporting Spanish origin." About 97 percent of persons of Spanish origin, about 99 percent of persons of Mexican origin, and 96 percent of persons of Puerto Rican origin were classified as white in the 1970 census; see: U.S. Bureau of the Census, *Selected Characteristics of Persons and Families of Mexican, Puerto Rican, and Other Spanish Origin: March 1971* (Washington, DC: U.S. Government Printing Office, 1971), p. 15. That only 3,678 Mexican immigrants should have been classified as Indians in 1970—coming as they do from a population deriving overwhelmingly from Indigenous gene stocks—should speak for itself. See Mörner, *Race Mixture in the History of Latin America.* Similarly, that only 1.9 percent (15,988 people) of the several-million-strong Mexican American population should be so categorized, is a travesty; refer to: U.S. Bureau of the Census, *Current Population Report: Characteristics of the Population by Ethnic Origin, November 1979* (Washington, DC: U.S. Government Printing Office, 1979).

97. Forbes, "Undercounting Native Americans: The 1980 Census and the Manipulation of Racial Identity"; U.S. Bureau of the Census, *Ancestry of the Population by State, 1980* (Washington, DC: U.S. Government Printing Office, 1983), p. 3.

98. For the official count, see U.S. Bureau of the Census, *General Characteristics of the Population, 1990* (Washington, DC: U.S. Government Printing Office, 1991), p. 9.

99. Even this instrument fails to go the whole distance, making no provision for naturalization by marriage, adoption, or petition. Moreover, it takes as its point of departure the Dawes Rolls: It explicitly excludes the descendants of Cherokee resisters who refused to move to Oklahoma from Arkansas, Missouri, Kansas, and Texas at the outset of the 20th century. Still, the present CNO constitution accords much more closely with actual Indigenous tradition than any other presently in existence. The constitution of my own Keetoowah Band follows not far behind, providing for enrollment based upon genealogy to anyone who can document it, but restricting voting, the holding of office, and receipt of benefits to those of one-quarter or greater blood quantum. The Band also makes provision for "Honorary Members" who demonstrate no genealogical connection, but who provide service/display loyalty to the group.

100. U.S. Bureau of the Census, *1980 Census of the Population, Vol. II, Subject Reports: American Indians, Eskimos, and Inuits on Identified Reservations and in Historic Use Areas of Oklahoma (excluding Urbanized Areas)* (Washington, DC: U.S. Government Printing Office, 1985), p. 99.

101. See 30 Stat. 495; named in recognition of Charles Curtis, the mixed-blood Kaw who became vice president of the United States (making him, contrary to claims recently made in behalf of Ben Nighthorse Campbell, the first American Indian to hold elected office in the federal government); see Unrau, *Mixed Bloods and Tribal Dissolution.*

102. Thornton, *American Indian Holocaust and Survival,* p. 200.

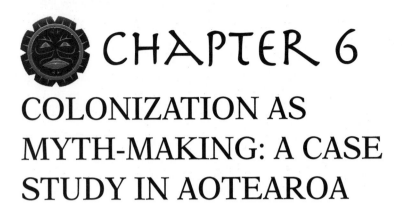

CHAPTER 6

COLONIZATION AS MYTH-MAKING: A CASE STUDY IN AOTEAROA

By Moana Jackson

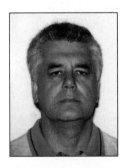

Moana Jackson belongs to the Iwi (tribal nation) of Ngati Kahungunu and Ngati Porou in Aotearoa/New Zealand. A graduate in law, he cofounded the Maori Legal Service in 1988, the country's first Indigenous community law centre. He is currently Director of the Maori Law Commission, an independent body established to research and revalidate the use of Maori justice processes and dispute resolution mechanisms. He works extensively in constitutional and treaty issues in Aotearoa and has chaired the Indigenous caucus at the United Nations Working Group on the Rights of Indigenous Peoples. He has also been a Visiting Fellow at the Law School, Victoria University of Wellington, and a founding tutor in the Maori Laws and Philosophy degree at the Iwi University Te Wananga o Raukawa.

Introduction

This chapter focuses on the politics and process of colonization. Rather than study a specific land dispute or analyze such consequences of colonization as the suppression of language and culture, it endeavors to chart the myth-making that surrounds the seizure and maintenance of political-economic power that is the base of all colonial endeavor.

All nations, of course, create or sustain myths from their past to make sense of a history and to provide a rationale for what now exists. In the story of the colonization of Indigenous peoples, the founding myths serve a particular purpose that is integral to colonization itself: They justify the current status quo by masking the reality or extent of dispossession that shaped the past and present. The myths become an exercise in absolution for the colonizer, and the basis for ongoing denial of the rights of the colonized.

Such absolution is both created and promoted by the agencies of colonizing power. The proselytizing church, the civilizing education system, the introduced media, and the interests of the commercial elite are all part of the hegemonic discourse; but the institution that provided the fundamental rationale and justification for the whole colonizing process is the law. In its symbiotic relationship with political power, the law is both colonization's architect of oppression and its instrument of denial. It is the chief myth-maker.

In New Zealand (Aotearoa) the present relationship between the Maori people and the State (or "Crown") is shaped by that myth-making. The myths have established a changing process of definition in which the State has altered its position on Maori rights and status to meet whatever it perceives to be its current political interests. It has seen the State give its own meanings to words: both to ignore and to claim to uphold treaty arrangements, to define and constantly redefine the classification of who or what it deems to be Maori, and to deny or reinterpret the facts of history.

In the annals of colonization, the New Zealand government is, of course, not unique in this regard; however, the myth-making of the last 150 years in Aotearoa does have particular features. It has enabled a perception of harmonious race relations to gain credence both domestically and internationally. This has grown largely out of the Victorian humanitarian myth that rendered the oppression of Maori as somehow more benign than that suffered by other Indigenous peoples, as if one could have comparative levels of oppression ranging from genocidal in one place (say, Australia) to enlightened in Aotearoa.

This myth not only diminishes the inherent horrors of all colonization; it also seeks to reduce State culpability. Thus when the State does seek to settle grievances, as the New Zealand government now claims to do, its liability and its response are both contextualized within the myths as recompense for determinable acts of injustice, rather than as reparation for the systemic injustice of the colonizing process itself. The actual forms of redress, shaped also by the myths, grant benefits to ensure economic equity rather than to recognize rights that would ensure economic and political sovereignty.

It is the purpose of this chapter to case-study this myth-making process and to analyze the continuing repression of Maori people that it seeks to deny. It, of course, will not be possible to do more than present a capsule of the history of the colonization of Aotearoa; however, enough history is provided to contextualize the myths, to chart their changes, and to illustrate the ongoing processes of colonization that they represent.

In essence, the chapter endeavors to illustrate that colonization and imperialism are more than tangible acts of land theft or physical genocide. They are also an accretion of intangibles that, in the words of Edward Said, "linger where they have always been, in a kind of general cultural sphere, as well as in specific political, ideological, economic and social practices."[1]

The Maori Nations in the Land Prior to 1840

Aotearoa was, and is, a country of Polynesia. The Indigenous Maori are related by kinship and history to the people of Hawaii, Tahiti, and other nations of the Pacific Ocean. Maori civilization in Aotearoa itself developed over centuries on a base of politically independent but genealogically and linguistically interdependent Iwi, or nations. Each nation had a clearly recognized territory (on land and water) and exercised political sovereignty or rangatiratanga throughout that territory. The land was called Papatuanuku, the earth mother, and the relationship sought with her was typically Indigenous, being based upon a need for harmony and balance.

Although the total land area of 66 million acres was not continually occupied, it was known and subject to a complex legal system determining its use, its maintenance, and its protection. Its importance is recognized in a proverb that says:

"Te oranga o te tangata, he whenua
Te marie o te tangata he ngahere
Te kopu o te tangata he kai"

("The land ensures the welfare of the people, the forest shade provides peace, and the bounty of both replenishes the body.")

Land was thus the nurturer of Maori cultural life, the base of economic security, and the nexus of political authority, but it was also much more than a political or economic resource that needed to be conserved and protected. The land itself was, and is, the source of life: the Earth Mother from whom we all come and to whom we all return. The placenta that nurtures us before birth and the land that provides nourishment in life are both called whenua.

The whenua provides its gifts to us as something that must be reciprocated. The exchange is an obligation to be Kaitiaki or guardian for all the earth so that her resources will continue to be available. With this obligation people and the land are interdependent and exist in harmony only as long as their relationship is in balance.

Maori did not walk the land to seek some Christian dominion over it. Rather, in the poet's words, we came to the land "barefoot, as befits a trembling lover"[2] and found our place in the interwoven pattern of life on the planet.

The values that sought protection of that place and defined meaning in that pattern were handed down from our ancestors. Maori law shaped the precedents that gave substance to those values and the exercise of Iwi sovereignty that gave them practical force.

Because the land could not be "owned" in a common-law sense by an individual, the authority of rangatiratanga was applied to ensure a balance between the just communal interests of the Iwi and the sustainable protection of Papatuanuku herself. The result was a system called "he waka eke noa," a process in which all can share and to which all must give protection.

The law that ensured this protection and balance was based on the precedents and wisdom of ancestral divines. The Law determined the care of the land, just as it sought to maintain the collective kinship relations of those who came from her. Maori were people of the land. As such, they lived not under a system of law, but with a set of legal proscriptions and prescriptions that governed the land and all things.

It is this complex society that the Dutch in 1642, and the British in 1769, first encountered. Increasing European incursions after that time were to lead to formal colonization by England from the 1830s and the development of justificatory myth-making from then until the present day.

Colonization and the Reason for Myth

The historian Michael Doyle has stated that colonization involves a "relationship . . . in which one state controls the effective political sovereignty of another political society. It can be achieved by force (or) by economic, social or cultural dependence."[3] Jacques Derrida has extended this definition to include a "violence of the letter," a process by which one culture subordinates and oppresses another in the "act of naming and leaving unnamed."[4]

In Aotearoa, the process involved a renaming: a reworking of events and their consequences that has resulted in an ongoing cultural and social oppression of Maori. It has led to a redefinition so profound that it has become mythologized into a received truth.

In this sense colonization is the construction of a particular reality. It is, in fact, a story of the imposition of a philosophical and myth-making construct, as much as it is a tale of economic and military oppression. The coercive reality of colonization flows inexorably from its theoretical ideals, which in turn continue to deny or delimit both the fact of its coercion, and the extant Maori constructs that it sought to destroy.

In Aotearoa today there is a grudging acknowledgment of the "facts" of colonization, but little recognition of their consequences, the myths which underpinned them, or the richness of Maori thought that they endeavored to eliminate. The horrors of massacres by colonial forces at Maori settlements such as Rangiaowhia are now accepted as causes of embarrassment, if not shame, but the forcible suppression of Maori religious beliefs is not. The eviction from and confiscation of millions of acres of land by the government, and the subsequent deportation of Maori "rebels," is regarded as wrong, but the dismissal of the complex jurisprudence of Maori law is not.

Within a colonizing culture framed by the ideals of 19th-century Christianity, it was axiomatic that there would be no room for Maori religion. The Christian notion of a monotheistic divinity dangling before humanity the hope or specter of eternal salvation or damnation (depending upon how individuals exercised their free will) dove-tailed nicely with the colonizing ideal. This ideal was therefore bound to see as a barrier to the civilizing ethos of colonization a belief that saw no need for promise or threat about the after-life, and that saw the exercise of individual free will as being limited by a person's collective responsibilities.

Likewise, the Victorian ethic of laissez-faire capitalism, which underpinned all colonial endeavors, could only be established with the destruction of the so-called "beastly communism" of Maori economic thinking. An English common law that protected the interests of capitalism and promoted the concept of individual culpability was bound to dismiss any legal thinking that sought responsibility in collective terms. Above all, a political system based on the racist notion of a right to rule through an indivisible sovereignty would not countenance any political theories that vested independent authority in institutions that were seen to question that right.

For colonization to succeed, both as "effective sovereignty" and in the "violence of the letter," it was therefore necessary to do more than physically take over the land and resources of Maori. It was, in fact, necessary to create levels of myth-making, to justify the physical and economic dispossession that underpinned the Western will to oppress. To hide the usurpation of political power, there needed to be a rhetoric of legal and constitution right; to disguise the spiritual and cultural costs of this genocide on Maori, there needed to be a myth-making that denigrated the worth of those ideals that were to be destroyed.

To salve the conscience of Victorian sensibilities, colonization, in fact, required a set of myths that reified (and frequently deified) the institutions and actions necessary to effect dispossession. To coerce unwilling Maori required a different set of myths that sought both to demean that which had to be destroyed and elevate as civilized and superior that which would replace it. In each instance the myths sought to present the racist human agency of colonial greed as something else: as immutable justice, as divine will, as manifest destiny, as benign civilization.

Colonization as Magic Fiction: Creating the Constitutional Myths

Colonization is often full of breathtaking exercises in illogic and legal gymnastics that the Indigenous American writer, Robert Williams, calls the "discourse of conquest,"[5] discourses that seek to construct new realities out of the facts of oppression and to legitimate the illegitimacy of colonial takeover.

In New Zealand the power-making machinery of the dominant culture maintains its unspoken right to dominate behind a set of ever-changing myths and rhetoric. The concept of discovery, the inherent authority of proclamation, and the confident assertion of Christian superiority have all helped establish a myth that the dispossession and subordination of the Maori are right.

The myth-making began in 1760 when Captain James Cook purported to "take possession" of Aotearoa. Although his secret admiralty orders required him to gain the "consent of the natives," he did not do so. Instead he "displayed the English colors (and) took formal possession of the place in the name of his Majesty."[6] In so doing, Cook, of course, was merely exercising the presumed right of a colonizing power to take Indigenous land—a right based in the beliefs of colonial law that heathen natives either did not have the capacity or right to "own" "territory," or that such capacity and rights could be extinguished by a colonizer.

Unaware that their land now "belonged" to Britain, Maori continued to occupy and exercise within the sovereignty that the colonizing rhetoric deemed them incapable of possessing. Even as a steady trickle mainly of English traders, whalers, and missionaries began to arrive after Cook's voyage, the de facto and de jure possession and authority remained with the Maori.

By the early 19th century, however, a population of about 2,000 Pakeha (White people) had made their base here, and they were calling for the establishment of some form of governmental structure. The existence of Maori governmental structures and legal processes was, of course, never deemed applicable to non-Maori. Although Englishmen always acknowledged the convention that they should accept the legal jurisdiction of other countries in which they resided, they did not accept that as part of the colonizing endeavor. Indeed a colonial convention arose that an Englishman always carried his law with him to "native" countries.

Calls for the formation of a White government were therefore inevitable. When they were combined with the development of a commercially backed "immigration scheme" in the 1830s, it was clear that the foundations for a colonizing enterprise in Aotearoa were being established.

In response to this movement, Maori leaders in 1835 issued the Declaration of Independence of the Iwi of New Zealand. While willing to access new technology, trade, and in many cases religion, Maori were very clear that their political authority and their relationship with the land should not be compromised. The Declaration in its English text thus states that "all sovereign power and authority is hereby declared to reside entirely and exclusively in the (Iwi) . . . who also declare that they will not permit any legislative authority to exist separate from themselves."[7] The Declaration was addressed especially to the King of England and was acknowledged by him. As a political document based within the certainties and precedents of Maori law, it remains for Maori a clear expression of self-determination, which our people expected to be respected.

To successive governments, however, it was merely a quaint artifact rendered invalid by the rules of imperial law. Indeed, for most colonizers the

Declaration seemed little more than Maori playing at being civilized, a fiction of sovereign power. And in pursuit of the fiction, the British issued a new proclamation of annexation in January 1840 that did not even mention the declaration. In Derrida's words it ceased to have meaning because it was "left unnamed."

A month later the Crown signed a treaty with the peoples it already claimed to have annexed. The Treaty of Waitangi signed between Iwi and the British Crown was also to be subsequently redefined or renamed in a way that changed it from a document of equal sovereignty to a device to pacify the natives to a new and contemporary form that sees it lauded as a document affirming Crown authority in a bicultural nation. To chart the changing Pakeha perceptions of the Treaty is to chart the myth-making process of colonization.

The Treaty is a bilingual document, the Maori text of which was signed by over 500 leaders of Iwi and the Crown representative Governor William Hobson. In the Maori text, the rangatiratanga or sovereignty of Maori is reaffirmed and the Governor is granted the right to govern the rapidly increasing (but minority) White population.

In the English text, which was not discussed at Waitangi, this right of governance over settlers is rendered as a "cession" of Maori sovereignty, and the rangatiratanga of Maori is rendered as "full exclusive and undisturbed possession of their lands and estates, forests, fisheries, and other properties."[8]

To Maori, the Treaty has always been an exercise of Iwi authority or nationhood, by which Britain was granted permission to enter Aotearoa and to impose authority upon immigrant settlers. It was also a reaffirmation of the sovereignty expressed in the Declaration of Independence, and many leaders declined to sign what they saw as a mere addendum to the Declaration. The English text received scant attention from Iwi, for whom any notion of giving away or ceding authority would be both unthinkable in cultural terms and impossible under Maori law.

Although such views were known and accepted by the British Colonial Office prior to 1840, they were inevitably subordinated to the constructs of absolute Pakeha power and their need to impose legal and political structures over all peoples within New Zealand. Just three months after its signing, the Treaty was discarded by the British with the issuing of a unilateral proclamation of sovereignty.

The proclamation read with due ceremony by the Governor, even while his officials were elsewhere gaining other Maori signatures to the Treaty, was deemed to give immediate right to the exercise of British authority over Maori. In an application of what may be termed the Doctrine of Imperial Petulance, the Maori people were to be British subjects because the British said so. The fact that Iwi did not participate in the Proclamation, did not consent to it, and in most cases did not even know about it, was irrelevant to the dominant discourse. Its efficacy required a suspension of disbelief, which the colonizers were willing to accept but which Maori still do not.

For the next 130 years, however, legal sovereignty was sourced in colonial rhetoric to the Proclamation, and the Treaty of Waitangi was literally hidden away to be almost destroyed by rats. In 1877 the courts created a legal precedent to annul the treaty in the case of *Wi Parata* v. *Bishop of Wellington*. In a remarkable piece of legal sleight of hand, the Chief Justice decided that the Treaty conferred no rights and established no constitutional arrangement, because it was "a simple nullity." It had no existence in law; therefore, it had no existence at all.

The sacred pact, which Maori had signed less than 40 years earlier, was clearly irrelevant to the colonizing discourse. Ironic meaning could now be ascribed to the words of a colonial Secretary that any treaty with natives was "a mere illusion and pretence." The reality of solemn prescription of rights was reduced to fantasy, to forgettable myth.

Constructing the Myths and Denying the Reality: 1840–1970

The commonalities of colonization known to all Indigenous peoples were meted out to the Maori. A rapid increase of settler numbers (from 2,000 to 1 million in 50 years), the introduction of new diseases, the preaching of a new religion, the imposition of a new legal system, and the expanding presence of a military force all helped the infrastructure for colonial takeover.

Each contributed also to the physical decimation of the Maori population; but, more importantly, they contributed to that awful decimation of the Indigenous soul, which is the spiritual cost of colonization and was a necessary precursor to the myth-making of a new social reality.

The soul of the people, the essence of their being, exists within the warmth of their culture; it is nurtured and sheltered by the wisdom of their history and philosophy. To oppress a people, to set in place the bloody success of colonization, it is necessary to destroy the soul.

For the Maori, the attack on their soul was to be so terrible that it would lead to a weakening of faith in all the things that had nourished it. The demeaning of the values that cherished it, the language that gave meaning to its soul, the law that gave it order, and the religion that was its strength were ultimately to affect the belief of Maori in themselves.

When colonization demanded the rejection of the actual institutions of Maori law, religion, education, economic distribution, and political authority, it removed those things that gave tangible expression to the Maori soul. In a sense it took away the structures and processes that gave meaning to the life of Maori. In so doing it began to capture the very processes of Maori thought and thus redefined what was henceforth to be the accepted worldview.

It thereby induced an agony into the Maori soul as it sought to survive under an increasing Pakeha domination that mocked it. In place of the surety of an ancient culture, colonization introduced an alien philosophy, an all-pervasive foreign ethos that would give meaning to all that was henceforth to be regarded as good.

The vehicle for much of the attack on the soul of Maori would be "the law": a law not seen as some impartial and culturally neutral set of theories, but as a manifestation of the same traditions that gave rise to the colonizing enterprise itself. The law of the colonizer has its roots in the Western Christian heritage, and its growth has been nurtured by the interaction of particular sociocultural and economic interests. Its definition of what is "legal" or "illegal," its definitions of "ownership," and its concepts of "property," are cultural artifacts linked by particular notions of political power. When that political power seeks suzerainty in a colonial context, the implementation and interpretation of the law becomes a political and ideological act. The law becomes a means of imposing and maintaining bonds of obedience and deference, of legitimizing colonial power, and of constantly recreating a structure of authority based on the taking and control of "property."

Rather than become what a former Prime Minister called a "pure and unpolluted stream," the law is actually part of the muddied pool of colonial domination. If the philosopher John Locke could state that "government has no other end but the preservation of property,"[9] the colonizing law could seek to legitimate the theft and redistribution of all properties held by those to be colonized.

The law was thus both the leitmotif on which colonization was predicated and the righteous indignation in which opposition to it was expressed. In Aotearoa, the indignation is illustrated by the ongoing process of placing Maori land under State control, which remains the most costly and tangible expression of the colonial imperative. The legal-political justifications of that process have in turn established the most enduring of myths.

The "Maori Wars," which were fought between Iwi and the Crown in the 1860s and 1870s, were both the prelude to and the aftermath of concerted efforts to clothe the theft of land in legal rhetoric. The eviction and deportation of people from their land was renamed and explained in the legislative myth-making of the Suppression of "Rebellion" Act, and the confiscation of millions of acres of land was rendered as something else in the New Zealand "Settlements" Act.

The Earth Mother was redefined as a property interest and became "Crown land." Her acquisition by White settlers, no matter how obtained, was legitimized in the Validation of Invalid Maori Land Sales Act, and her subsequent description as "private" land rendered it inviolable and beyond claim by Maori. The guardianship ties that Maori had with the land were broken, and a new tenure system changed Maori from the children of the earth with communal obligations to vested "owners" with individual title. Dispossession was masked and redefined in legal myth to appear as something other than theft. Yet by 1900 the State-defined estate of Maori land was less than one-twentieth of its original area.

These wars and laws were actioned by the representative "settler government" established by an imperial statute, the 1852 New Zealand Constitution Act. No longer directly responsible to Britain, the elite of White society could impose their own version of capital self-interest and Indigenous subordination. If opposition arose, new myths could be created to nullify it, as in the New Zealand Settlements Act 1863, which redefined to the large-scale confiscation of Maori land as "settlement."

The law in effect redefined what was happening to Maori and helped create both a new reality and a determining set of understandings and interpretations to underpin that reality. To shore up the new construction and to ensure Maori subordination, colonization had to constantly assert the rightness of what was happening and to apparently ameliorate the consequences of genocide, land theft, and the social and cultural dislocation that still determine the lives of Maori today. The diseases of poverty, the internalized violence born of oppression, and the despair among the young shaped by an unemployment rate of nearly 60 percent are all products of the dispossession wrought by colonization.

Yet Maori have survived and now claw back cultural and spiritual imperatives of language, religion, customs, law, and history; and this survival exposes the myth of harmonious race relations born of a time when Maori were invisible in the struggle to live. It exposes also a more potent myth: the assumed right of Whites to rule this land. The changing nature of that myth is seen in the recent history of the Treaty of Waitangi.

The Born-Again Treaty: Myth-Making Rampant

For a major part of this century, Maori sought solace and protection from the pain of colonization in political quietude. Largely restricted to isolated rural areas, the people sought to take advantage of new technologies, access the new literacy, nourish the battered soul, and cherish the dreams invoked by the Treaty of Waitangi.

Colonization, of course, continued. Land alienation occurred under various legislatively enshrined confiscators such as the Maori Affairs Act, which permitted confiscation for roads and other "public developments." Maori children were punished for speaking the Maori language, and Maori adoption and marriage procedures were prohibited. Where deemed necessary, military power could still be used, as it was in the attack on the religious community of Maungapohatu in 1916.

Through the exercise of power by its now established political apparatus, the State could thus proclaim its ability and right to subordinate the Maori. Through the other institutions of the law such as the Courts, that subordination could be framed within a legalistic rhetoric that both evidenced and legitimated its assumed sovereign authority.

Peaceful Maori opposition and protest against State usurpation did not die out but gathered momentum in the 1960s as Maori began to move to the cities and voice discontent in forums beyond the rural home-base. Mass returns to the land (defined as "illegal occupations" by the State), protests seeking reaffirmation of the Treaty, and the articulation of a self-determination dialectic by many Maori thinkers and activists contributed to a new sovereign movement that by the mid-1970s could not be ignored or forcibly repressed.

The Crown response was to introduce a new policy and create a new mythology. In the 1970s and 1980s the government announced that it would acknowledge the wrongs done to Maori and would seek practical ways in which the issues could be "defined, faced and solved. Ignorance and apathy should not deter or delay a proposed solution."[10] The new policy was seen by many as a genuine attempt to deal with a legacy of colonial oppression. The strategies and processes developed to implement the new dawn exposed a new face on the old myths.

The baseline of the policy remained the assertion by the State of its right to rule and the denial of any right to question that assumption. What changed, though, was the basis upon which the state now made the claim to sovereignty.

The Crown, in essence, rediscovered the Treaty of Waitangi. Century-old treaty petitions by Maori to parliament, and even directly to the sovereign in England, which were previously rebuffed, were now regarded as "pointers to resolution." Court decisions, which had previously dismissed the Treaty, were redefined as "judicial aberrations." Arguments based on a notion of treaty rights that had previously been taken by one judge to simply evidence that a council had been driven to desperate straits,[11] were now to become the basis of serious academic and political debate. The simple nullity was to become a binding constitutional document, but it was to be a document redefined as a treaty of cession. Maori perceptions of the Treaty as an argument signed, in the words of one Iwi, in terms of "self-determination . . . of the enduring right to govern ourselves,"[12] were to be dismissed.

Rangatiratanga, the concept and expression of that right to govern, was redefined as an "especial interest" in land. But even that interest, described in the Treaty as "full and exclusive," was to be reclassified as an interest delimitable by the Crown. The Treaty would indeed no longer be a discarded nullity in the rhetoric of the Crown, but it would remain a device to pacify the natives in the processes that lay behind the rhetoric.

A myth was born in which the Treaty was to be the justification and base for the Crown sovereignty. The 1840 proclamations of annexation and sovereignty were shuffled to the margins of constitutional thinking and replaced by the Treaty as the raison d'être for Crown authority. Reflecting New Age sensitivities, this revivified Treaty was to be different from other oppressive or discarded arrangements of the colonizing era. The Treaty of Waitangi was now held to have created a unique concept of partnership in which the State must recognize the particular interests of its junior Maori partner. To ensure the "good faith" recognition of that partnership, reference was not to be made to the Waitangi Treaty, but rather to a set of Treaty "principles."

Within the contest of this new Treaty awareness, the Crown has come to be seen as facing up to the difficult decisions of finding just solutions for Maori without creating new injustices for Pakeha. While constantly reassuring the majority White electorate that "very little is actually being done," the apparatus of the State constructs the new reality of a progressive government seeking to redress wrongs of the past. An agency of the Crown, the Waitangi Tribunal, was established in 1975 to hear Maori grievances. Bound by its parent statute to equally consider both texts (exit the contra proferentum rule) and to find resolution based on treaty principles, the tribunal has been a major component of the myth. In spite of the honest endeavors of tribunal members, its statutory ability only to recommend resolution to government has meant that its work has helped shape the myth without delivering any substantive change for Maori in terms of the sovereign power assumed by Pakeha in colonization. Its junior role in the judicial hierarchy has also meant that it is bound to accept Court interpretations of the Treaty and Court pronouncements on sovereignty.

Since 1987 the courts have dismissed the Wi Parata decision and begun analyzing the Treaty's principles in a new jurisprudence that draws heavily upon the colonial law doctrine of aboriginal title, which recognizes the validity of native title to land. The doctrine, however, countenances no authority but that of the colonizing State and reserves to that State the right to extinguish native title. In its most important pronouncement of the 1987 Maori Council case,[13] the Court of Appeal legitimated Crown sovereignty (and, hence, subordinated Maori) by simply stating that the Treaty, while no longer a nullity, was nevertheless a bargain in which the "Queen was to govern and the Maori were to be subjects" (Cooke, P), and that neither "the provisions of the Treaty . . . nor its principles are . . . a restraint on the legislative supremacy of Parliament" (Somers, J).

In less than 20 years this reaffirmation of Maori nonsovereignty has been refined into a myth of judicial compassion and state good faith. Maori challenges to that myth and Maori perceptions of the Treaty are dismissed or redefined to maintain the illusion of a just and legitimate colonial authority. The socioeconomic and cultural pain that resulted from the land loss and diminution of Maori values is now variously attributed to Maori laziness, inability to cope with the "modern" world, or even to some genetic inferiority.

While the imposed law no longer rejects a notion of Maori rights, it redefines those rights and thereby sources them within a pluralistic common law, rather than in Maori authority. Pakeha lawyers, judges, and institutions no longer dismiss the concept of Maori authority of rangatiratanga; they capture and emasculate it. Pakeha academics frame the whole discussion of Maori rights within a pluralistic jurisprudence of the spirit that is consistent with the law. Overseas experts laud the "advances" and hold up the Waitangi Tribunal as a model for other Indigenous Peoples. But the Tribunal and the Courts do not, cannot, question the political dynamics that established and maintain them. And the new wave of bicultural sensitivities of state policy cannot disguise the reality of ongoing colonization: the removal of political power from the people being colonized.

What they do achieve, however, is the construction of a powerful new myth: that New Zealand leads the world not only in the benevolence of its actual colonization, but also in the way it now seeks to redress the wrongs of its past.

Such is the power of myth. Such is the force of the colonizing imperative that a treaty entered into with good intent, and then dismissed, can now be resurrected as an instrument of deception.

Conclusion: Deconstructing the Myth

The process of colonial myth-making makes the oppression of others justifiable in the eyes of the colonizer and justifiable in the minds of the colonized who are its victims. In its present-day manifestation in Aotearoa, what has been erected for the majority Pakeha is a good faith partnership in which any challenge by Maori is perceived as an ungrateful threat to racial harmony. For many Maori a seemingly necessary trust has been engendered in the efficacy and ability of the dominant culture to recognize and facilitate Maori self-determination.

The myths have, in fact, created a Gramscian hegemony in which the colonial-constructed reality persuades Pakeha to believe their own mythology and Maori to live within parameters of political and economic expression determined by the State. The only reality Maori are permitted to define and inhabit is a "cultural" construct of language, music, art, and custom. At best such a construct offers comfort and spiritual protection to Maori; at worst it is confined by State perceptions of safe colonial expression and by a Christian historiography of what is acceptable custom.

If Maori are to reclaim the right to define both the cultural and the political expression of sovereignty, the myths of colonization need to be challenged from within the social reality of Maori culture. That will lead to a new reality in which Maori are again the namer of names and will inevitably change the belief systems that colonization has imposed to ensure our subordination and acquiescence; for whenever Indigenous peoples have been able to break free from the state that many writers have called the "colonization of the mind," their new freedom to think and believe differently has also led to different societies and different structures of power. So it will be with the Maori.

In Aotearoa many Maori are striving to establish new ways of believing that focus not on the determinable grievances of the past but on the systemic injustices of colonization itself. Such a process involves identifying the myths that permeate and maintain colonization as the first step in its deconstruction. It will inevitably lead to practical strategies in which Maori can reconstruct Maori reality for the 21st century and thus reclaim effective sovereignty. In so doing they will fulfill the hopes expressed by a Maori leader, Te Ataria, in 1892: "What has happened since the Treaty is all confusion . . . the loud voices and strange silences of others hide our loss . . . our children will need to break the silence and tell our stories once again."[14]

NOTES

1. Edward Said, *Culture and Imperialism* (New York: Random House, 1993), p. 8.
2. ARD Fairburn, *Collected Poems* (London: Oxford Press, 1963), p. 42.
3. Michael W. Doyle, *Empires* (Ithaca: Cornell University Press, 1986), p. 45.
4. Jacques Derrida, *Of Grammatology* (trans.) (Baltimore: Johns Hopkins University Press, 1976), p. 123.
5. Whaton, ed., *Cook's Journals*, entry 15, November 1769 (1893).
6. J. Hight and W. Bawford, *The Constitutional History of New Zealand* (Whitcources, 1914).
7. *The Declaration of Independence of the Maori People of New Zealand*, Waitangi, 1835.

8. Article 2, Treaty of Waitangi, 1840.
9. John Locke, *The Second Treatise of Government* (Library of Liberal Arts Edition, LAE Press, 1952), p. 72.
10. Geoffrey Palmer, Policy Statement of NZ Labour Party, February 2, 1984.
11. John Jeffries, *Portrait of a Profession: A History of the New Zealand Law Society* (Wellington: New Zealand Law Society, 1969), p. 68.
12. Submission to NZ Parliament of Te Kotahitanga o Te Tai Tokerau, July 1987.
13. *New Zealand Maori Council* v. *Attorney General* (1987), 6NZAR (New Zealand Appeals Report).
14. Diaries of te Ataria Rarer, Ngati Kahungunu, family archives.

PART III

Indigenous Philosophy and Activism

CHAPTER 7
FROM SOVEREIGNTY TO FREEDOM

By Taiaiake Alfred

Taiaiake Alfred is a Mohawk orator, writer, and professor. He was raised in the community of Kahnawake. He was educated by Jesuits at Loyola High School in Montreal and served in the U.S. Marine Corps infantry from 1982 to 1985. He graduated from Concordia University in 1989 with a bachelor's degree in history, and in 1994 he received a Ph.D. in comparative government and political thought from Cornell University. Taiaiake is the Indigenous Peoples Research Chair at the University of Victoria. He was the founding director of the University of Victoria's Indigenous Governance Programs, and prior to that, a professor of political science at Concordia University. He has lectured at more than 30 universities and colleges in North America, Europe, and Australia. His publications include *Heeding the Voices of our Ancestors* (1995), a history of Mohawk militancy and nationalism, and *Peace, Power, Righteousness* (1999), an essay on Indigenous ethics and leadership. Since 1987 he has worked as an advisor and strategist for Indigenous governments across North America. He is also an award-winning journalist known for his incisive social and political commentary.

Introduction

Sovereignty—the word, so commonly used, refers to supreme political authority, independent and unlimited by any other power. Discussion of the term *sovereignty* in relation to Indigenous peoples, however, must be framed differently, within an intellectual framework of internal colonization. Internal colonization is the historical process and political reality defined in the structures and techniques of government that consolidate the domination of Indigenous peoples by a foreign, yet sovereign, settler state. While internal colonization describes the political reality of most Indigenous peoples, one should also note that the discourse of state sovereignty is and has been contested in real and theoretical ways since its imposition. The intercounterplay of state sovereignty doctrines—rooted in notions of dominion—with and against Indigenous concepts of political relations—rooted in notions of freedom, respect, and autonomy—frames the discourse on Indigenous "sovereignty" at its broadest level.

The practice of history cannot help but be implicated in colonization. Indeed, most discussions of Indigenous sovereignty are founded on a particular and instrumental reading of history that serves to underscore internal colonization. From the earliest times, relations between Indigenous peoples and European newcomers vacillated within the normal parameters that characterize any relation between autonomous political groups. Familiar relations—war, peace, cooperation, antagonism, and shifting dominance and subservience—are all to be found in our shared history, yet the actual history of our plural existence has been erased by the narrow fictions of a single sovereignty. Controlling, universalizing, and assimilating, these fictions have been imposed in the form of law on weakened but resistant and remembering peoples.

European sovereignties in North America first legitimated themselves through treaty relationships entered into by Europeans and Indigenous nations. North American settler states (Canada and the United States, with their predecessor states, Holland, Spain, France, and England) gained legitimacy as legal entities only by the expressed consent, through treaty, of the original occupiers and governors of North America. The founding documents of state sovereignty recognize this fact: All Dutch and French treaties with Indigenous peoples, the Treaty of Utrecht, the Articles of Capitulation, and the Royal Proclamation (made in a context of military interdependency between the British and Indigenous nations) all contain explicit reference to the independent nationhood of Indigenous peoples. As the era of European exploration and discovery gave way to settlement, with its concomitant need for balanced peaceful relations with Indigenous nations, the states' charter documents made clear reference to the separate political existence and territorial independence of Indigenous peoples.

None of this historical diversity is reflected in the official history and doctrinal bases of settler state sovereignty today. Rather, Canada and the United States have written self-serving histories of discovery, conquest, and settlement that wipe out any reference to the original relations between Indigenous peoples and Europeans. This post facto claim of European "sovereignty" is limited by two main caveats. The first is factual: The mere documentation of European assertions of hegemonic sovereignty does not necessarily indicate proof of its achievement. European control over actual territory was tenuous at best; and the political existence of European settler states was a *negotiated* reality until well into the 19th century (and not completely achieved, even in colonial mythology, until the end of the 19th century in the United States and, to this day, in Canada).

The second limitation is theoretical: The discourse of sovereignty upon which the current post facto justification rests is an exclusively European discourse; that is, European assertions in both a legal and political sense were made strictly vis-à-vis other European powers, and did not impinge upon or necessarily even affect in law or politics the rights and status of Indigenous nations. It is only from our distant historical vantage point, and standing upon a counterfactual rock, that we are able to see European usurpations of Indigenous sovereignty as justified.

If sovereignty has been neither legitimized nor justified, it has nevertheless limited the ways we are able to think, suggesting always a conceptual and definitional problem centered on the accommodation of Indigenous peoples within a legitimate framework of settler state governance. When we step outside this discourse, we confront a different problematic, that of the state's "sovereignty" itself and its actual meaning in contrast to the facts and the potential that exists for a nation-to-nation relationship.

The Critique from Within

Indigenous scholars have focused on this problematic concept with profound effect. Russel Barsh and James Henderson, for example, explored the process of intellectual obscurantism in close detail in *The Road: Indian Tribes and Political Liberty*. Barsh and Henderson concentrated on the United States and the creation of a historical narrative that completely ignored basic principles of natural law and the philosophical underpinnings of American notions of liberty and equality. They traced the evolution of the doctrine of tribal sovereignty in United States (U.S.) law through judicial decisions and demonstrated the ways in which the process misrepresented the true potential of liberal principles—and even the U.S. Constitution—to accommodate notions of Indigenous nationhood.

The Road is a landmark work. It embarked on a critique from within, arguing for recognition of Indigenous peoples' rights *within* the historic and legal frame of state sovereignty. Ultimately, Barsh and Henderson subjected the rationale for Indigenous or "tribal" liberty to criteria defined by the framers of the U.S. Constitution. The problem, they argued, was the subjection of principle to politics and unprincipled decisions by the state judiciaries. Barsh and Henderson designed a "theory of the tribe in the American nation" (p. 205), and in doing so advanced the theoretical notion of a coexistence of Indigenous and state sovereignty that was hamstrung as a conceptual tool by the weight of skewed legal precedent and the reality of the political context. In this sense, *The Road* follows the trajectory of Native sovereignty within and in relation to state sovereignty, first set forth in the 1830s in the Cherokee decisions, which suggested that tribes were "domestic dependent nations."

The entanglement of Indigenous peoples within the institutional frame of the colonial state, of course, went beyond legal doctrines. The practice of sovereignty in the structures of government and the building of institutional relationships between Indigenous governments and state agencies offered another forum for the subordination of principle. In two volumes, *American Indians, American Justice* and *The Nations Within*, Vine Deloria, Jr., and Clifford Lytle first outlined how the legal denial of Indigenous rights in the courts was mirrored in governing structures that embedded the false notion of European superiority in indigenous community life. The example of the U.S. usurpation of Indigenous nationhood clarified how the state generally uses not only political and economic but also certain intellectual strategies to impose and maintain its dominance. Such linking of the intellectual and structural forms of colonialism has produced some of the deepest analyses of the issue.

In considering the question of the "sovereignty" of Indigenous peoples within their territorial borders, the state takes various positions: The classic strategies include outright denial of Indigenous rights; a theoretical acceptance of Indigenous rights combined with an assertion that these have been extinguished historically; and legal doctrines that transform Indigenous rights from their autonomous nature to contingent rights, existing only within the framework of colonial law. Scholars have documented fully the manifestation of these strategies in the various policies implemented by settler states in the modern era: domestication, termination, assimilation.

With the minor concession that in both Canada and the United States the federal government itself has maintained and defended its powers over Indigenous peoples vis-à-vis states and provinces, the potential for recognition of Indigenous nationhood has gone unrealized. There have been total theoretical exclusion and extinguishing of Indigenous nationhood, leading to what a recent United Nations Human Rights Commission study labeled the unjust "domestication" of Indigenous nationhood.

Indigenous peoples, nonetheless, struggled to achieve a degree of freedom and power within the intellectual and political environment created out of a colonial domestication project and settler state sovereignty. For generations, Indigenous peoples fought to preserve the integrity of their nations and the independent bases of their existence. They were successful in countering the colonial project to the extent that they survived (a monumental human achievement, given the intensive efforts of two modern industrial states to eradicate them). Yet by the late 1980s, the increasing erosions of tribal governing powers in the United States, and failed attempts to enshrine a recognition of Indigenous nationhood in the Canadian constitution, made it clear that the governments of Canada and the United States were incapable of liberalizing their relationships with "the nations within."

The New Approach:
Deconstructing the Architecture of Colonial Domination

As they regained their capacity to govern themselves and began to reassert the earlier principles of the nation-to-nation relationship between Indigenous peoples and states, Indigenous people began to question seriously the viability of working within the system, of considering themselves "nations within." The questioning often came out of models—tribal and band councils dependent upon and administering federal funds, for example—that recognized Indigenous sovereignty, yet always subsumed it to that of the state. A new intellectual approach began to emerge in the critique of the fundamental pillars by which the United States and Canada claimed legal authority over Indigenous peoples and lands. Reflecting critical trends in other academic disciplines, legal scholarship began the project of deconstructing the architecture of colonial domination. Perhaps the two most important strategies to reachieve a political plurality in the face of the dominance of state sovereignty have been woven together: on the one hand, the assertion of a prior and coexisting sovereignty, and, on the other, the assertion of a right of self-determination for Indigenous peoples in international law.

The most thorough and illuminating of the critical legal studies of the Indigenous–state relationship is Robert Williams's *The American Indian in Western Legal Thought*. Its description of how law, embodying all of the racist assumptions of medieval Europe, has served as the European colonizers' most effective instrument of genocide destroys the arguments of those who would defend the justice of the colonial state. Williams shows how the deep roots of Europeans' belief in their own cultural and racial superiority underlie all discussions of the interaction between whites and Indigenous peoples on the issue of sovereignty. After Williams's critique, any history of the concept of sovereignty in North America must trace the manipulation of the concept as it evolved to justify the elimination of Indigenous peoples. By examining the deep history of European thought on Indigenous peoples—what he calls the "discourse of conquest"—Williams showed how the entire discussion of sovereignty in North America represents the calculated triumph of illogic and interest over truth and justice.

After the end of the imperial era and the foundation of the North American states, in no instance did principles of law preclude the perpetration of injustice against Indigenous peoples. In Canada, the rights of Indigenous peoples were completely denied in the creation of the legal framework for the relationship. In addition, the U.S. Supreme Court's definition of tribal sovereignty, made by Chief Justice John Marshall in a series of 19th-century decisions centered on *Johnson* v. *McIntosh*, merely gave legal sanction to the unilateral abrogation of treaties by the United States and denial of the natural law rights of Indigenous peoples. As Williams argues, "*Johnson's* acceptance of the Doctrine of Discovery into United States law preserved the legacy of 1000 years of European racism and colonialism directed against non-Western peoples."[1] Recent assertions of prior and persistent Indigenous power have come from two places: first, the intellectual and historical critiques of state legitimacy, and second, the revitalization of Indigenous communities. Using "remnant recognitions" in colonial law, Indian critics have sought to deconstruct the skewed legal and institutional frame and to focus directly on the relationship between Indigenous peoples and state sovereignty.

Core to this effort is the theoretical attention given to the entire notion of sovereignty as the guiding principle of government in states. What Canadian philosopher James Tully calls the "empire of uniformity" is a fact-obliterating mythology of European conquest and normality. Tully recognizes the ways in which injustice toward Indigenous peoples is deeply rooted in the basic injustice of normalized power relations within the state itself. In his *Strange Multiplicity,* Tully considers the intellectual bases of dominance inherent in state structures, and he challenges us to reconceptualize the state and its relation with Indigenous people in order to accommodate what he calls the three post-imperial values: consent, mutual recognition, and cultural continuity.

Taiaiake Alfred, in his *Peace, Power, Righteousness,* has engaged this challenge from within an Indigenous intellectual framework. Alfred's "manifesto" calls for a profound reorientation of Indigenous politics and a recovery of Indigenous political traditions in contemporary society. Attacking both the foundations of the state's claim to authority over Indigenous peoples and the process of co-optation that has drawn Indigenous leaders into a position of dependency on and cooperation with unjust state structures, Alfred's work reflects a basic sentiment within many Indigenous communities: Sovereignty is inappropriate as a political objective for Indigenous peoples.

David Wilkins's *American Indian Sovereignty and the United States Supreme Court* amply illustrates the futility and frustration of adopting sovereignty as a political objective. Wilkins traces the history of the development of a doctrine of Indian tribal sovereignty in the U.S. Supreme Court, demonstrating its inherent contradictions for Indian nationhood. From the central Marshall decisions in the mid-19th century through contemporary jurisprudence, Wilkins reveals the fundamental weakness of a tribal sovereignty "protected" within the colonizer's legal system.

Wilkins's exhaustive and convincing work draws on postmodern and critical legal studies approaches to the law. Examining the negative findings of the Court, he deconstructs the façade of judicial objectivity, demonstrating that in defining sovereignty,

> justices of the Supreme Court, both individually and collectively, have engaged in the manufacturing, redefining, and burying of "principles," "doctrines," and legal "truths" to excuse and legitimize constitutional, treaty, and civil rights violations of tribal nations.[2]

In the United States, the common law provides for recognition of the inherent sovereignty of Indigenous peoples, but simultaneously allows for its limitation by the U.S. Congress. The logic of colonization is clearly evident in the creation of domestic dependent nation status, which supposedly accommodates the historical fact of coexisting sovereignties, but does no more than slightly limit the hypocrisy. It accepts the premise of Indigenous rights while at the same time legalizing their unjust limitation and potential extinguishment by the state.

Rejecting Sovereignty—Regaining Nationhood

Scholars and Indigenous leaders, in confronting the ignorance of the original principles in politics today and in the processes that have been established to negotiate a movement away from the colonial past, have usually accepted the framework and goal of "sovereignty" as core to the Indigenous political movement. New institutions are constructed in communities to assert Indigenous rights within a "tribal sovereignty" framework, and many people have reconciled themselves to the belief that we are making steady progress toward the resolution of injustices stemming from colonization. It may take more energy or more money than is currently being devoted to the process of decolonization, but the issue is always framed within existing structural and legal parameters.

But few people have questioned how a European term and idea (*sovereignty* is certainly not Sioux, Salish, or Iroquoian in origin) came to be so embedded and important to cultures that had their own systems of government since the time before the term *sovereignty* was invented in Europe. Fewer still have questioned the implications of adopting the European notion of power and governance and using it to structure the postcolonial systems that are being negotiated and implemented within Indigenous communities today.

These are exactly the questions that have become central to current analyses of power within Indigenous communities. Using the sovereignty paradigm, Indigenous people have made significant legal and political gains toward reconstructing the autonomous aspects of their individual, collective, and social identities. The positive effect of the sovereignty movement in terms of mental, physical, and emotional health cannot be denied or understated. Yet this does not seem to be enough: The seriousness of the social ills that do continue suggests that an externally focused assertion of sovereign power vis-à-vis the state is neither complete nor in and of itself a solution. Indigenous leaders engaging themselves and their communities in arguments framed within a liberal paradigm have not been able to protect the integrity of their nations. "Aboriginal rights" and "tribal sovereignty" are, in fact, the benefits accrued by Indigenous peoples who have agreed to abandon autonomy to enter the state's legal and political framework.

Yet Indigenous people have successfully engaged Western society in the first stages of a movement to restore their autonomous power and cultural integrity in the area of governance. The movement—referred to in terms of Aboriginal self-government, Indigenous self-determination, or Native sovereignty—is founded on an ideology of Indigenous nationalism and a rejection of the models of government rooted in European cultural values. It is an uneven process of reinstituting systems that promote the goals and reinforce the values of Indigenous cultures against the constant effort of the Canadian and U.S. governments to maintain the systems of dominance imposed on Indigenous communities during the last century. Many communities have almost disentangled themselves from paternalistic state controls in administering institutions within jurisdictions that are important to them. Many more are currently engaged in substantial negotiations over land and governance, hoped and believed to lead to significantly greater control over their own lives and futures.

The intellectuals' rejection of the co-optation of Indigenous nationhood and the creation of assimilative definitions of "sovereignty" in Canada and the United States followed years of activism among Indigenous peoples on the ground. That activism was the direct result of the retraditionalization of segments of the population within Indigenous communities—rejection of the legitimacy of the state and recovery of the traditional bases of Indigenous political society. In Canada, the movement has taken the form of a struggle for revision of the constitutional status of Indigenous nations, focused on forcing the state to break from its imperial position and recognize and accommodate the notion of an inherent authority in Indigenous nations. In the United States, where a theoretical, redefined, and arbitrarily limited form of "sovereign" authority still resides with Indian tribes, the movement has focused on defending and expanding the political and economic implications of that theoretical right. In comparison, the struggles can be seen as philosophical vis-à-vis Canada and material vis-à-vis the United States.

There has been a much more substantive and challenging debate in Canada (linked to the struggles of Indigenous peoples confronting the Commonwealth legal tradition in Australia and New Zealand), where actual political and legal stature is being contested, as opposed to the United States, where Indigenous peoples tend to rely implicitly upon the existing legal framework. In Canada, Indigenous peoples have sought to transcend the colonial myths and restore the original relationships. It is this effort to transcend the colonial mentality and move the society beyond the structures of dominance forming the contemporary political reality that will drive future activism and scholarship on the question of Indigenous peoples' political rights and status in relation to states.

In spite of this progress—or perhaps because of it—people in many Native communities are beginning to look beyond the present, envisioning a postcolonial future negotiated at various levels. There are serious problems with that future in the minds of many people who remain committed to systems of government that complement and sustain Indigenous cultures. The core problem for both activists and scholars revolves around the fact that the colonial system itself has become embedded within Indigenous societies. Indigenous community life today may be seen as framed by two fundamentally opposed value systems, one forming the undercurrent of social and cultural relations; the other, structuring politics. This disunity is the fundamental condition of the alienation and political fatigue that plague Indigenous communities. A perspective that does not see the ongoing crisis fueled by continuing efforts to keep Indigenous people focused on a quest for power within a paradigm bounded by the vocabulary, logic, and institutions of sovereignty will be blind to the reality of a persistent intent to maintain the colonial oppression of Indigenous nations. The next phase of scholarship and activism, then, will need to transcend the mentality that supports the colonization of Indigenous nations, beginning with the rejection of the term and notion of Indigenous "sovereignty."

A Postsovereign Future?

Most of the attention and energy thus far has been directed at the process of decolonization: the mechanics of escaping from direct state control and the legal and political struggle to gain recognition of an Indigenous governing authority. There has been a fundamental ignorance of the end values of the struggle. What will an Indigenous government be like after self-government is achieved? Few people imagine that it will be an exact replica of the precolonial system that governed communities in the past. Most acknowledge that all Indigenous structures will adapt to modern methods in terms of administrative technique and technology. There is a political universe of possibility when it comes to the embodiment of core values in the new systems.

The great hope is that the government systems being set up to replace colonial control in Indigenous communities will embody the underlying cultural values of those communities. The great fear is that the postcolonial governments being designed today will be simple replicas of non-Indigenous systems for smaller and racially defined constituencies with oppression becoming self-inflicted and more intense for its localization, thereby perpetuating the two value systems at the base of the problem.

One of the main obstacles to achieving peaceful coexistence is, of course, the uncritical acceptance of the classic notion of "sovereignty" as the framework for discussions of political relations between peoples. The discourse of sovereignty has effectively stilled any potential resolution of the issue that respects Indigenous values and perspectives. Even "traditional" Indigenous nationhood is commonly defined relationally, in contrast to the dominant formulation of the state: There is no absolute authority, no coercive enforcement of decisions, no hierarchy, and no separate ruling entity.

In his work on Indigenous sovereignty in the United States, Vine Deloria, Jr., has pointed out the distinction between Indigenous concepts of nationhood and those of state-based sovereignty. Deloria sees nationhood as distinct from "self-government" (or the "domestic dependent nation" status accorded Indigenous peoples by the United States). The right of "self-determination," unbounded by state law, is a concept appropriate to nations. Delegated forms of authority, like "self-government" within the context of state sovereignty, are concepts appropriate to what we may call "minority peoples" or other ethnically defined groups within the polity as a whole. In response to the question of whether or not the development of "self-government" and other state delegated forms of authority as institutions in Indigenous communities was wrong, Deloria answers that it is not wrong, but simply inadequate. Delegated forms do not address the spiritual basis of Indigenous societies:

> Self-government is not an Indian idea. It originates in the minds of non-Indians who have reduced the traditional ways to dust, or believe they have, and now wish to give, as a gift, a limited measure of local control and responsibility.

Self-government is an exceedingly useful concept for Indians to use when dealing with the larger government because it provides a context within which
negotiations can take place. Since it will never supplant the intangible, spiritual,
and emotional aspirations of American Indians, it cannot be regarded as the
final solution to Indian problems.[3]

The challenge for Indigenous peoples in building appropriate postcolonial
governing systems is to disconnect the notion of sovereignty from its Western,
legal roots and to transform it. It is all too often taken for granted that what
Indigenous peoples are seeking in recognition of their nationhood is at its core
the same as that which countries like Canada and the United States possess
now. In fact, most of the current generation of Indigenous politicians see politics
as a zero-sum contest for power in the same way that non-Indigenous politicians do. Rather than a value rooted in a traditional Indigenous philosophy,
Indigenous politicians regard the nationhood discourse as a lever to gain bargaining position. For the politician, there is a dichotomy between philosophical
principle and politics. The assertion of a sovereign right for Indigenous peoples
is not really believed and becomes a transparent bargaining ploy and a lever for
concessions within the established constitutional framework. Until "sovereignty" as a concept shifts from the dominant "state sovereignty" construct and
comes to reflect more of the sense embodied in Western notions such as personal sovereignty or popular sovereignty, it will remain problematic if integrated within Indigenous political struggles.

One of the major problems in the Indigenous sovereignty movement is that
its leaders must qualify and rationalize their goals by modifying the sovereignty
concept. Sovereignty itself implies a set of values and objectives that put it in
direct opposition to the values and objectives found in most traditional Indigenous philosophies. Non-Indigenous politicians recognize the inherent weakness
of a position that asserts a sovereign right for peoples who do not have the cultural frame and institutional capacity to defend or sustain it. The problem for
the Indigenous sovereignty movement is that the initial act of asserting a sovereign right for Indigenous peoples has structured the politics of decolonization
since, and the state has used the theoretical inconsistencies in the position to its
own advantage.

In this context, for example, the resolution of 'land claims' (addressing the
legal inconsistency of Crown or state title on Indigenous lands) is generally seen
as a mark of progress by progressive non-Indigenous people. But it seems that
without a fundamental questioning of the assumptions that underlie the state's
approach to power, the bad assumptions of colonialism will continue to structure the relationship. Progress toward achieving justice from a Indigenous perspective made within this frame will be marginal, and indeed it has become
evident that it will be tolerated by the state only to the extent that it serves, or at
least does not oppose, the alter Indigenously defined interests of the state itself.

In Canada, to note a second example, recognition of the concept of "aboriginal rights" by the high court is seen by many to be such a landmark of progress.
Yet those who think more deeply recognize the basic reality that even with a
legal recognition of collective rights to certain subsistence activities within cer-

tain territories, Indigenous people are still subject to the state's controlling mechanisms in the exercise of these inherent freedoms and powers. They must conform to state-derived criteria and represent ascribed or negotiated identities in order to access these legal rights. Not throwing Indigenous people in jail for fishing is certainly a mark of progress, given Canada's shameful history; but to what extent does that state-regulated "right" to fish represent justice when you consider that Indigenous people have been fishing on their rivers and seas since time began?

There are inherent constraints to the exercise of Indigenous governmental authority built into the notion of Indigenous sovereignty, and these constraints derive from the myth of conquest that is the foundation of mainstream perspectives on Indigenous-White relations in North America. The maintenance of state dominance over Indigenous peoples rests on the preservation of the myth of conquest and the noble-but-doomed, defeated nation status ascribed to Indigenous peoples in the state sovereignty discourse. Framing Indigenous people in the past allows the state to maintain its own legitimacy by disallowing the fact of Indigenous peoples' nationhood to intrude upon its own mythology. It has become clear that Indigenous people imperil themselves by accepting formulations of nationhood that prevent them from transcending the past. One of the fundamental injustices of the colonial state is that it relegates Indigenous peoples' rights to the past and constrains the development of Indigenous societies by allowing only those activities that support its own necessary illusion—that Indigenous peoples do not today present a serious challenge to the legitimacy of the state.

Indigenous leaders have begun acting on their responsibility to expose the imperial pretence that supports the doctrine of state sovereignty and White society's dominion over Indigenous nations and their lands. State sovereignty can only exist in the fabrication of a truth that excludes the Indigenous voice. It is, in fact, antihistoric to claim that the state's legitimacy is based on the rule of law. From the Indigenous perspective, there was no conquest and there is no moral justification for state sovereignty—only the gradual triumph of germs and numbers. The bare truth is that Canada and the United States "conquered" only because Indigenous peoples were overwhelmed by imported European diseases and were unable to prevent the massive immigration of European, African, and Asian populations. Only recently, as Indigenous people have learned to manipulate state institutions and have gained support from others oppressed by the state, has the state been forced to incorporate any inconsistencies.

Recognizing the power of the Indigenous challenge and unable to deny it a voice, the state's response has been to attempt to draw Indigenous people closer. It has encouraged Indigenous people to reframe and moderate their nationhood demands to accept the fait accompli of colonization, to help create a marginal solution that does not challenge the fundamental imperial premise. By allowing Indigenous peoples a small measure of self-administration, and by forgoing a small portion of the moneys derived from the exploitation of Indigenous nations' lands, the state has created an incentive for integration into its own sovereignty framework. Those Indigenous communities that cooperate are

the beneficiaries of a patronizing faux altruism. They are viewed sympatheti-
cally as the anachronistic remnants of nations, the descendants of once-inde-
pendent peoples who by a combination of tenacity and luck have managed to
survive and must now be protected as minorities. By agreeing to live as artifacts, such co-opted communities guarantee themselves a mythological role and
thereby hope to secure a limited but perpetual set of rights.

An Indigenous Alternative

Is there a Native philosophical alternative? And what might one achieve by
standing against the further entrenchment of institutions modeled on the state?
Many traditionalists hope to preserve a set of values that challenge the destructive, homogenizing force of Western liberalism and materialism: They wish to
preserve a regime that honors the autonomy of individual conscience, noncoer-
cive forms of authority, and a deep respect and interconnection between human
beings and the other elements of creation. The contrast between Indigenous
conceptions and dominant Western constructions in this regard could not be
more severe. In most traditional Indigenous conceptions, nature and the natural
order are the basic referents for thinking of power, justice, and social relations.
Western conceptions, with their own particular philosophical distance from the
natural world, have more often reflected different kinds of structures of coercion
and social power.

Consider these different concepts of power as they affect one's perspective
on the relationship between the people and the land, one of the basic elements
of a political philosophy, be it Indigenous nationhood or state sovereignty.
Indigenous philosophies are premised on the belief that the human relationship
to the earth is primarily one of partnership. The land was created by a power
outside of human beings, and a just relationship to that power must respect the
fact that human beings did not have a hand in making the earth; therefore, they
have no right to dispose of it as they see fit. Land is created by another power's
order; therefore, possession by man is unnatural and unjust. The partnership
principle, reflecting a spiritual connection with the land established by the Creator, gives human beings special responsibilities within the areas they occupy,
linking them in a natural and sacred way to their territories.

The form of distributive or social justice promoted by the state through the
current notion of economic development centers on the development of industry and enterprises to provide jobs for people and revenue for government
institutions. Most often (and especially on Indigenous lands) the industry and
enterprises center on natural resource extraction. Trees, rocks, and fish become
resources and commodities with a value calculated solely in monetary terms.
Conventional economic development clearly lacks appreciation for the qualitative and spiritual connections that Indigenous peoples have to what developers
would call "resources."

Traditional frames of mind would seek a balanced perspective on using
land in ways that respect the spiritual and cultural connections that Indigenous
peoples have with their territories, combined with a commitment to managing
the process respectfully, and to ensuring a benefit for the natural and Indige-

nous occupants of the land. The primary goals of an Indigenous economy are the sustainability of the earth and ensuring the health and well-being of the people. Any deviation from that principle, whether in qualitative terms or with reference to the intensity of activity on the land, should be seen as upsetting the ideal of balance that is at the heart of so many Indigenous societies.

Unlike the earth, social and political institutions were created by men and women. In many Indigenous traditions, the fact that social and political institutions were designed and chartered by human beings means that people have the power and responsibility to change them. Where the human-earth relationship is structured by the larger forces in nature outside of human prerogative for change, the human-institution relationship entails an active responsibility for human beings to use their own powers of creation to achieve balance and harmony. Governance structures and social institutions are designed to empower individuals and reinforce tradition to maintain the balance found in nature.

Sovereignty, then, is a social creation. It is not an objective or natural phenomenon, but the result of choices made by men and women, indicative of a mindset located in, rather than a natural force creative of, a social and political order. The reification of sovereignty in politics today is the result of a triumph of a particular set of ideas over others—no more natural to the world than any other man-made object.

Indigenous perspectives offer alternatives, beginning with the restoration of a regime of respect. This ideal contrasts with the statist solution, still rooted in a classical notion of sovereignty that mandates a distributive rearrangement, but with a basic maintenance of the superior posture of the state. True Indigenous formulations are nonintrusive and build frameworks of respectful coexistence by acknowledging the integrity and autonomy of the various constituent elements of the relationship. They go far beyond even the most liberal Western conceptions of justice in promoting the achievement of peace, because they explicitly allow for difference while mandating the construction of sound relationships among autonomously powered elements.

For people committed to transcending the imperialism of state sovereignty, the challenge is to de-think the concept of sovereignty and replace it with a notion of power that has at its root a more appropriate premise. As James Tully has pointed out, the imperial demand for conformity to a single language and way of knowing has, in any case, become obsolete and unachievable in the diverse (ethnic, linguistic, racial) social and political communities characteristic of modern states. Maintaining a political community on the premise of singularity is no more than intellectual imperialism. Justice demands a recognition (intellectual, legal, political) of the diversity of languages and knowledge that exists among people—Indigenous peoples' ideas about relationships and power holding the same credence as those formerly constituting the singular reality of the state. Creating a legitimate postcolonial relationship involves abandoning notions of European cultural superiority and adopting a mutually respectful posture. It is no longer possible to maintain the legitimacy of the premise that there is only one right way to see and do things.

Indigenous voices have been consistent over centuries in demanding such recognition and respect. The speaker of the Rotinohshonni Grand Council,

Deskaheh, for example, led a movement in the 1920s to have Indigenous peoples respected by the members of the League of Nations. More recently, Indigenous leaders from around the world have had some success in undermining the intellectual supremacy of state sovereignty as the singular legitimate form of political organization. Scholars of international law are now beginning to see the vast potential for peace represented in Indigenous political philosophies. Attention focused on the principles of the Rotinohshonni *Kaienerekowa* (Great Law of Peace) in the international arena, for example, suggests the growing recognition of Indigenous thought as a postcolonial alternative to the state sovereignty model. James Anaya, author of the most comprehensive and authoritative legal text on Indigenous peoples in international law, writes:

> The Great Law of Peace promotes unity among individuals, families, clans, and nations while upholding the integrity of diverse identities and spheres of autonomy. Similar ideals have been expressed by leaders of other indigenous groups in contemporary appeals to international bodies. Such conceptions outside the mold of classical Western liberalism would appear to provide a more appropriate foundation for understanding humanity . . .[4]

The state, however, is not going to release its grip on power so easily. The traditional values of Indigenous peoples constitute knowledge that directly threatens the monopoly on power currently enjoyed by the state. Struggle lies ahead. Yet there is real hope for moving beyond the intellectual violence of the state in a concept of legal pluralism emerging out of the critiques and reflected in the limited recognition afforded Indigenous conceptions in recent legal argumentation. In a basic sense, these shifts reflect what many Indigenous people have been saying all along: Respect for others is a necessary precondition to peace and justice.

Indigenous conceptions, and the politics that flow from them, maintain in a real way the distinction between various political communities and contain an imperative of respect that precludes the need for homogenization. Most Indigenous people respect others to the degree that they demonstrate respect. There is no need, as in the Western tradition, to create a political or legal hegemony to guarantee respect. There is no imperial, totalizing, or assimilative impulse. And that is the key difference: Both philosophical systems can achieve peace, but for peace the European demands assimilation to a belief or a country, while the Indigenous demands nothing except respect.

Within a nation, one might even rethink the need for formal boundaries and precedents that protect individuals from each other and from the group. A truly Indigenous political system relies instead on the dominant intellectual motif of balance, with little or no tension in the relationship between the individual and the collective. Indigenous thought is often based on the notion that people, communities, and the other elements of creation coexist as equals—human beings as either individuals or collectives do not have a special priority in deciding the justice of a situation.

Consider the Indigenous philosophical alternative to sovereignty in light of the effect that sovereignty-based states, structures, and politics have had on

North America since the coming of the Europeans. Within a few generations, Turtle Island has become a land devastated by environmental and social degradation. The land has been shamefully exploited, Indigenous people have borne the worst of oppression in all its forms, and Indigenous ideas have been denigrated. Recently however, Indigenous peoples have come to realize that the main obstacle to recovery from this near total dispossession—the restoration of peace and harmony in their communities and the creation of just relationships between their peoples and the earth—is the dominance of European-derived ideas such as sovereignty. In the past two or three generations, there has been movement for the good in terms of rebuilding social cohesion, gaining economic self-sufficiency, and empowering structures of self-government within Indigenous communities. There has also been a return to seek guidance in traditional teachings and a revitalization of the traditions that sustained the great cultural achievement of respectful coexistence. People have begun to appreciate that wisdom and much of the discourse on what constitutes justice and proper relationship within Indigenous communities today revolves around the struggle to promote the recovery of these values. Yet there has been very little movement toward an understanding or even appreciation of the Indigenous tradition among non-Indigenous people.

It is, in fact, one of the strongest themes within Indigenous American cultures that the sickness manifest in the modern colonial state can be transformed into a framework for coexistence by understanding and respecting the traditional teachings. There is great wisdom coded in the languages and cultures of all Indigenous peoples; this is knowledge that can provide answers to compelling questions if respected and rescued from its status as a cultural artifact. There is also a great potential for resolving many of our seemingly intractable problems by bringing traditional ideas and values back to life. Before their near destruction by Europeans, many Indigenous societies achieved sovereignty-free regimes of conscience and justice that allowed for the harmonious coexistence of humans and nature for hundreds of generations. As our world emerges into a postimperial age, the philosophical and governmental alternative to sovereignty and the central values contained within their traditional cultures are the North American Indian's contribution to the reconstruction of a just and harmonious world.

NOTES

1. R. A. Williams, Jr., *The American Indian in Western Legal Thought: The Discourse of Conquest* (New York: Oxford University Press, 1990.), p. 317.

2. D. E. Wilkins, *American Indian Sovereignty and the U.S. Supreme Court: The Masking of Justice* (Austin: University of Texas Press, 1996), p. 297.

3. V. Deloria, Jr., and C. M. Lytle, *The Nations Within: The Past and Future of American Indian Sovereignty* (Austin: University of Texas Press, 1984), p. 15.

4. S. J. Anaya, *Indigenous Peoples in International Law* (New York: Oxford University Press, 1996), p. 79.

CHAPTER 8

SHE MUST BE CIVILIZED:
SHE PAINTS HER TOE NAILS

By Sharon Venne

Sharon Venne (Old Woman Bear) is a Cree from the Treaty 6 area of Great Turtle Island. She has been involved with Indigenous issues for more than 30 years, working at national and international levels. Sharon has written numerous essays and articles for publication around the world. Her Master's of Law thesis, entitled "Our Elders Understand Our Rights—Evolving International Law regarding Indigenous Peoples," was published by Theytus Press in 1998. At present, Sharon is working with the Akaitcho Dene to implement their treaty over 468,000 square kilometers in the northern part of Canada.

Introduction

Christopher Columbus' disoriented arrival on the shores of Indigenous America inaugurated a war of survival for the Indigenous peoples. Indigenous lands and resources have been and continue to be used by the colonizer states of Indigenous America. During the longest war of survival, Indigenous peoples have been subjected to genocide, slavery, diseases, population transfers, and other acts designed to depopulate their territories to make way for the colonizers. Despite all the depopulating actions by the colonizers, some Indigenous peoples have continued to survive. Why do Indigenous peoples continue to survive? Indigenous peoples were to fall before the wheels of colonization. The war against Indigenous peoples has moved from unabashed destruction to more insidious attempts to diminish the Indigenous nations into manageable units. In the United States, Indigenous peoples are to be part of the melting pot, while in Canada, part of a mosaic. Each aim effects the same end: Indigenous peoples and nations are not to exist as separate units. The colonizers want to erase the Indigenous presence on Great Turtle Island. Only when this action has been completed can the colonizers feel safe in their illegal occupation of Indigenous America.

Being "Indigenous" is a political identification and not a racial indicator. Indigenous peoples identify with their lands and territories. It is not the color of the skin or the state government's racial criteria that make an Indigenous person. Being Indigenous comes from the heart and the mind as the elders have said on so many occasions. Colonizer states, like Canada and the United States of America, have used racial criteria to decide and register Indigenous peoples. The colonizer's criteria are based on blood quantum designed to rob Indigenous peoples of their inherent right to decide their citizenship.

The domestic legislation of colonizer states has attempted to subject Indigenous nations to criteria based on race. Identification based on race has been universally rejected by the United Nations' Declaration on the Elimination of All Forms of Racial Discrimination. Why classify Indigenous peoples by racial identity? As the years move onward and intermarriage continues to occur between the nations, eventually no one group will have the necessary blood quantum to meet the colonizer's quota. Under these kinds of rules, in time Indigenous peoples will legally disappear. If there are no "legal" Indigenous peoples, then the lands become "terra nullius"—lands belonging to no one. Then the lands can be open for the colonizer to occupy and use without obstruction.

Why would the colonizers spend so much time trying to determine who is an Indigenous person? Why try to control the Indigenous nations? It gives a false sense of security for the colonizer to control their environment. If the colonizer's legal system can define who is an Indigenous person and who is not, then control of lands and territories is the next step. Those Indigenous peoples not recognized by the colonizer cease to have any legal rights to their lands and territory, leaving the lands open for use by the colonizers. The colonizers can rest easy. The collective guilt of colonization will have been dispelled. The colonizers would not have eliminated the Indigenous peoples. Natural laws of reproduction would have eliminated their presence. Underlying these programs and policies is the glaring face of racism. This essay is about the myth meeting the reality. Indigenous peoples have survived 500 years by knowing who we are and our role in relation to the Creator. It is a role as old as time and as new as tomorrow.

Colonizer's Model of Indigenous America

From the colonizer's point of view, Indigenous peoples were to disappear. Indigenous peoples would vanish before a supposedly more "superior civilization." The progress of civilization would naturally overcome the more traditional societies. As Blaut wrote: "Europeans are seen as the 'makers of history.' Europe eternally advances, progresses, modernizes. The rest of the world advances more sluggishly, or stagnates; it is 'traditional society.'"[1] Indigenous peoples were the traditional societies that would not survive European colonization. The historical record written from the colonizer's point of view must be challenged and uprooted. Indigenous peoples continue to assert their rights to their lands and territories, thus remaining a threat to the colonizers. It is not a physical threat but a mental and psychological threat.

To acknowledge that Indigenous peoples have been colonized and continue to be colonized is to call into question the whole history of Indigenous America. Since Indigenous peoples assert their land and territorial rights, the occupation of Indigenous America remains suspect. Within a colonizer's model, the only viable way for Indigenous peoples to survive is to live under the preconditions and structures established by the colonizers. In this model, only the outward manifestations of indigeneity should be seen. These should be superficial and decorative. If it happened that an Indigenous person survived, the nations could not survive. It was expected that, as individuals, Indigenous people had to be satisfied and fulfilled to dance and sing for the colonizers. Indigenous peoples, however, cannot survive as individuals outside the collective. It is from the collective that the individual is recognized and protected. The collective responsibility of the group is to the lands and territories that the colonizers want to destroy. The attempt to impose individualistic values on Indigenous peoples via educational, political, social, and cultural systems has led to alienation of Indigenous peoples from their own peoples and lands. Putting an individual ahead of the group gives a false presumption that the individual could exist without the whole. When this has occurred, Indigenous peoples have been lost to their culture, their history, and their land, which is the ultimate goal of the colonizer.

Within an Indigenous nation, if an individual did something that could harm the group, that person could be banished from the group. As an individual the person's chances of survival were greatly diminished. These days it is more difficult to banish an individual, but there is still a strong law of ignoring or shaming the person. In a community a person is shunned by the community for unacceptable behavior. While the colonizer's society prizes the right of the individual above all else, Indigenous societies know that the collective must be protected for the future generations. Often, the Elders remind the young people to think not of themselves but of the future generations. When one is commanded to think in those terms, the needs of the immediate are put into perspective. The colonizer society, however, dictates immediate satisfaction. Perhaps this is the reason that less than 10 percent of the world's population consumes more than 60 percent of the world's produced goods. A colonizer society built entirely on consumption and greed cannot understand the rights of Indigenous peoples to protect their territories and lands. The colonizer mentality, of instant pudding solutions for instant gratification, makes thinking about the consequences of an action difficult.

In order to defeat the collective rights of Indigenous peoples, Indigenous peoples must become a "minority" people within their own territories. In international law terms, minorities do not have rights to lands and territory. Minorities have a right to speak their languages, wear their traditional costumes, and practice their religion. In 1992 the General Assembly of the United Nations passed Resolution 47/135 accepting the Draft Declaration on Minorities. The declaration does not include minority political rights or their rights to lands and territories. It recognizes their ethnic, religious, and linguistic characteristics. In numerous studies leading to the drafting of the Declaration on Minorities, Special Rapporteurs of the United Nations had concluded that Indigenous peoples were not minorities.

Indigenous peoples' rights are based on principles of collective rights: the right to land, government, laws, and self-determination, which have a collective application to a people. These collective rights function contrary to the Eurocentric notion of individual rights that protect the right of the individual over those of the collective. However, this is not always the case, since there are collective rights that Nation-States have promoted to protect themselves. For instance, enacting legislation for the "public good" protects the collective right of the State. Nevertheless, it has been a consistent challenge for Indigenous peoples to promote their collective rights within the national and international community.

The aim of Indigenous peoples is not to be assimilated into the State that has colonized and dispossessed them but to persist as Indigenous peoples within their territories. It is generally held in international law that the main difference between Indigenous peoples and minorities is that the former have the right to self-determination and the latter do not. The difficulty for Indigenous peoples has been to obtain the rights that have been applied and accepted as rights of peoples: that is, to add *Indigenous* to *Peoples*. Peoples have a right to their lands, territories, laws, government, and self-determination. Colonized peoples have a right to decolonize themselves. These rights have been accepted and applied worldwide but not in Indigenous America. Why not?

Indigenous peoples, by maintaining their rights as nations, undermine the colonizers' objective: to assimilate them into the state and forget their inherent rights. Indigenous peoples are allowed to sing, to dance, and to speak their languages. Indigenous peoples are to be a caricature, wearing feathers, beads, and buckskins; it is less threatening to the colonizers. Columbus' legacy has been to dehumanize the populations as their lands and territories are used by the colonizer. Indigenous peoples who protect their lands and territories are portrayed as "radicals," "dissidents," "mad," "angry," and several other unfavorable names. It is still a war that dehumanizes and disenfranchises for the colonizer's consumption.

Indigenous peoples have to overcome the stereotypes and the negative impressions to press their case for their lands and territories. The land, which is at the center of their existence, is the primary responsibility of Indigenous peoples. This was part of the original instructions given by the Creator: The lands and territories of Indigenous America belong to the Indigenous peoples, not to the colonizers. The colonizers' political agenda dictates that Indigenous peoples can be seen at powwows wearing traditional clothes, saying opening prayers in their languages, but Indigenous peoples should not be allowed to have their traditional territories and their wealth. In the colonizer's model, it is totally unacceptable for Indigenous peoples to speak out and advocate their political and legal rights. These rights are things of the past—best forgotten. The struggle for political identity is a struggle against the prejudices of the colonizers' false history. There are many dimensions to the struggle for Indigenous peoples. A major hurdle for Indigenous peoples to overcome is the perception of being frozen in time. To freeze Indigenous peoples in time is to deny their existence. It is entirely possible to discuss the rights of Indigenous peoples without wearing buckskin, beads, and moccasins.[2] Freezing Indigenous peoples into a period, however, produces no threat to the colonizers.

Lands and Territories

Often it is written that Indigenous peoples have a spiritual relationship to their territories. This is not a myth. The myth is that Indigenous peoples can survive without their lands and territories. Once Indigenous peoples are removed from their territories, they begin to lose their identity with their territories. The Elders say that the land is our mother. From the land and territories, the knowledge of the relationship to all things is learned. From the land, children are taught their place in the creation. When an Indigenous person meets another Indigenous person, the question is asked: "Where are you from?" There is no interest in a particular city but in a land base. It is the saddest thing for an Indigenous person to give the name of a city rather than the territory. Part of the colonization process is to remove the identity with the lands, thereby destroying the link to the ancestors.

The creation story of each Indigenous nation on Great Turtle Island relates to the territory. Indigenous peoples were not created somewhere else and migrated here. Indigenous peoples are not the first settlers of Great Turtle Island; they are the original caretakers of the island with a shared responsibility to care for all creatures. It is not one individualistic goal; it is a collective consciousness to protect the lands and territories of the ancestors.

Kari-Oca

The collective obligation to care for the earth is not only a goal and aspiration of the Cree or Blood Peoples but of all Indigenous peoples as evidenced by the Kari-Oca Declaration (also known as the Indigenous Peoples' Earth Charter). The Declaration was adopted at an Indigenous peoples meeting held before the United Nations Conference on the Environment and Development (UNCED) in 1992 in Rio de Janeiro, Brazil. Indigenous peoples who were struggling to maintain their link to their lands and territories were excluded from UNCED meeting by the State governments. In response, Indigenous people organized their own conference to address issues related to the environment and, in the process, drafted their own declaration:

> We, the Indigenous Peoples, walk to the future in the footprints of our ancestors.
>
> From the smallest to the largest living being, from the four directions, from the air, the land and the mountains, the creator has placed us, the Indigenous Peoples, upon our mother the earth.
>
> The footprints of our ancestors are permanently etched upon the land of our Peoples.
>
> We, the Indigenous Peoples, maintain our inherent rights to self-determination. We have always had the right to raise and educate our children, to our own cultural identity without interference.
>
> We continue to maintain our rights as Peoples despite centuries of deprivation, assimilation and genocide.
>
> We maintain our inalienable rights to our lands and territories, to all our resources—above and below—and to our waters. We assert our ongoing responsibility to pass these on to the future generations.
>
> We cannot be removed from our lands. We, the Indigenous Peoples, are connected by the circle of life to our lands and environments.
>
> We, the Indigenous Peoples, walk to the future in the footprints of our ancestors.

When accepting the Declaration, Indigenous peoples came forward and put their hand to the paper or put a mark on the paper signifying their acceptance. While Nation-State governments were spending millions of dollars in Rio determining how to destroy the environment, Indigenous peoples were effectively putting in place a strategy to save the earth from destruction: not from greed but from the collective responsibility to the future generations—for those children yet unborn. The Kari-Oca Declaration was significant for several reasons: First, Indigenous peoples did not give up when excluded from the UN meeting. They went on to organize their own meeting to deal with the issue. Second, Indigenous peoples did not threaten disruption of the main UN forum but simply chose to hold their own forum. In addition, when the Kari-Oca meeting was proceeding without the help of the United Nations, the officials in charge of the UNCED formally requested that Indigenous peoples present their finding to the plenary. Finally, Indigenous peoples from around the world could decide their own agenda without waiting to see what State governments were doing. The Kari-Oca meeting went ahead without the need to request the colonizer States' permission. It was a significant step because Indigenous delegates have been oppressed and assimilated by colonizer State governments. The meeting was a time to liberate their minds to make decisions for future generations as directed by the Creator. Each delegate has witnessed the colonization process that has led to the destruction of the lands and territories of his or her ancestors. It was time to stand up to take care of the lands and territories for the future generation. This action is unacceptable to the colonizers. The Kari-Oca Declaration reminds them of their own failure to care for the earth. In an attempt to reduce the impact, the declaration was called "radical." In trying to degrade the Declaration, non-Indigenous peoples pointed out their own shortcomings.

Recently, the Canadian Federal Environmental Department, in a study covering 16 chapters, reported that two earths are required to meet the needs if every person on earth were to live like the typical Canadian. The report says that the average Canadian uses the equivalent of nearly 25 liters of gasoline per day, which is the highest per capita consumption of any country. The average Canadian uses 360 liters of fresh water for household use. In addition, the average Canadian produces 1.8 kilograms of garbage a day, one of the highest per capita levels in the world. The report made no clear recommendations for the governments. It did urge consumers to consider the environmental consequences of their daily actions but recognized the limitations of such a request. Consumers want the products and their two baths a day. Instant pudding solutions lead to environmental destruction.

In a separate study, the Canadian Wildlife Service and Parks Canada reported that the clear-cut logging in the parkland regions occurred at a rate five times higher than the global average. The rapid deforestation of the parkland, the wildlife-rich transition zone between prairie and boreal forest, will lead to a loss of habitat for animals and birds. Also, the deforestation will lead to more soil flowing into lakes and streams, causing problems for fish. The land is being killed for greed. On the eastern slopes of the Rocky Mountains, Cheviot Mines, a U.S. company, has proposed the development of an open-pit coal mine 23 kilometers long and 3.5 kilometers wide. The coal will be used in the Asia markets. On the other hand, the mine will destroy wildlife habitats and damage populations of grizzly bears, elk, moose, and various types of fish when their habitat is filled with the debris from the mine. Finally, the mine is within 1.8 kilometers east of the Jasper National Park. Any opposition to the mine by the environmentalists is unfortunately not realistic. Tourism is not an option when mining pays up to $22 an hour as opposed to wages of $6 to $8 an hour. When the mine is finished and the environment is destroyed in 20 years, what will happen? The miners will leave the town and move to another mining spot. The land will be destroyed. The grizzly bears, elk, moose, and fish will be gone. This is not the future that Indigenous peoples want to leave for the future generations. The Kari-Oca Declaration points out that all the environment must be protected for the future, not just for 20 years. Indigenous peoples do not view the earth as a short-term goal. It seems that the evidence supports the view of Indigenous peoples that the Earth as our mother is being destroyed by greed.

One non-Indigenous writer wrote that the Kari-Oca Declaration was radical and should be ignored. What is radical? That Indigenous people determine their own future? What is radical? That Indigenous peoples drafted a document without the help and participation of multinational corporations or non-Indigenous people? What is radical? That after 500 years Indigenous peoples still possessed the ability to decide their own future? What is radical? That Indigenous peoples can think? That Indigenous peoples were still alive? That is radical! As one of the drafters of the Kari-Oca Declaration, let me set the record straight—the Declaration is a prayer, an Indigenous prayer for all creation. Is it radical to speak to the Creator about your responsibility? Is it radical to point out that acts of genocide have been committed against our peoples? More than 1,200 Indigenous nations from Great Turtle Island have disappeared since the arrival of Columbus. Is it radical to point out such facts? Is it radical to want to survive on our homelands? Apparently, our survival is contrary to the goals and objectives of the colonizers. Indigenous peoples were to disappear and/or be good little nonpolitical Indigenous peoples who had been tamed by the forces of the colonization.

For example, the Human Genome Diversity Project has estimated that another 700 Indigenous nations will disappear in the next 75 to 125 years. What is radical? The project was developed by the scientific colonizers. The stated goal is to link Indigenous America to Asia. Science with its political agenda tries to deny that our existence began and ends on Great Turtle Island. In the last 160 years, they have been unable to prove their theories about the Bering Strait. It is entirely possible that the people of Asia once lived on Great Turtle Island and migrated to Asia. Why does it have to be the other way around? The colonizers want to believe that Indigenous peoples were the first settlers of North America and that they themselves were the second settlers. In this way they can deny our rights to land and territory. When Indigenous peoples claim that the Creator placed us on Great Turtle Island, the first-settler theory lacks credibility. At every turn, the colonizers continue to find evidence showing them the folly of the argument. Indigenous peoples have been occupying Indigenous America longer than their theories.

If the stated purpose of the Human Genome Diversity Project is to link Indigenous peoples to Asia, why is the project planning to patent the genes of Indigenous peoples? Is it radical to point out the facts to the colonizers who continue to use our territories and resources without our consent and have now moved to harvest our body parts, including the genes? What is the purpose of patenting our genes? Recently, the media have reported that Crees and Cherokees possess a genetic predisposition against Alzheimer's disease. Will the scientists want to patent Cree genes to make money on the cure for Alzheimer's disease? Genetic codes are given by the Creator, not to be discerned by the science world. There is an overriding preponderance of the scientific world to explore and harvest our genes, just as our lands and territories have been explored and destroyed. The same reasons that were used to justify the exploitation and use of our lands and territories are being used by the proponents of the Human Genome Diversity Project. Scientists believe Indigenous peoples

should be interested in promoting new discoveries for diseases and genetic mal-
functions. Indigenous peoples who protest against the project are painted as
being against development as if harvesting the body is development!

It is radical for Indigenous peoples to point out the historical relationship of
the colonizer and the colonized. Any Indigenous person who attempts to put
the record straight must be a fanatic. If not, then a person has a serious mental
problem in need of correction. The following is one example to illustrate the difficulty facing Indigenous peoples correcting 500 years of colonial history and
myths.

Teaching Human Rights

In 1992 the Institute of Human Rights in Strasbourg, France, invited me to
present five lectures on the history of Indigenous peoples' struggle to have their
rights recognized by the international community. It was the first attempt by the
Institute to present such material in its annual human rights course.[3] The Institute acknowledged that after 500 years of colonization some human rights
material related to Indigenous peoples should be presented. Indigenous issues
were becoming a major issue at the United Nations, the European parliament,
and many other public forums. The Institute requested an outline of the lectures
and a reading list for the students. Following the submission of the materials, an
hour-and-a-half conversation took place on the methodology of the lectures.
The general practice was for the lectures to be read to the students. However,
Indigenous peoples have an oral tradition that makes speaking rather than
reading more culturally appropriate. Finally, it was determined that an oral presentation based on the written material would be acceptable to the Institute. The
written lecture notes were published by the Institute for the students to read
before the lectures. The Institute published the material to promote discussion
in the lectures on the material. In theory, if students read the material before the
class, they have more opportunity to consider and ask questions. It is only a theory since subsequent events showed that the Institute did not want to have such
discussions.

To teach the reasons for the present situation of Indigenous peoples and
their struggle for international recognition, there is a need to begin with the colonization of Indigenous America and the continued colonization of their lands
and territories. Along with the colonization and the development of the doctrine of discovery, there needs to be a history of the effects of the colonization,
including the acts of genocide, murder, slavery, and other gross human rights
violations. If this history is unknown, how can students understand the reasons
for Indigenous peoples' needing to seek redress outside the State? At the first
lecture several human rights students from Canada and the United States
protested to the Institute about the content of the course material. They did not
want to be reminded that they lived in colonizer States that oppress Indigenous
peoples. Students of human rights wanted to hear about other situations but not
about their own backyards. They signed a letter requesting that the Institute terminate the lectures. During the second lecture, the director of the program

stopped the lecture when many students tried to disrupt the class. Some students were requesting that the other side of the story be told (one assumes the colonizer's history). One African student wanted to know the other side of genocide or slavery. It was an interesting discussion on rights and the perception of rights. The class was suspended, and a meeting was held between the Director of the program and the President of the Institute.

At the meeting there was a general request to stop the lectures and change the lectures to a discussion of education, health, and social issues. These are rights that flow to minorities and not to peoples. It is not possible to discuss minority rights when the rights of peoples are at stake. It would not have been possible in the five days given to get into an adequate discussion of social rights without some context. The Director wanted me to leave. I wanted them to ask me to leave. Out of respect to my ancestors, I could not deny their existence and acquiesced to the Director's request. At one point the President of the Institute, a former European Human Rights Judge, informed me that I was "civilized" and did not need to raise these issues. I was shocked! On further inquiry, I learned that I was viewed as "civilized" because I did not wear my traditional dress and had painted toenails. In an attempt to point out the blatantly racist statements by the President of a human rights institute, it was suggested that clothes and painted toenails do not bar an Indigenous person from advocating his or her rights. It was firmly suggested that since I rode on airplanes, used the telephone, and wore their clothes, I had lost any rights to claim my indigeneity.

It was lost on the human rights Director and President that their assumptions about Indigenous peoples were a good reason for such a course at their institute. After an hour-and-a-half discussion, it was decided that the lectures would be read in class. These same notes that had been previously submitted to the Institute and published would be edited and approved by the Director before the class. In addition, I was to discourage the students from engaging in any discussions on the issues. I was to give a simple, straightforward lecture without pauses, dry but sufficient for human rights students. No need to bog them down with the details. In order keep the peace, I agreed to their terms. When I left the meeting, many students from other parts of the world were waiting outside the door. They demanded to know what was happening. Why was the lecture stopped? It had been the most interesting lecture of the four weeks.

It was explained to the students that the lectures would be read to them and no questions were allowed during the class. The format was used on the following day. At the end of the lecture, many students protested that the Institute was violating their human rights. Further, the students requested that the lecture continue in an oral manner with students asking questions. If not, then the students were going to the media to inform them about the Institute's denying them their fundamental human right of free speech. The 100 American and Canadian students were overruled by the 300 remaining students who saw that the colonization of Indigenous peoples was a serious issue in need of discussion. Because of the intervention by the students, the last two lectures were in the oral tradition. At the end of the week, the students in the class purchased a glass vase made "illegally" by the Palestinian peoples in occupied Israel. The vase is a constant reminder of the students who were prepared to stand in solidarity with Indigenous peoples against the colonizers. As a final note, no other Indigenous person, to my knowledge, has been asked to give lectures at the Institute. One person in 500 years is a sufficient contribution to the understanding of violations of Indigenous peoples' rights.

During the confrontation with the Institute, the Elders who had passed away were always on my mind. What would they have done? Would they have denied their indigeneity to survive? If you have to deny your identity to survive, what future is left? This was not a confrontation about one person with painted toenails, but of Indigenous peoples fighting against racism.

Many lessons were learned in Strasbourg that summer. Racism against Indigenous peoples is pervasive. At a human rights institute dedicated to the elimination of racism and the promotion of human rights, there was a general failure to recognize that Indigenous peoples suffer the most basic racism and denial of their rights. The denial of rights can be directly linked to ignorance. The colonizers' history has been very effective. Historical records need to be corrected. However, how can the record be corrected if Indigenous peoples are not allowed to speak out and change the record? It is not possible for the colonizers to recognize the wrongs of their ancestors unless such wrongs are pointed out. It must be Indigenous peoples, who are the objects of the racism, who point it out. The President of the Institute did not see anything wrong in pointing out the kind of dress as a symbol of civilization. My style of dress was a bar to any discussing of political rights. Since I was benefiting from Western clothes, there was a general assumption that Indigenous rights could not and should not be discussed. One was to be a good Indigenous person to accept the ultimate fate. Putting on a dress or painting toenails was an automatic symbol of giving up an identity as an Indigenous person. Another myth. If you must look, dress, and sound like their image of an Indigenous person to be accepted, then the battle has been lost.

Recently during a lecture tour in Italy, one of the students asked about my costume: Why was I not wearing a full traditional dress to give the lecture? She was disappointed to meet me wearing dress pants and a suit jacket. She was concerned that I could not speak authentically about clear-cut logging, pollution, diamond mines, land struggles, and death of the Indigenous peoples. Personally, I am not prepared to put on a buckskin dress and feathers to appease an audience. If only the surface is important, then trying to discuss our rights on a more fundamental level is never going to take place. Wearing the beads, feathers, and buckskin gives in to the stereotype, allowing the audience to think that things are not that bad because Indigenous peoples can still dance, sing, and wear buckskin.

Laws of the Creator

In order to make a buckskin dress, you need the hides of the animals. Before colonization, animals were plentiful and available for clothing. Now, having a dress made of hides is a luxury item. Since the number of animals has been greatly diminished by the loss of habitat, overhunting by non-Indigenous hunters, and disease, hides for clothes are not a priority. Trying to keep the animals alive is a priority. When the Creator placed Indigenous peoples on Great Turtle Island, the food that was provided was to be taken in a certain way. When an animal is taken for food, an offering must be left for the Creator and the spirit of the animal whose life has been given to help humans survive. An animal can only be killed for food. It is against the laws of the Creator to kill an animal for any other reason. When we were young children, the Elders told us that to kill for no reason is a crime against the Creator; anything that is killed must be used. There should be no waste, so children are taught not to kill even a small bird for any reason. Children are to respect the Creation. When we see non-Indigenous hunters kill for the horns or a part of the animal, we see the destruction and the waste. The Creator entrusted these animals to our care. Now it is a multimillion-dollar business for hunters and fishermen to use our relatives for their own sport. In many cases, our own peoples cannot hunt, trap, fish, and gather because the lands and territories are controlled by the colonizers.

The Elders tell us that if we do not leave an offering for the spirit of the dead animal, that spirit returns to the Creator and never returns again. This is how the Elders explain the disappearance of the animals, fish, and other relatives. The laws are taught to the young people. The relatives must be respected. Everything is part of the circle. Since man is the last of creation, all of creation is the older and wiser. Humans must respect their Elders. It is part of the laws.

Children Learning the Laws

An Indigenous child is a gift from the Creator. Children do not belong to their parents. Children are lent to parents, who are given a responsibility to raise them to be healthy and productive adults. Indigenous children belong to a nation. There is a collective responsibility to educate that child within the large extended family of aunts, uncles, and grandparents. It is usually a close relative who takes the child under his or her wing to teach the child the essential elements of the society. All persons within the community are responsible for teaching and educating the child through example, experience, ceremonies, storytelling, praise, rewards, and recognition of the norms of the community. It is through these methods that children grow up to know their responsibility to themselves and their community. Often a child is told to think about wanting something. Where does the item come from? What has gone into making that item? Does the child really need that particular item? From an early age, a child knows that the future must be considered.

It is in this setting that children are raised to become adults and learn the essential elements of their identity. In the naming ceremonies and other ceremonies, children learn their place in the circle of life and their responsibility to the circle. As children grow, they are exposed to different people. Some children meet spiritual Elders who know about the spiritual aspects of Indigenous life; other Elders know about the history of the community; and still other Elders know the history of the nation vis-à-vis other Indigenous nations; finally, some Elders know the relationship between the colonized and the colonizer. No one Elder knows everything. There is only one being who knows everything: the Creator. No human being would claim to know everything. Often we have witnessed experts coming into our communities and meeting with people. Later we read their material and had a good laugh. Many times they have interviewed the tricksters—individuals who have been put on the earth to create mischief. Once, an uncle was approached by a man who wanted to fish in a lake near the community. This man had seen an Indigenous person walking down the road and asked for permission to fish. My uncle told him that the lake was not good for fishing. The man just wanted to know if he could put his boat in the water and try to catch a fish. My uncle told him that he would not catch a fish. The man took that as a challenge and wanted to fish. Well, my uncle told him that if he wanted to try, he could. The man put his expensive motor boat in the water and cruised around all day. At the end of the day uncle was standing at the shore. The man informed him that he did not catch any fish. My uncle acknowledged that he would not have caught any fish in that lake. The man was undeterred. He wanted to come back another day. My uncle did not stop him. Since the man did not ask why he would not catch any fish, my uncle did not tell him that the lake was an alkali lake with no fish. Often, people come to the communities with a preset idea and do not know what questions to ask. In addition, our people are reluctant to tell any outsider about the internal workings of the communities. Knowledge is power, and there is a preference to keep that knowledge to ourselves. After all, the Creator gave us that knowledge to survive for the future generations.

Telling stories is an important aspect of the educational process. It is through stories that the history, culture, traditions, laws, and values are taught. In this essay, several stories have been related to the reader. Within the oral tradition, storytelling is an important skill, while in the written world the story loses some of its texture and style, especially in the English format. But the essential elements are transmitted to the reader. Indigenous peoples from Indigenous America have been colonized and continue to be colonized. The history of colonization is a painful history for both sides. On one side is the reality of the colonization process, and on the other side is the whitewashed version of superiority and imposed values. To correct the record, the colonized must tell their history and its effects on their peoples. It is an obligation to the hundreds of nations that have disappeared since the arrival of the colonizer. It is a responsibility to the future generations as they carry the traditions left by the ancestors into the future.

Conclusion

Now, State governments, through UN officials, have been saying that Indigenous peoples should move away from dealing with legal instruments and lawyers and move toward social scientists with anthropology backgrounds. They think the rights struggle relates not to legal issues but to the social, cultural, and linguistic characteristics—rights that have traditionally flowed to minorities. Another myth of the colonizer is to decimate the Indigenous population, making them a numerical minority in their own territory. Diminishing the population does not take away Indigenous peoples' rights as nations. The Elders have told us that even if only one Indigenous person remains on the land, protecting the land, then that person is part of a nation with a right of self-determination and inherent rights to the lands and territories.

Since Indigenous peoples are still doing ceremonies on the land for the future generations, there are still Indigenous peoples. Indigenous peoples have struck too close to the core of the colonizer by calling into the question the very legal system that oppresses them. Indigenous peoples are not supposed to have the intellectual capability to question their oppressor; we are supposed to just accept. In 500 years, we have never accepted the idea that Columbus discovered Indigenous America. Why should we accept anything else? Painted toenails do not diminish the questions that need to be asked. Painted toenails give an excuse to the colonizer not to answer the questions. It is an old tactic. When you do not want to answer, attack the person asking the questions. Rarely do these attacks have any effect other than to expose the extreme racism of the colonizers.

In the mindset of the colonizer, in order for Indigenous peoples to claim rights to their lands and resources, they would have had to remain in the same condition as when colonization began. If any technological changes have occurred, then Indigenous peoples have no right to press their claims for their lands and territories. Indigenous peoples dancing in the powwow give a false sense of security to the colonizers. As we watch Indigenous peoples dance their dances and sing their songs to the Creator, we are watching the survival of the peoples. This is a political act—an act of identity that cannot be diminished by the colonizers.

NOTES

1. James M. Blaut, *The Colonizer's Model of the World: Geographical Diffusionism and Eurocentric History* (New York: Guilford Press, 1993), p. 1.
2. In 1994 at the University of Alberta, a program director hired to work with Indigenous law students asked whether I wore my beads and feathers when speaking on the rights of Indigenous peoples. When I asked why, I was told that by my wearing them the audience would know that I was Indigenous. There is no need to wear beads and feathers to know that one is Indigenous.
3. Each year the institute puts on a four-week course on human rights. Different people are requested to make presentations in their areas of expertise for approximately 400 international students.

PART IV

Culture-Ways of Being

CHAPTER 9

THE LESSONS OF COYOTE AND THE MEDICINE TREE

By Arleen Adams

Arleen Adams is Salish and Kootenai of the Confederated Salish and Kootenai Tribes of Montana. She holds a bachelor's degree in Native American Studies from the University of Montana with a minor in Anthropology. Arleen is currently in pursuit of her Master's in Public Administration, Collaborative Administration, and Tribal Governance via Evergreen State College, Washington. She has served in various capacities as a teacher, board member, and administrative assistant for Salish Kootenai College, Two Eagle River Tribal School, and the Confederated Salish Kootenai Tribes (CS&KT). She is certified Class Seven Native Bilingual Instructor. Arleen has an extensive history of working for the preservation of Salish and Kootenai languages and culture.

Introduction

As a child I grew up with the name Weenie. I had a good childhood and have many good memories. With the name Weenie, there were many teasers and my dad called me Ween-dog. My Ya-Ya, which means "great grandmother," left me with most of the memorable good memories. Hollering "Weenie" from the huckleberry patches at Bellmore Sloughs, she would call me to help with emptying her full bucket. Being stooped over, sitting uncomfortably and not able to move well, she would always give this faraway holler. The name Weenie slowly faded out and now only a few people still call me this, and it really makes me feel good when they do, in that good ol' days sort of way.

The many huckleberry patches, the many dry meat racks, the many tanned hides, the many fishing holes, the many pall mall cigarettes, the many pow-wows, the many campsites—so many things to think about, so many things to remember. To write about cultural resilience, I think of what it means in the context of a ceremony of life. As I now walk in this ceremony of life, I have been given the name Indian Paint Brush (Thunder Sparks) and reflect upon the many lessons of Coyote.

I am of the Salish and Kootenai nations, with traces of Cree, Shawnee, Cheyenne, and Nez Perce ancestry. My name Indian Paint Brush, when said in Salish, means Thunder Sparks. As a child I was raised hearing Coyote stories or Creation stories that taught me the value of life. I find it very entertaining to read and listen to Coyote stories, not only from my own Salish/Kootenai cultures but from other surrounding tribal cultures as well. There are an incredible number of similarities that many nations have on how life and the earth were created. The focus of this paper will be to explain what Coyote stories mean to me, to discuss who Coyote is and the values generated and passed down by his teachings, and, most importantly, to weave together a Creation story and speak to the importance of protecting the sacred Medicine Tree site near present day Darby, Montana.

It is very important that cultures prompt the interest in gathering legends of their people for the transmitting of important aspects of tribal and cultural heritage. Creation stories were told to me by Elders during the early years of my life. The Elders gave me the assurance of continued identity as a tribe by keeping alive the history and traditions of my culture. Through storytelling by the Elders, which is highly respected, generation upon generation learned lifelong values, concepts, religion, beliefs, songs, dances, ceremonies, and legends. At the same time, Elders have their special role in the family structure; everyone has a vital role in maintaining the well-being of families. Elders are our very own way of life, our most precious natural resource, which we need to love and respect for our very existence. They are our historians, teachers, and guardians of all tribal and cultural knowledge. Our science and society are greatly appreciative for their existence and special role in our lives.

Creation stories, in which Coyote is the main character, teach us right from wrong. A time before mankind, all animal people had human-like personalities.

Coyote, known to the Salish/Kootenai people as Sncle and Skinkuc, appears in various forms in order to teach the ideals of good and evil, as ordered by He-Who-Sits-On-The-Top to prepare the nations for the coming of mankind. He-Who-Sits-On-The-Top is seen as the superior being, Creator of the universe. Coyote's adventures were given to Indian people to explain how things came to be the way they are. These stories provide knowledge and experience to guide our existence and welfare as human beings, and all the initial values of humans that came into being, respecting all stages in life, all walks of life, and all behaviors of life. Coyote stories teach the best means of survival such as what foods to eat; where to find them; how to cook, prepare, and store such foods. Most importantly, the stories also teach the care of wild game, how to prepare and store for seasons, and how to make and use weapons for hunting and warfare.

In addition to lifelong learning of survival, Coyote stories are entertaining and fun to listen to; and one never grows tired of learning about Coyote. Coyote's bad deeds are very valuable, but, much more importantly, he protected all animal life and mankind by combating the existence of powerful monsters and serpents that threatened the lives and well-being of Coyote's relatives and nations. Coyote uniquely possesses a multiple nature—that of man, animal, and creator—and is prone to make misjudgments. He has all physical capabilities, needs, strengths, and weaknesses of man. As animal he is a natural hero who existed in a magical time before the coming of man—when animal people possessed the earth. Then all animals could speak and had great powers that they could freely use in protection of their existence. Coyote, as Creator, was granted superior and divine powers, from He-Who-Sits-On-The-Top, in order to carry out his missions, but he was not given clear-cut guidelines. Because of this his human-like passions and curiosity sometimes got in the way of his mission, thus creating a human value that is passed on. In some cases, Coyote appears in animal form as a Hare, Raven, and Spider in some stories and is more commonly known as the Old Man Coyote and Trickster.

The Salish Indians believe wholeheartedly in the land and all that it provides. They give thanks for all of creation and respect the ways of the forefathers. There were many instances in time when the Salish were faced with obstacles beyond their control. They adhered to their ancestors and gave thanks and dedication to the old ways, as passed down through the generations. With the religion as given by the Creator and the stories of history, song, and dance, the Salish are able to sustain a traditional way of life. One of the most important of the oral traditions is storytelling and the preservation of the origin histories. In these histories the people are told where we came from, how the stars were created, where we discovered fire, how light became divided from darkness, and how death originated. "It is through these stories we obtain the basic tools and ways of knowledge with which to survive in the world: healing ceremonies, prayers, dances, games, herbs, and models of behavior."[1] Through creation stories, as with the Salish Coyote stories, I am able to hold on to the valuable lessons of creation and what it means.

A Coyote Tale

Long ago before there were humans on this earth, there were animal people. The Creator sent Coyote to this land to prepare the vast territories for the coming of man. Coyote was to protect all life and destroy monsters and evils that threatened life. One day Coyote was walking along looking for something to do when he stepped on a meadowlark. "I had some important and good news for you, but since you broke my legs, I cannot tell you this important news." Coyote knew she was the carrier of great news, so he mended her legs with sinew, leaving markings on her legs to this day, and in no time meadowlark was walking again. Coyote picked her up to see if she could walk, and she could. Then she told Coyote there was a monstrous bighorn sheep over the ridge killing all the animals who passed this way. Coyote knew that this was the only crossing for many people, through the Bitterroot Mountains, and if he didn't destroy this monster, everyone was in danger. Coyote approached the mountain and could see the big horn sheep in a great rage. He challenged Coyote and the fight was on. Coyote challenged him to ram a big pine tree, and in the process the Big Horn Sheep got his head stuck in the tree. Coyote worked as fast as he could with his powerful flint knife to cut the body of Big Horn Sheep down, leaving the rammed head stuck into the tree. Coyote said from that day forward, for generations to come, when there are humans on this land, this will be their Medicine Tree. They will come here in prayer and goodness, and all their wishes will be granted.

Winter is the time for teaching through Coyote stories. It is also the time to prepare items for spring- and summertime lodges, ceremonies, celebrations, and the basics for survival. This is the time for women to teach sewing, mending, beading, and how to make clothing and dolls, and for men to teach how to make tools, crafts, toys, and basic protections of the family structure. Coyote stories are told orally and often along with sign language. Stories are only told in the wintertime because it is said, "If they are told after the snow melts, the monster or serpent will get you." Stories adhere to a protocol of how they are to be told and of visiting sacred sites where they should be told. These protocols are essential in teaching basic fundamentals of life as well as essential to the survival of Coyote and his stories.

Protecting Sacred Sites and Sacred Knowledge

In preserving cultural ways of knowing, Indigenous peoples need to work together to protect our sacred sites for generations to come. The sacred Medicine Tree site of the Bitterroot Valley, sometimes referred to as the Ram's Horn Tree, stands near Darby, Montana, on the east bank of the Bitterroot River. This site has been threatened by the U.S. highway department because it stands in the way of development and progress. No matter what one defines as development or progress, there is no need for definition when it comes to a sacred site. Because Western culture misconceives that all we need to do is cut the tree down and plant another one someplace else, they ask, "What is the problem?"

It's the equivalent of saying, "Let's bulldoze the Vatican; it's preventing the development of a major highway."

In the early 1900s, it was questioned whether the actual tree was indeed the sacred Medicine Tree. Many people witnessed several rams' horns in trees and landowners cut some of them down, thinking they would sell the embedded horns to museums because of the "medicine." There are stories of other trees that were sacred and cut down; in fact, there was once a Medicine Tree on the edge of Mount Jumbo, in Missoula, Montana, that old Indians talked about. The tree was cut down because the Indians used to come from miles to gamble and make trade with the Suyapi (whites). Some Indians, on occasion, after making a wish to the tree, went back to gambling and then took all the money home. Nonetheless, the question of whether the Medicine Tree in the Bitterroot Valley near the Bitterroot River is actually the true one has never been in doubt for the Salish people. There have been others, but from far back in time the Salish people have traveled to the Bitterroot River to make their offerings. It is said that even other tribes never doubted the power of the Medicine Tree:

> It seems that a Nez Perce, on his way to hunt buffalo with a party of Flatheads (a Suyapi name for the Salish), boastingly demonstrated his scorn of the tree by firing a rifle ball into its trunk. Directly afterwards, while running some buffalo on the plains east of the mountains, his horse fell and he was killed. The Flatheads said it was because the Nez Perce had spoiled his luck by mistreating the Ram's Horn Tree.[2]

The Medicine Tree, near present-day Darby, Montana, for the Salish is one of many sites in the United States impeding the progress of transportational development. Several years ago there was a threat that the tree would be cut down because it sat right next to the highway and the highway department wanted to widen the road. At the very mention of threatening the life of the Medicine Tree, the Salish people made a stand. Even the farmers in the area surrounding the tree came to the Salish defense. The highway department said that they had tried every means of rerouting the existing road, but there were no alternatives. As it turned out, the highway department was unable to purchase the land the tree sits on; in fact, negotiations are still being held for the highway department to purchase the land from the landowner and give it to the tribes. It didn't matter what anyone had to say about the origin of the tree and what it stands for; the highway department needed a bigger and better highway. There was even a threat made that maybe someone or something would lurk in the night and the tree could be cut down. These things never bothered the Salish; this kind of treatment has been going on for years. After all, has there ever been any indication that it would end? As long as we continue to stand our ground in honor of our Creator and all He provides, and in the strength of our ancestors, we will continue to endure.

Ever since I can remember, my Ya-Ya (great-grandmother), now deceased, told us the story of the Medicine Tree, and every year (sometimes twice a year) we would travel to make our offerings and wishes for the coming new year. Then after she passed on, her son took us and now my father carries the tradition, along with myself. It is very important to me that my children know and carry the oral traditions of the Salish people. My role for the future is carrying on the best way I know how, to ensure that oral traditions are passed on. Coyote is very important for the survival of our culture, and the lessons go far beyond any teachings of the Western culture.

> . . . [T]hey are laughing at the way Coyote does things, and at the way the story is told. Many things about the stories are funny, but the story is not funny. If my children hear the stories, they will grow up to be good people; if they don't hear them, they will turn out to be bad . . . If Coyote did not do all those things, then those things would not be possible in the world.[3]

Coyote and the Medicine Tree will always live on. In terms of development and progress, the Medicine Tree has been given an age of 340 to 400 years old, which has been determined by the ages of trees in the area surrounding the Medicine Tree. Development and progress continue to mull over the fact that it could be older, but to the Suyapi, "What's the problem?" The problem is development and progress. Yet why should it be said we are not making progress and that development is the answer or key to making things faster and better? There is now renewed hope, and it's high time that through the Native American Graves and Repatriation Act, the Indigenous peoples of this continent be protected from the exploitation that comes with development and progress. It is time to stand our ground and protect what little we have left that hasn't already been stripped from us, dug up, dumped on, contaminated, polluted, wasted, corrupted, or destroyed; and still the list goes on. Western culture continues to talk about preserving the land and getting in tune with the native worldview, yet our lands continue to be mistreated. Indigenous peoples believe that "as long as the grasses grow, the rivers flow and the mountains endure," we shall continue to take care of our land, and in turn the land will take care of us. As Ada Deer, Assistant Secretary of Indian Affairs has stated, "I am an extension of this land; it is fundamental to being Indian."[4] It is through the hope of the peoples of today that our extension to the land will be protected and guarded as sacred for generations to come in the preservation and passing of our sacred creation stories.

The experience of Coyote (creation) stories has not changed my concept of life. Every time I am told a story or read one, I reflect heavily on what it means to me to have been given such a great part of Salish/Kootenai culture as Coyote stories, and to be given the opportunity of passing them on for generations to come. My concept of life has not changed as a result of learning about Coyote; my concept of life remains a constant through the world of knowledge and experience as passed down by my ancestors. Life will always be sacred, shared, and given to be cherished by means that are to be at one with mother nature. As a child I was raised with Coyote stories that taught me the value of life and all that life holds. Those values generated and passed down through Coyote teachings weave together a creation story to protect the importance of sacred sites and all life from one generation to the next.

Coyote Tales of the Montana Salish, published in 1974, was the only book closest to the stories I was raised with as a child.[5] The Elder of this book, and a translator of Coyote stories, was Pierre Pichette. He was a blind Salish Indian who lived in the Arlee, Montana, area until sometime before the 1970s. At the time of this work, when Mr. Pichette was interviewed in the early 1950s, Pierre told the stories to Harriett Miller and Elizabeth Harrison, authors who later transcribed and adapted them for publication. I asked my father, Louis Wilbur Adams, about the book and about this man, Pierre Pichette. My father told me this was a remarkable man who taught my father many Coyote stories. My father said that after reading the book, and after being raised with Pierre Pichette (they called him Pete), it seemed the book left out much of the story as my father had remembered it. My father said he never liked the idea of publishers' changing the story once it was told: "They always leave out much of the most important parts of a story."[6]

Pierre Pichette, reluctant at first, believed in prompting the interest in gathering legends of his people for the transmitting of important aspects of tribal and cultural heritage. My father remembers his stories took all night. He said that, when he was a little boy, his parents would take him to Pete's house to listen to the whole Creation story. How the connection of the creation stories took place, from ocean to ocean, and the stories would last all night long. My father said that, when he was a little boy, he would try his best to stay awake. The next day his father would tell him, "Pete finished around five this morning."

The connection I made with the stories in relation to the location of the Medicine Tree today did not always seem to fit the stories written in the book. My father clarified much of this for me. He told me about the stories Pete used to talk about that the book left out. He said Pete used to say that the Ram's Horn Tree story was a recent story, full of power. The tree was given to the Indian people because so many other things were being destroyed. It provides a belief beyond the Suyapi control. When Coyote left the Medicine Tree for the people, it was never questioned by the people; it always held power. My father said he remembered Pete and the rest of the families making the trek to Darby and Pete told the story of the legendary Chief Joseph of the Nez Perce, when he ran from the government. He said Pete used to laugh when he told how Chief Charlo sent three men, John Delaware and two of his brothers (Moses, Narsiss, or Louie), to help Chief Joseph from Fort Fissle to the Bitterroot Valley. The government never knew that Joseph and his people snuck past them and made it to the Medicine Tree in the Bitterroot Valley. When Chief Joseph arrived, he sent his bands' medicine man to the Medicine Tree to see what they had to do. Upon his return he told Joseph that they had to leave them to make it to the Canada border. Joseph reluctantly agreed and said they needed to rest for a few days first, for everyone was too tired and needed rest. It has been said that that was why he never made it to Canada; he never left when he was told. Now there has never been a doubt for me about the power of the Almighty. No matter how recent the Medicine Tree story may be or what the age of the tree is, the belief in what it stands for will always remain. The story of Chief Joseph, it is said, is how the Salish and Nez Perce intermarried and became relatives. Chief Charlo said, "We will help you and your people, but we will not fight." When Chief Joseph left for Canada, many of his band stayed with the Salish.

I will always be grateful for the value and knowledge of Coyote stories, as well as all stories, told by my father, my Elders, and all the ancestors who so graciously passed them on. The values of respecting self, life, land, sky, water, animals, family, and cultural tradition are greatly instilled in all stories. The values of disciplines in nature, plants, animals, and human behavior are greatly impressed upon us as well. Great human, physical, emotional, and moral values as a tribe are given to us through the legendary histories of Sncle, or Skinkuc.

I am sharing a way of life I could have lost if it weren't for my YaYa. My parents raised a family of 10 in an era of transition when the Indian people were at the very edge of making a major breakthrough in history (to be accepted as being Indian). My parents were raised in a time when Indian people were being assimilated to very modern times and forced to attend Catholic or government boarding schools. My father has an eighth-grade education, from the Old Valley Creek School, north of Arlee, Montana, and some education from the Arlee public school system. He was hit, spanked, and humiliated for speaking his native tongue—the only language he knew at the time, although he did know some English. In the first grade at the Arlee school system, a second-grade teacher, Miss Hartman, caught my father and Peter Pierre speaking their native language in the hall. She got a yardstick and broke it over Peter's head and took the other half and hit my dad; she said, "Now you boys know the rules." She took them both to the principal's office, and he said, "The next time you boys don't follow the rules, you'll get this" (showing them a big leather belt). When my father went home, he told his parents what happened, and they said, "You do their rules and do what they say; when you're playing with other kids away from where you can be heard, you speak your language."

My mother was sent to boarding schools where she received a high school education and was not taught her native language. According to stories told by my parents, when they were being raised, language and culture were secretly done, or families (such as my father's) took their children and kept them from the agencies (the government body directed to assimilate native peoples) and hid out in the mountains or in and around their homes. My YaYa took care of us as much as possible while my parents worked, and my father didn't teach us much language because he said he thought he was protecting his children from what he went through in his educational experience. He did not see much change in the school systems; therefore, my YaYa gave us as much as she could in his place. All through my schooling days, language or tribal culture was not taught in the schools.

The Lesson of One Elder

A long time ago my YaYa gave me something that no one can ever take away: an education. That education in her lifetime remains a way of life today. Through her cultural and spiritual strength, and overall resilience, her educational knowledge was passed on. It is through her resilience that I am able to carry what educational knowledge I have obtained. The cultural and spiritual resilience is what has allowed everything to happen, thus far, for me. I am overwhelmed by the amount of knowledge still to be learned, yet this is only the beginning. My YaYa's resilience to keep cultural, spiritual, and educational knowledge alive has allowed me to carry myself in such a way as to keep my eyes, ears, and mind open. When I reflect on what it means to be one of the first major Native American Studies degree program graduates, I think of my YaYa's resilience.

The Creator laid out the path for us to walk. This path has not always been smooth; there have been many rough spots. Those rough spots have allowed me to see and hear things with greater clarity. Every time I was knocked down and stepped on, physically or emotionally, I would pick myself up and continue on.

Walking the Path of Education

My YaYa's resilience has allowed me to walk the path of education. The education I have attained at the University of Montana is the beginning to the next step on my path. I look at the path. I am not allowed to see what lies ahead, but I am allowed to see each step I take. I am able to make decisions based on those steps and learn from everything, including the rough spots.

Every step I have taken has been very challenging. As one of the first Native American Studies Major degree program graduates, I have received a tool to allow me to do all that I can to help in the preservation, protection, and passing on of the cultural knowledge that our children need to know about and to help in the process of educating about the past and present state of Indian affairs in Indian country, particularly (for me) on the Salish and Kootenai Reservation.

It has long been my desire to write the Elders' stories and children's language books and to develop curricula and educational materials in native languages and history, develop a native song and dance recording studio, and most importantly develop and operate my own cultural camp year around. The Native American Studies degree allows all of these doors to open up. With all the educational resources and knowledge I have obtained during my university education, I can make these things happen.

I am very proud to have had the opportunity to be educated by such a great group of professors, instructors, advisors, administrators, and friends. They have all allowed my walk on this path of education to be difficult, challenging, encouraging, and fun. There were also times I was angry and wanted to give up. The diverse knowledge I have received about many different worldviews, though, has enabled me to maintain my balance and identity. At various times along this educational path, I have heard other Indian students say, "In order to go to college I had to put my culture aside." This was something I could never figure out. Without my culture I would not be where I am today.

Though cultural resilience passed down from my YaYa and all or ancestors has helped me to flourish, without all the challenges and encouragement, my balance and cultural identity would not have flourished. Through the various areas of study my identity has persevered and has been shared through the expression of who I am culturally. The importance of who I am, where I came from, and where I am going has blossomed, and I have come to understand that while on this educational path my cultural knowledge and understanding of life have also survived. So when I hear "I had to put my culture aside," I have to disagree.

I had once been asked to talk with the Diversity Council and Faculty Senate about diversity on campus. I had to be very honest with them and I said: "What diversity on campus?" While I have heard a lot of talk with good intentions, I have never seen diverse groups of people do things together, work together, or help organize any one event. In retrospect, diversity did exist on campus. It came in many forms, one of which was learning about various diverse world-views. It was that learning that helped to sharpen my knowledge and tolerance, rather than get angry over racist remarks or attitudes that existed on campus.

Some might say that racism doesn't exist or they might be naïve to the fact that on university campuses racism exists. I have directly observed racism in classes where the instructors have at times said that everything that Indians say about their culture and creation is myth, not founded on fact. I have learned to be tolerant of such attitudes, but at the same time I've wondered why these people were even teaching the subject matter in the first place. There were students, as well, who held racist attitudes. I experienced this once when I was run into and knocked down by a biker. He picked himself up, gathered his books, and took off riding. When he got across the parking lot, he yelled, "You f—en Indian." On another occasion I was standing in line at the campus store. Not realizing I needed to move forward, three cowboys (hats, wranglers, boots, and chew hanging out of their lips) cut in front of me, at the same time saying "She's just a f—en Indian." When it was their turn to pay, the cashier said, "Excuse me; I believe she was next." Yes, racism exists, not only on this campus but everywhere we go, just the same as diversity exists in many shapes, sizes, and forms. Through those racist attitudes, I have learned and striven to be as diverse as I can in walking on this educational path. The two worlds we all strive to live in do not always work together. There were many times when I had to make big decisions about which way to go. I have always gone with asking the Creator to guide me, and things have always seemed to work out.

There is something that I will always hold in my heart that I heard a young lady say on two separate occasions. The second time it was said, it stuck with me. She said:

> There's a reason for everything. There's a reason why we are all here today, and why some people are not. There's a reason why you have to be first in blazing a trail and there are reasons why people need to hear what you have to say, at this moment. There's [sic] reasons why people struggle and go through hard times, and there's [sic] reasons why things work out at every turn you take.[7]

The Creator has allowed me to hear this because there are reasons why I need to be doing what I am doing. When my YaYa held my hand and put me on her path, she had faith that the Creator would take my hand and continue me on that path. I have experienced many great and wonderful people on this educational path. So many have taught me how to continue on this path. They have helped me learn not to be afraid to write from my heart. They have given me new perspectives on how to teach what needs to be taught. They have taught me how to be a professional and to use the so-called "language of empire." They have allowed me to maintain my cultural balance, even through all the rough spots. They have taught me the importance of holding on to and getting an education. They have taught me how to write and express myself in ways I never thought were possible. Most importantly they have allowed me to be me, culture and all, and showed me that it is important for me culturally to be who I am and always to be a part of my native community no matter where I am or where that may be within this ceremony of life.

Conclusion

My cultural upbringing, traditional values, and education are of great meaning to me. I do not look back with blame on anyone for what has happened to our Indian people. I can only go forth and hope that there might be an instilling of respect for the importance that Indigenous cultural values can bring to us all, and that we all nurture whatever unique cultural traditions we possess for generations to come. The traditions of Coyote give me a great love for being an Indian person as a whole—to have a culture so rich and fulfilling!

NOTES

1. Peggy V. Beck, Anna Lee Walters, and Nia Francisco, eds., *The Sacred* (Arizona: Navajo Community College Press, 1990), pp. 57–58.
2. George Ferdinand Weisel, *The Ram's Horn Tree and Other Medicine Trees of the Flathead Indians* (Helena, 1951), p. 8.
3. Beck, Walters, and Francisco, p. 61.
4. Ada Deer, Henry Mann Lecture Series, Spring, NAGPRA series (1996).
5. Harriet Miller and Elizabeth Harrison, eds., *Coyote Tales of the Montana Salish*, from tales narrated by Pierre Pichette (Rapid City, South Dakota: Tipi Shop, Inc, 1974).
6. Louis Adams, Personal Communication, Polson, Montana (May 1997).
7. Iris Heavy-Runner, Health Conference speech (April 1997).

CHAPTER 10
MAYAN WAYS OF KNOWING: MODERN MAYANS AND THE ELDERS

By Victor Montejo

Victor Montejo is Professor and Chair of the Native American Studies department, University of California—Davis. He has a Ph.D. from the University of Connecticut (1993) and an MA from the State University of New York, Albany (1989). Victor's areas of interest include ethnohistory; ethnography; oral traditions and folklore; indigenous literatures; native knowledge; Indigenous people of Mesoamerica (Mayan); and human rights, particularly in the area of refugees. He has written and published numerous books and articles, including: *El Q'anil: The Man of Lightning* (1984, 1999, 2001); *The Elders Dreamed of Fire: Religion and Repression in the Guatemalan Highlands* (1990); and *Tying Up the Bundle and the Katuns of Dishonor: Maya Worldview and Politics* (1993).

Introduction

> "Oh, our sons! we are going, we are going away; sane advice and wise counsel we leave you. And you, also, who came from distant country, oh our wives!" they said to their women, and they bade farewell to each one. "We are going back to our town; there already in his place is Our Lord of the stags, to be seen there in the sky. We are going to begin our return, we have completed our mission [here], our days are ended. Think, then, of us, do not forget us. You shall see your homes and your mountains again; settle there, and so let it be! (*Popol Vuh*)[1]

It has become evident that in every Native community of our continent, the Elders have complained about the difficulties of performing their sacred rituals and of continuing Native knowledge as a result of modernization. But despite these barriers, the Elders have managed to continue and transform their identities within the dominant culture that has ruptured Native worldviews and cosmologies for over 500 years. In other words, despite the little space left for the expression of their own ways of life, they have managed to pass on their oral histories and help younger generations to root their identities in the land.

As a Jakaltek (Mayan) I have experienced these changes, transformations, and the revival of Mayan culture in the highlands of Guatemala, and I have recognized the role of the Elders in this sociocultural process of continuous changes and accommodations. Obviously, not all Mayans value the teachings of Elders since there are those who neglect the Elders and consider their roles as irrelevant (Sandoval 1992). No doubt some Elders are very concerned about our future and they too understand that we Mayans are linked to the outside world, so they have encouraged modern Mayans to maintain their Mayan-ness against the forces that tend to assimilate them. It is then clear that this distinctive way of life has been inherited from the ancestors, and it is the responsibility of new generations of Mayans to nourish and maintain it with transformations that are necessary for our survival in this highly technological and globalizing world.

In the space that follows I will discuss some of the issues that I believe are of vital importance for the continuous creation, recreation, and maintenance of the great Mayan tradition. First, as a Mayan I have always considered my culture with respect and not just as a field of research or the expression of an ancient world shattered into folkloric pieces. In addition, there is a necessity for modern Mayans to revitalize and promote our culture for the future, and to do so we must understand the roots of our Mayan tradition and show a genuine interest and pride in promoting it for the future. Third, we recognize that if we have to leave our stamp on history for the future, we must take into account the teachings of the Elders and build our strength from Mayan ideology, politics, and epistemology. In Mayan culture, the Elders are respected and consulted on delicate issues such as marriages, the sale of land, religious ceremonies, and communal histories (Salazar Tetzaguic 1992).

In my discussion I will refer to the ways in which the Mayans are linked to the outside world and how the Elders have complained about the unequal social relations that their people have endured for centuries. To illustrate these points (respect, communal solidarity, open-mindness, and cultural identity), I will refer to the most important legend of the Jakaltek-Mayan: *El Q'anil: The Man of Lightning* (La Farge 1931, Montejo 1984) and other Mayan parables from which we can distill the essence of the Elders' knowledge and ways of teaching. In other words, this is not just an anthropological analysis or interpretation of Mayan culture but the "presentation" of the dynamics of modern Mayan life in the Cuchumatán highlands of Guatemala described from an Indigenous experiential or empirical perspective.

Oral Histories and the Elders

At the turn of the 20th century (1900), Mayan communities were still almost undisturbed by major technological innovations such as roads, electricity, radio, telephones, TV, and so forth, and relied more heavily on the oral tradition to pass on to new generations their sacred beliefs and traditions. The Mayan ways of life during the first half of that century rested essentially on the concepts of respect and communal solidarity that gave Mayan communities their distinctiveness and the means for their corporate survival (Farriss 1984, Lovell 1985, Cox de Collins 1980).

In the Cuchumatan towns of Jakaltenango, Santa Eulalia, Todos Santos, and Santiago Chimaltenango of western Guatemala, the maintenance and the practice of Mayan religion such as the Year Bearer ceremony was very important as a unifying force in these communities (LaFarge 1931, 1947, Oakes 1951, Wagley 1950). In 1929, Oliver La Farge marveled to observe how the ancient Year Bearer ceremony was still practiced among the Jakaltek and Q'anjob'al people whom he visited in the Cuchumatan highlands of Guatemala.

Unfortunately, a few years after La Farge's visit and the publication of his ethnography *The Year Bearer's People* (1931), the Year Bearer's ceremony came under intense attack by the Ladino (Spanish speakers) and the Catholic missionaries of the region. In Jakaltenango, the person held responsible for the eradication of the Year Bearer ceremony was Father Pablo Sommer, a Maryknoll priest, who was considered an assiduous enemy of Mayan culture by the inhabitants. During those years (1930–1950) many Mayan priests (*Ah B'eh*) were punished for promoting what the Ladino authorities and missionaries have labeled a primitive and backward culture.[2] La Farge has mentioned the case of Antil, an *Ah B'e* (diviner) whom La Farge interviewed for information on the Mayan calendar.

> The man has twice been in jail, at times when Indians were civil Alcaldes, on complaint of witchcraft. He concluded from our note-taking that we had been sent by the President of Guatemala to spy on him, and was dead scared of being sent to prison, perhaps away at Quetzaltenango. (La Farge 1931: 155)

The public ceremony of the Year Bearer was abolished in 1947, so my generation did not have the chance to witness and experience the ceremony as our parents did. But we continued to learn about it from the Elders and through the oral tradition. Thus, considering the importance of the transmission of traditional knowledge for the continuity of the Mayan culture, I will now discuss the ways in which the Elders communicate their oral histories.

The Storytelling Method

There are several techniques that the storytellers use to communicate their stories to an audience. Among these discursive methods we can mention the process of personalization of the stories, as a way of inducing the listeners to be part of the stories and experience a direct contact with their roots and heritage. For example, some storytellers would start telling stories by insinuating that such an event occurred "here" in *Xaqla'-Jacaltenango*,[3] and it may occur again in the future since history follows a cyclical pattern. The storyteller makes the event more personal and timeless, as the listener finds herself or himself belonging to the place and the people who have performed such incredible deeds. In a sense it is providing young people with the elements that are basic or primordial in maintaining their underlying Mayan ethnic identity or Mayan-ness. These communal values are preached by the Elders and expressed in everyday life through the repetition of stories, fables, myths, and legends that enhance values such as respect, communal solidarity, and the relationship of humans with their environment. Thus, following the Elders' and *Principales'*[4] teachings, we find it useful to tell our stories to the world, not because we are "exotic" people with "strange" stories, but because Mayan traditions are the expression of our Maya-logical world that has been fading away for the past 500 years. The *Chilam Balam* makes reference to the Elders' lamentations concerning this loss of Mayan knowledge.

> Should we not lament in our suffering, grieving for the loss of our maize and the destruction of our teachings concerning the universe of the earth and the universe of the heavens? (*Chilam Balam*, transl. Makemson 1951: 4)

Among the Elders that I had the chance to talk to, I will mention, with respect, señor Antun Luk.[5] He was one of these Elders who did not hesitate to share with me his thoughts about our Mayan heritage whenever I asked him to talk about it. Antun Luk was the most expert bonesetter in town, and he would walk any distance to help anyone who asked him a favor and he never charged for his service. He followed the tradition of "serving the community" because the "gift of curing" according to him was given by God, and a person born with this ability must serve the people without asking for a fee. I came to his house one day in 1975 when my ankle was twisted from playing soccer. He provided me with help, and since then we both became very good friends and he visited my house frequently.

In January 1976, Antun Luk came to visit me as usual on a Sunday morning. He was concerned about the latest developments in Guatemala, particularly the announcement by President Kjell E. Laugerud Garcia (1974–1978) that every able Guatemalan man should be ready to enlist in the army's reserve in case

Guatemala should declare war against England in defense of Belize, then a Guatemalan-claimed territory.[6] Antun Luk did not know how to read or write, but he heard the news from other people who listened to the development of this conflict on the national radio TGW. As a traditional bonesetter and a caring man, he understood that it was suicidal to declare war against one of the world's military superpowers without having matching weapons. He then mentioned the legend of *El Q'anil: The Man of Lightning* (Montejo 1984), a Jakaltek-Mayan hero who decided to give his own life in order to save his people and his community from destruction because of a war. This is how Antun Luk repeated to me his version of this legend that every Jakaltek knows from childhood. As he retold the legend, he put special emphasis on the fact that the invaders fought from the sea with strange weapons, and our heroes defeated them by turning themselves into lightning. The legend is summarized as follows:

El Q'anil: The Man of Lightning

One evening Jich Mam, our First Father, came forward in great majesty to tell the people of Xajla' the following news: "Brave sons of Xajla', I bring you a heavy heart and a strange story. Men have come to me from people far away who fight invaders hidden in the sea, who from that impossible battlefield destroy armies and raze whole villages with weapons no one has ever seen. Before long a whole people will have died. From their land these proud people have followed our name, the word of our courage a star guiding them. These men have brought us their hope and prayer, asking us to share the wealth of our hearts, honoring us with their confidence. We'll go to them and to the bloody war that waits for us and we'll return unbeaten."

Jich Mam chose the bravest and the strongest, but the sorcerers said that they were the best since they knew the darkest power that would stop the strange weapons of the invaders by the sea. "I shall become a wasp and sting them. I shall become a snake and sting them. I shall become a lion and tear out their throats," they said. The sorcerers went to the war and took with them two young men to be the carriers of their sleeping mats and jars. Then the young porter Xhuwan became concerned about the faith of the sorcerers. He went to the lightning guardians or their sanctuaries in the hills around the town to ask for power. He visited several of these lightning men's sanctuaries, but only Q'anil acceded to his petition.

"Tomorrow my brothers will go to fight a war for a dying people far from here. Their messengers followed our fame to Xajla'. Their enemy fights only from the sea protected by the waves and strange weapons. Our battalion that leaves in the morning is not warriors but sorcerers. They can turn themselves into vicious beasts and strange pests, but what will they be on the beach but more targets for the invader's arms? We will all lose our lives by that sea. Father Q'anil," Xhuwan begged, "I want to save them. I want to prove the people of Xajla' cannot be beaten. I don't care if my blood runs on the sand or if I never return. Give me those powers I must have because tomorrow we leave with the morning star."

This is how Q'anil shared his powers of lightning with Xhuwan. On their way, the sorcerers ordered the two porters to fetch water and this is when they discussed the danger of going to war with unmatched weapons. Xhuwan shared the power with the other porter and started to practice with the huge pine trees. But they did not reveal their secret to the sorcerers. They continued to walk for a long time until they reached that place of war.

When they arrived at the site of the battle, the sorcerers became fearful and wanted to go home. Then Xhuwan and the other lightning companion took care of the battle by turning themselves into thunderbolts. During the battle, the brothers from Chiapas came to help them to defeat the enemy. Then the king that invited our fighters wanted to celebrate the victory with gifts to our heroes. But then our warriors answered: "Do not think of us. We are thankful to have fought as promised. We ourselves think only of returning home." So our men turned back tributes and honors, preferring the peace of humility to all the world's feasts and celebrations.

On the way back to Xajla', Xhuwan and his companions told the rest: "You will return to Xajla' without us. We who used our power in that cruel slaughter can never live again among our people. We have promised never to return, not to Xajla', not to our families. You must tell them that we are well and that the powers we used forbid us return. We shall hide ourselves and our gold arrows in the great southern mountain of El Q'anil. We shall live with our father who gave us our power and look down on all Xajla'. When danger comes our banners shall fly in the clouds and our voices speak in the wind, day and night, year after year, always."

All this the old ones know and have told us out of the aching memory of the past. And so they passed it on to their children and to their children's children, until it came to us who live today in Jakaltenango (Montejo 1984).[7]

Rooting Our Identities

As I have mentioned earlier, each Jakaltek child grows up knowing about the cultural hero El Q'anil. In other words, this is the story that parents, grandparents, and the Elders in town tell their children in order to establish at an early age a strong connection with the past. Recognizing that the Jakaltek share a common root and origin with the cultural hero makes them proud of being connected to the ancient past, and this helps to maintain unity and solidarity among the people. It is like saying, "We are Jakalteks and this is the legend of our people." In this way, Mayans become rooted to the land because the landscape or sacred geography becomes the resting place or sanctuary of the ancestors. This is the case of *Xajla'* (Jakaltenango), which is surrounded in every direction by thunderbolts or guardian angels that protect the town from danger. The founding father decided to protect his people by placing lightning bolts or guardians to protect them from the dangers of war.

> Jich Mam, faithful to God's design, surrounded the settlement with the K'ues, the man-angels who are the thunder and lightning, our protectors every hour and day and every season of the year. (Montejo 1984: 17)

This is how *Q'anil*, meaning the "yellow power or emanation," who is one of the most powerful lightning protectors, was placed at the southwestern part of the Jakaltek territory as a guardian by *B'alunh Q'ana*, the founding father who is also a Man of Lightning. Oliver La Farge (1931) recognized the importance of this legend and also the difficulties of obtaining a full version of it. Briefly, La Farge said:

> A very interesting legend is that of Juan Mendoza [Xhuwan Q'anil], and one which we had some difficulty in obtaining. Shuwan Manel admitted frankly that he was afraid to tell it to us for fear of its hero who today inhabits the big hill that dominates the western view. (La Farge 1931: 118)

Unfortunately, the Year Bearer ceremony and other religious practices that were the reason for the religious gathering of the major towns of the Kuchumatan were abolished during the decade of 1940 to 1950. With this attack on a major religious ceremony, such as the Year Bearer, which provided unity and solidarity among the people and the surrounding villages, the Elders were more cautious in telling their stories to foreigners. As a consequence, the cult to Q'anil became less relevant through the years until 1990 as a result of the revitalization of Mayan culture in Guatemala.

From 1975 to 1976, Juvenal Casaverde worked and studied the politico-religious hierarchy among the Jakalteks and provided more systematic information about the nature and the attributes of the lightning guardians surrounding the town. According to Casaverde, Q'anil

> [i]s one of the Jacaltec stock founding ancestors; he is a protector war deity; and he is one of the four Year Bearers of the traditional calendar . . . The alcaldes rezadores [Prayer Makers] of the stock Niman Conob' must regularly visit K'anil's shrine, in relation with the traditional calendar, to perform rituals asking for his protection. (Casaverde 1976: 33)

Despite the elimination of the Year Bearer ceremony as a communal celebration, the Elders continued to go to the Q'anil sanctuary and ask protection for their children whenever they were drafted (most of the time, forcibly) for military service far away in distant Guatemalan cities. This is why Antun Luk was particularly disturbed by the news about a possible military confrontation between Guatemala and England mentioned earlier. Although he did not understand international politics and the threats of a nuclear war between superpowers during the 1960s and 1970s, the unmatched weapons and the poverty of the young Mayan, drafted forcibly to serve in the army were his major concern. The people of these Indigenous communities were also very concerned about the situation and feared that thousands of people would die if such a war were to occur. Fearing massive destruction, the Elders recalled the Q'anil legend and revived their faith in the ancestors and heroes. Antun Luk said that even if they couldn't handle the lightning bolts as in the legend, the children would be protected if Q'anil were remembered in his magnificence and was asked for his protection.

According to the legend, whenever there is an imminent danger threatening the town, a yellow or red flag would appear at dusk on the peak of the Q'anil mountain or volcano of war, signaling the presence and readiness of our mythical heroes to protect the town. One late afternoon during this time of high anxiety, a red nylon flag appeared at dusk on top of the Q'anil mountain. Someone wanted to make fun of the Elders' belief and went up on top of the mountain to tie a red nylon on top of a tree. Obviously, the Elders were very disgusted by the disrespectful attitude of young people to their beliefs and traditions.

Then, the conflict between Guatemala and Great Britain escalated at the end of January 1976. But suddenly, during the early hours of February 4, 1976, an earthquake shook the earth, causing the death of some 20,000 Guatemalans in just a few seconds. Again, Antun Luk came to visit me and he said that God must have been angry at the world and at Guatemala in particular; that is why he had allowed the "world bearers" to remove the load on their back, provoking the earthquake.[8] There was already a lot of violence and internal problems at home, and now the government was getting into more trouble by challenging a military superpower. Antun Luk, who claimed to be a descendant of Q'anil himself, said: "K'anch'an anma meb'a, axkam ha'tik'a xkamopaxoq tato ch'okoq hune howal ti'." (Pity to the poor people since they will be the first to die if this war were to occur.) He was referring to the Mayan young men who are the first to be drafted forcibly to join the army and be sent to war.

It was nice to listen to the Elder, Antun Luk. He was part of the Mayan political and religious cargo system that was abolished 50 years ago in Jakalte-nango.[9] As a member of this cargo or politico-religious office, Antun Luk could recite by memory the ancient Mayan sacred prayers in the traditional Mayan literary devices of couplets and triplets.[10]

Because of his knowledge and understanding of the conflicts that have affected Mayan life and the sufferings that they have endured in this ever-changing world, I asked him in 1981 what he thought about the current political situation in Guatemala. He said that this was a question to be asked of a politician and not of a traditional bonesetter: "To those who offer too many things to the communities and never fulfill their promises, just as Rios Montt," he said.[11] Certainly during his presidential campaign in 1974, General Rios Montt came to the Cuchumatan communities and offered roads, schools, potable water; but later, when he became president by a coup d'état in 1982, he did not fulfill his promises. Instead, he implemented his scorched earth policy that he called "Bullets and Beans," a policy of murder and genocide.[12] As a Mayan peasant and a traditional healer, Antun Luk did not want to deal with outside politics. His politic was that of communal life, care for nature, and respect for the super-natural world. "We are related to the outside world," he said, "but not in a good way. We have being [sic] destroyed by those outsiders, and bad Ladinos that only think of us as ignorant and backward people. Unfortunately we cannot handle the lightning in our hands and do not have other Q'anil who could lead us to freedom and get rid of this misery that we have endured for centuries."

Then, during the violence of the early 1980s, the people in Jakaltenango were fortunate to have a native Catholic priest who worked hard to keep the people united during those difficult days of armed confrontation between the army and the guerrillas. The priest preached in the Popb'al Ti' language to the people during his Sunday sermons and used Mayan anecdotes and parables to teach the people to value their culture. In an effort to explain out-side politics, the priest used the ways of teaching of the Elders and told the following story:

> There was a boy who went to fetch firewood in the forest, and when he was tying up the firewood to be carried home, a group of furious wild pigs came running to attack him. Fearing for his life the boy avoided the danger by climb-ing a tree nearby. The wild pigs started to circle the tree making a huge noise to scare down the boy. After a while and seeing that the boy was clinging to the tree with no intention to come down, the wild pigs got tired and laid down at the foot of the tree waiting for the boy to come down. The time went by and then the boy needed to pee desperately. Since he couldn't come down, he started to pee from the tree wetting the head of one of the pigs. When the other pigs woke up, the smell irritated them and they attacked the pig that had been urinated upon. The boy watched this happen from the tree and proceeded to urinate on all of the pigs that were waiting for him on the ground. Soon they all smelled so bad that they attacked each other, until some were dead and others ran off still fighting among each other.[13]

The priest who told this story explained that this is a parable of how we Mayans have been living under alien rule and domination. "Mayans have always lived in communal life and their social solidarity has been essential in the maintenance of their worldview and Mayan traditions." The priest was careful and did not get involved in the political situation, but from his message in the Mayan language people could draw their own conclusions. His words could refer to the violence that people were experiencing in the Cuchumatan at that time when people were turning against each other. In fact, we could say that "up there" the deceiving Ladino rulers have somebody urinating on their heads and they get angry and destroy our culture. Or they have tried to turn us against one another, such as the case of the civil patrol and the soldiers who killed and massacred their own people. The soldiers and civil patrollers were indoctrinated in such a way that they could kill their own relatives without remorse. Up there the military commanders who urinate on their heads make them get mad, so they get crazy and kill.

Mayan Politics, Cosmology, and Epistemology

With the distinctive ways of explaining local politics in relation to the outside world, we can recognize that the Elders have advocated for a politico-religious system that promotes respect for life and communalism in which every individ-ual is important in the maintenance of the corporate community (Wolf 1957). This type of Mayan polity finds its major expression in the cargo system, a Mayan politico-religious office that is accessible to every individual in the com-munity (Cancian 1969, Vogt 1969).

> In Mayan politics, people in positions of power and authority are constantly reminded of their communal or public responsibilities. An excellent example is the election of a leader in the cargo system. The leader must be someone who has worked for his people and is recognized by the community. His authority is

confirmed by the Mayan political institution called Lah-Ti',[14] meaning to compare discourses and to come to a common consensus during a public assembly. (Montejo 1993: 106)

Generally, those who are elected and achieve the status of *principal* or *alkal txah*, the highest office in the modern Mayan politico-religious hierarchy, are those who have given their time to the service of the community and are expected to continue their communal service without individualism or personal interest.[15] For example, among the Ixil, "after a person has served as *b'aal mertoma*, he then becomes a lifelong member of the Elders (*Principales*)" (Colby & Colby 1981: 39–40). Antun Luk said that, more frequently, those who occupy this position end up being poor because they cannot use this civic-religious position to benefit themselves or to take advantage of others. The cargo system is a burden to be carried for the duration of your time (one year) in office, which implies full-time service to the community without remuneration. If the elected Alkal Txah uses his position to enrich himself or to cause problems to his community, he is immediately thrown out and criticized and disgraced by the community. As Antun Luk spoke, I thought about the difference between Mayan political systems and those of the corrupt rulers of Guatemala and Latin America.

The Mayan system has worked for the Mayans to maintain cohesiveness and solidarity in the community and to nourish and maintain their links with the natural and supernatural world. That is why we modern Mayans are anxious again to learn and continue the Elders' knowledge and to maintain our Mayan worldviews and politics. This cosmic link and solidarity between humans and the natural and supernatural world is expressed in Mayan creation myths. According to the *Popol Vuh:*[16]

> Great were the descriptions and the account of how all the sky and earth were formed . . . how it was partitioned; and the measuring-cord was brought, and it was stretched in the sky and over the earth . . . by the Creator and the Maker, the Mother and Father of Life. (Recinos 1983: 80)

This is then the link with the divinity that some Elders who are prayer-makers want to maintain with their prayers and ceremonies. That is why the Mayans say that they have been placed on the navel of earth as in the case of the Chamulas (Gossen 1984), or the Jakaltek, whose mythology placed them at the navel of sky. In the same way the Yucatek Mayans maintained a story of the "*Kusansum*," which was prevalent until the Spanish invasion of the 16th century.[17] This legend reinforces the idea of a cosmic link, since "the Mayans believed that a sacred umbilical cord, through which nourishment flowed in both directions linked heaven and earth" (Farriss 1984: 287). In other stories of the Yucatek Mayans, it has been called *Sak b'eh:* "It was a road suspended in the sky, and connected to the Mayan centers of Uxmal, Tulum and Chichén Itzá" (Bricker 1981: 166). But this link was ruptured by the Spanish conquest and by destruction of Mayan sanctuaries and sacred places.

These ancient stories have continued in modern Mayan oral traditions, and Mayans recognize the importance given to the umbilical cord or the afterbirth and some modern Mayans still perform rituals for its disposal. When a Mayan child is born, the placenta is ritually buried in the ground at a specific place (usually near a water spring). The place holds a special meaning for the Mayans, since it is where the individual is symbolically "planted" in the ground to root his or her Mayan identity.[18] In this way, Mayan religious traditions root them to the land at the moment of birth and it is hoped that the person will not become individualistic or selfish, but an integral part of the community, nature, and the universe.[19]

The persistence of religious belief systems among the Mayans demonstrates that they have a different way of explaining their knowledge and representing the world around them. Also, Mayan ceremonies are related to the ancient Mayan calendar (a unifying element of the great Mayan tradition), which is also threatened to disappear, and this worries the Elders. For example, among the Jakalteks the Mayan calendar b'isom tz'ayik, which is the instrument for counting and recording the time q'inal, was almost totally destroyed in 1947. Following the ancient calendar, the names of the days q'inh were used for divination and for naming children after birth. To maintain their sacred beliefs, the permanence of the Mayan calendar is essential, since now most Mayans depend on the Gregorian calendar for counting time.[20] That is why the Elders have been afraid that the Mayan calendar would disappear forever, since up to the 1980s it was not used openly in the Cuchumatan region. But, as a response to the quincentenary commemoration, the Elders decided to revive their hidden Mayan rituals, and for the first time in modern history 200 Mayan priests from different linguistic communities congregated at the Mayan sites of Zaculeu and Iximche, Guatemala, to perform their Mayan ceremonies in public. The same type of ceremony was performed when the members of the Academy of Mayan Languages of Guatemala took office on December 1992. A ceremony was performed by the spiritual Elders from different ethnic groups. In this way they have ruptured the silence imposed on them and have began to perform their ceremonies without fear of being called brujos, or witch doctors, but as Mayan priests and experts in the ancient Mayan calendar and sacred knowledge. But Mayan revival is not easy in a country like Guatemala, where the countryside has been militarized. As I worked as a schoolteacher in the Cuchumatan highlands for 10 years, I witnessed the difficulties that the Elders have confronted in performing their ceremonies. In July 1982, when the civil patrol was formed in the Mayan villages of northwestern Guatemala, the Elders could not practice their religious ceremonies with the usual burning of candles and incense (pom) at night for fear of being accused of being guerrillas.

The attacks on the fundamentals of the Mayan culture have been constant, but not everything is lost. The Mayans are reviving and recreating their ceremonies, and they are telling the world that they are still alive after five centuries of denigration of their cultural heritage. Despite being accused of being viejos supersticiosos (superstitious old men) the spiritual leaders and Elders who perform Mayan rituals have continued their mission of telling the world that Mayan culture is not evil, but another way of life that the West does not understand (Montejo 1993). For example,

[w]hen we Mayans say that we respect nature, we are sincere, because we live what we say; we feel a unity with other living creatures on earth. It is not only that we are "close to nature" but that we recognize the value of life, and we respect others. The Mayan cosmology and world view are centered on communal practices in which all elements that promote life—cosmic elements (e.g., sun, wind), humans and the environment are interrelated. Our world view also informs the politics of how we must act and react when this communalism is threatened by outside forces. (Montejo 1993: 104)

It has become necessary for Mayans to know how this cosmic unity (human-nature-supernatural) is built and maintained. In the past, when a campesino (peasant) cleared a piece of land to plant corn, he talked to the trees. He asked permission to the "Giver of Life" to cut down the trees for the cornfield, because he also needed to nourish himself and his family. The Mayan world used to be different, and there was a true respect for life.[21] There are prayers and ceremonies that precede each activity in which earth and the life on it may be affected. For example, among the Yucatek Mayans, the tortoise is believed to help the men to ask for rain during the times of drought. That is why this animal is protected when the *campesinos* prepare their lands for corn planting.

When the bush is kindled at the time of burning, the pious agriculturalist does not fail to call out, "Save yourselves tortoises! Here comes the fire!" (Hoceneex acob, He cu tal le kake!). (Redfield and Villa Rojas 1964: 207)

Speaking from the K'iche'-Mayan tradition, Rigoberta Menchú has said that we Mayans "ask pardon to Mother Earth when we cause a destruction on her face."[22] This appreciation and respect for life is the prime teaching among Native peoples of our continent. For example, practicing his beliefs, the patriarch of the Lacandon Mayans of Chiapas, Mexico, Chan Q'inh, has cried desperately against the deforestation of the Lacandon jungle by loggers. Looking at the huge mahogany (caoba) trees being felled, he was saddened and reminded us all that

the roots of all living creatures are linked. Every time a powerful tree falls, a star falls from the sky. Before cutting down a caoba tree, permission should be asked to the lord of the forest, and to the lord of the stars. (Perera 1982: cover jacket)

This philosophy of life that "those who cut trees for pleasure shorten their lives" (Montejo 1991: 62) is constantly expressed in the daily activity of Native people. But again, it is difficult to continue with the teaching of the ancestors and Elders if there is oppression in every moment of our lives. Similarly, our ways of teaching and learning are not recognized as viable ways. To have a dialogue with a tree may sound absurd to Western rationality, but humans' link to nature and the supernatural world has been very important in Mayan beliefs and rituals.[23] In other words, Mayans have their own knowledge system, a particular way of expressing their worldviews from different epistemological grounds. But how can Mayans continue with their cultural beliefs and sacred knowledge with relation to earth if their land has been taken for the expansion of coffee plantations and cattle ranches? In Guatemala the campesino cannot live without the land. For Indigenous people "the land is the property of the ancestors and people live on it without owning it" (Bunzel 1981:52). For this reason, the landscape serves as a sanctuary for religious rituals and offerings to God and all his manifestations. That is why,

> On the top of the highest mountains we render cult to the absolute Being, that is why the volcanos, the mountains and the highest hills occupy a privileged place in our Mayan rituals. (Matul 1989: 22)

Thus, the major dream and desire of a Mayan *campesino* is to have a piece of land to cultivate his corn (the metaphor for humans) because corn is life itself and corn has an important place in Mayan culture. Unfortunately, the encroachment on their communal lands has forced Mayans to stop performing some essential religious ceremonies. It is then difficult for a campesino to get involved in ceremonies of planting and harvesting if he is a landless peasant.[24] This was particularly relevant during the "scorched earth" policy of Rios Montt in 1982, when hundreds of villages and cornfields were burned and the inhabitants of the most isolated villages were forced into exile by the Guatemalan army (Montejo 1987, Manz 1988, Carmack 1988, Falla 1992).

Histories of the Mayan people are communal histories, and the philosophy of life that has guided their lives stems from their religious beliefs and cosmology. A Mayan priest has said that the "spirituality of the Mayans is life itself . . ." (Mijango 1990:4) and this life is expressed in communalist ways. Having participated in communal works in my town, I have come to understand and value this Mayan way of life. One of the forms of Mayan social organization that has helped to maintain Mayan identities is the form of communal work called Wayab'[25] as part of a larger Mayan theory of corporate survival that I will call Komontat.[26] Unfortunately, this type of communal activity was not able to continue when the army settled the barracks in the Cuchumatan highlands. Whenever men and women came together for communal purposes, they were suspected of organizing and making plans against the government (Manz 1988).

But, as in ancient times, the destruction of Mayan villages was also prophesied by the Elders in the Cuchumatan highlands (Montejo 1992). I remember that in 1965 an elderly man called Kaxh Manel commented to a group of people gathered, as usual, in the corridor of his house to listen to his stories. There were no roads in the region, and no car had yet entered the town at that time. Then the people started to ask for a road until a dirt road was constructed communally, and with the help of a Maryknoll missionary the town became linked to the rest of the country. As this modernization came to the region, the Elders were also concerned about the price that the people had to pay for such conveniences. This is when Kaxh Manel said: "Don't be joyful when the first car will come to town; instead, be sorrowful since it will be the sign of tragedy and sadness in our lands." Indeed, when the Transversal del Norte (1980–1981) was being built in northwestern Guatemala, army patrols started to enter Mayan communities, bringing morally unacceptable social problems and behaviors such as rape, kidnapping, torture, and killings.

This is what happened in the community of *El Limonar* on January 5, 1981. The men in the community were constructing the house of one of the villagers in their accustomed communal way when the army arrived. The soldiers surrounded the village where the men were singing and giving thanks to God after finishing their communal work. The soldiers raped the women and ordered the 16 men captured to kneel and in this position and then they shot them in the head (Montejo & Akab' 1992). The town life was once again disrupted and Mayans started to have dreams from the ancestors, who gave advice on how to defend and protect their children. In 1980 even before the counterinsurgency war reached its most extreme levels, some people recounted and told me their dreams. The Elders dreamed that our ancestors passed through the sky in a procession that headed towards Mexico. Others dreamed that the patron saints abandoned their chapels and crossed the border into Mexico (Montejo & Akab' 1992). The dream of the Elders proved true. When Mayan villages were bombed and burned during what the army called the "Black August" in 1982, this displaced one million Guatemalans, among them the 46,000 refugees who went to seek refuge in Chiapas, Mexico, carrying with them the wooden images of their patron saints.[27]

Conclusion

In Guatemala, despite the systematic destruction of Native cultures, the revival of Mayan ethnic identities has become very strong, and there are interethnic movements of recreation and redefinition of a pan-Mayan identity. These efforts of deepening the roots of our Mayan heritage are political acts of reaffirming our presence, stronger than ever. The revival of Mayan culture(s) is inevitable despite the efforts of some sectors of the Guatemalan elite to uproot the Mayan from their sacred beliefs and knowledge. For this reason Native values and politics are important for the construction and maintenance of Native people's worldviews.

> Thus, Mayan political movements have developed, in a restricted way, by rupturing the established non-Mayan frameworks, names and images created for native inhabitants. This is a continuous task. If we are to promote our values and world view into the future of our continent, we have to eliminate the denigrating images that were imposed on us and reaffirm our Mayan identity. (Montejo 1993: 110)

For the past 500 years, Mayans have been neglected and persecuted instead of having a free environment in which to express their creativity and to promote their Mayan-ness. The complaints and lamentations of the Elders concerning the destruction of Mayan knowledge are stated in the books of the *Chilam Balam* as follows:

> We complain in great sorrow, in loud voices . . . and death. Our grief is torment. We are pierced with a great longing to read the books of wood and the writings on stone, now in ruins. They contain the seven well-springs of life! They were

burned before our eyes at the well. At noon-day we lament our perpetual burdens. (*Chilam Balam*, transl. Makemson 1951: 5)

Against this "perpetual burden" and aggression, Native people of the continent are building an Indigenous internationalism for the purpose of getting rid of the denigrating images and representations that have portrayed Mayans and Native peoples negatively. With the recharging of our Mayan cultural traditions and the emergence of a Mayan unity with plural identity, we are making sure that the voices of our ancestors and Elders are becoming louder and louder again. We must struggle to maintain our life where our placenta has been planted, since the land is essential for our lives and provides our communal spirituality.

Finally, it is my hope that we may learn to value and recognize Indigenous knowledge expressed by the Elders when they explain Mayan beliefs and spirituality with emphasis on values: such as the respect that links humans, nature, and the supernatural world. By knowing and valuing these ways of life, we will understand the suffering that Indigenous people have endured for the past five centuries. In other words, the major concern of Guatemalan-Mayans at the present is their cultural survival in a world that has encroached upon their worldview, not only through exploitation but with ethnocidal wars that tend to keep them apart from their dreams of creating and recreating a pan-Mayan ethnic identity. We hope that Mayan culture will be practiced without restrictions and as it has been prophesied by the *Chilam Balam:*

> As soon as they have departed we will no longer need to speak exceedingly softly when we cast our lots. And in the day there will be no more violent disputes. *Our good fortune will unite us.* We will be able to look at ourselves in the mirror without sadness. We will amuse ourselves once more when that day comes. (*The Jaguar Priest, Chilam Balam*, transl. Makemson 1951: 8, my emphasis)

At the present, modern Mayans are engaged in the revitalization of Mayan culture. Meanwhile, the teachings of the Elders must continue and modern Mayans must draw their strength from their wise words. In 1982 Antun Luk communicated to me his hope for the continuity of our Mayan religious traditions: "Oxhoqwal stoh st'inhb'akoq sb'a yala' tatoh xtxum sb'a sk'ul k'ahole, kutz'ine." (Translation: "Hopefully our ways will be continued and strengthened in the future if our sons and daughters retake our paths.") And this is happening now. We modern Mayans are responsible for this task of cultural recreation and revitalization of Mayan culture, and we have to fight for our rights as significant people with a millenarian history in the Americas.

NOTES

1. From the translation of Adrian Recinos, 1983, pp. 204–205.
2. See La Farge 1931.
3. The original Mayan name of this town was *Xaqla'*, but it was renamed as Xacaltenango (Jacaltenango) by the Nahuatll speaking allies of Pedro de

Alvarado (Aztecs and Tlaxcaltecs) during the invasion of Guatemala in 1524.

4. The *Principals* are the Elders who have served in the cargo system of politico-religious office and hierarchy in Mayan communities. Their role has become that of the "advisers" and guides to the people, since they are the most knowledgeable and made sacred by means of serving in this cargo or politico-religious office.

5. Antun Luk (R.I.P) died in 1983, one year after I went into exile. I did have the chance to see him after we talked about *El Q'anil: The Man of Lightning* (November 1982), but he wanted me to return to town and stay with my people.

6. As Belize struggled for independence from England and Guatemala, General Kjell Eugenio Laugerud Garcia wanted to keep this *departamento* as an integral part of Guatemala, as it has been historically. In the struggle, England threatened to destroy the Guatemalan army if it attempted to thwart the decision of Belize to be independent.

7. An enlarged edition of *Q'anil: The Man of Lightning* was published by University of Arizona Press (1999) with the Mayan text.

8. According to Jakaltek mythology, the earth is carried by the four bearers, and the earthquakes are produced when they remove the porter's strap to rest their foreheads. Another Elder (Mat Tiyes) has said that one of the bearers constantly asks for his birthday, but God does not tell him the date to avoid making him too excited because then he might remove his load violently, causing earthquakes.

9. The Mayan political and religious cargo system is a civic-religious office in Mayan communities. It should be performed with religious commitment, as a genuine service to the community.

10. This Mayan literary device is used particularly in sacred songs and prayers and is called *ninhq'omb'al.*

11. Rios Montt was a presidential candidate for the Christian Democratic party of Guatemala in 1974. Later he became a president by a coup d'état in 1982. In 1999 Rios Montt's political party, the Frente Republicano Guatemalteco (FRG), won the elections and Ríos Montt became the president of Congress.

12. During Efraín Ríos Montt's short term in office, some 440 villages were razed to the ground and produced one million displaced Guatemalans. Currently, there are some 46,000 Guatemalan refugees in Southern Mexico.

13. The story was told by a Jakaltek-Mayan (Catholic priest) during a Sunday mass in town.

14. A Mayan political and democratic form of electing the communities' leaders. This is a communal meeting in which everybody is encouraged to voice their concerns and to reach communal consensus (from *Lah* = equal, *ti'* = mouth).

15. This is the highest hierarchy in the cargo system. The *alkal txah* is the Prayer Maker, or head of the civic-religious Mayan ceremonies.

16. This K'iche' Mayan ethnohistorical document has been named by scholars as the *Popol Vuh*, recently, K'iche' Mayan speakers have renamed it *Pop Wuj*,

while it is also named differently in other Mayan languages. For example: *Popb'al Hum,* from *Popb'al Ti'* (the Jakaltek-Mayan language).

17. From the Yukatek Mayan language, *kusansum* means a rope that gives life, symbol of the umbilical cord.

18. Victor Montejo, *The Elders Dreamed of Fire: Religion and Repression in the Guatemalan Highlands,* Challenge, vol. 1, no. 3 (1990).

19. The process of syncretization of traditional Mayan beliefs with tenets of Christian doctrine occurred over centuries, resulting in a dynamic and complex system of faith and view of the world.

20. The Mayan regular calendar, composed of 18 months of 20 days, plus five sacred days, made up a year Hab'il of 360 days.

21. These traditional forms of knowledge and respect for other living beings are not clearly observed now by young Mayans in most Mayan communities.

22. Rigoberta Menchú, film: *When the Mountains Tremble,* 1984.

23. Recent experiments by U.S. and Japanese scientists have shown that a plant has a "feeling." The plants respond differently to the intensity of sounds directed toward them. They say that plants grow if you say nice things to them, as was shown by the waves emitted by the plants registered in the spectrographs.

24. This is the case of the Mayan refugees in Mexico who have become landless peasants struggling to survive in an alien territory since 1982.

25. This is a Mayan concept of mutuality. This has been a communal and moral responsibility of caring for the survival of each member of the community through mutual help.

26. A Mayan theory of cosmic unity. A philosophy of life based on the consensus of communalism.

27. On January 20, 1992, the first repatriation or retorno took place when 2,800 refugees returned to northern Guatemala to build a new community that they called Victoria 20 de Enero.

CHAPTER 11

TARARUA IS MY MOUNTAIN

By Rachael Selby

Rachael Selby is a Māori woman from New Zealand. She is a senior lecturer in social policy, Māori history, and research at Massey University, Palmerston North. She works in Māori development and research and works extensively within her tribal area, promoting higher education. Rachael is editor of Te Ukaipo, a journal published by a tribal college, Te Wananga o Raukawa, in which all contributors are women from the tribal confederation. Her research interests are currently focused on oral history, Māori women and education, Indigenous women's issues, and social work in schools. She is the author of *Still Being Punished* (1999) a collection of stories of Māori people punished at school for speaking the Māori language.

Introduction

Ko Tararua toku maunga

Ko Hokio toku awa

Ko Ngāti Raukawa toku iwi

Ko Ngāti Pareraukawa toku hapü

Ko Ngātokowaru toku marae.

Tararua is my mountain

Hokio is my river

Ngāti Raukawa is my tribe

Ngāti Pareraukawa is my subtribe

Ngātokowaru is my marae, my ancestral home.

On a slight rise beside the Hokio stream facing east into the rising sun stands my ancestral meeting house, Ngātokowaru. This house, completed in 1978, replaced the old Ngātokowaru that had stood there since 1900. Both were built in the traditional style of Māori meeting houses—a single room with a veranda in the front and a single-door opening onto the veranda. At Ngātokowaru the door opens to face the Tararua ranges to the east, and in the early morning one looks from the doorway across the pasture, the headstones in the cemetery, the misty waters of Lake Horowhenua to the hills, snow-capped in winter, colors changing throughout the seasons from deep dark blues and purples to the greens and grays of winter.

When the clouds roll down over the Tararua ranges, the hills are obscured behind thick blankets, and when the clouds lift, Tararua stands majestic with many peaks and hills, valleys, and bush, with waterfalls and streams making their way down to the flatter pastures of the Horowhenua to the towns and farms nestled between hills and sea.

From Lake Horowhenua, the Hokio Stream meanders west past the meeting house to join the sea, 10 miles west of the lake. We call the sea that wraps around our coastline Te Moana o Raukawa, the sea of Ngāti Raukawa. Ngāti Raukawa are the people who descend from Raukawa, chieftain and ancestor who lived 14 generations ago. Ngāti Pareraukawa is the subtribe located beside the Hokio Stream, the people who descend from Pareraukawa—my maternal ancestor from whom I descended and am separated by seven generations of women.

Pareraukawa's descendants, who are my family and who form the subtribe Ngāti-Pareraukawa (the descendants of Pareraukawa), gather at Ngātokowaru throughout each month and each year as our parents and grandparents have for the past 50 years since moving away from living at the marae to live in suburbia. We identify as a family, as a subtribe. We are bound to one another by our common ancestry, our genealogy, our obligations to one another in times of trial and difficulty as well as in times of celebration. Pareraukawa's descendants number in the thousands now, and we are spread throughout Aotearoa (New Zealand), Australia, and the rest of the world.

It was Pareraukawa's descendants who were the seven original owners of the block of land on which our marae stands. Ema Hapai was my great-grandmother, and it was she who lived and farmed beside the stream with her husband and children and her grandchildren, one of whom is my mother. Granny Ema Hapai lived at the turn of the 20th century and foresaw the changes that would happen as the land became occupied by the non-Māori white immigrants known to us as the Pākehā people. She warned against selling the land to the Pākehā. The land is Papatuanuku, the earth mother from whom sustenance comes. How could one sell one's mother? We use the land while we are here, and we then leave it for our children and our grandchildren to sustain them, to provide them with the fruits of the earth. After the railway was built from the city of Wellington in the south to meet with the railway coming from the city of Auckland in the north, more and more people arrived to settle between the lake and the Tararua ranges. They built a town and brought modern society, modern technology, sewage and tuberculosis, asthma and medicines, hospitals and schools, motorcars and pollution.

After the Second World War, as our family grew and urbanization moved families from the land to the towns, the extended family formed the Ngātokowaru Tribal Committee to represent the people. My grandfather Hohepa Jacob was elected chairman of the committee at its first meeting on the 7th of July 1946; my grandmother Lucy Atareti Jacob, daughter of Ema Hapai, was elected to the committee. She proposed that families be levied two shillings and sixpence (25 cents) per month to provide finance for the committee's activities. The committee met monthly in those postwar days in the meeting house at the marae on the rise beside the Hokio Stream. Their main concerns in the first year were the education of their children, access to health professionals for families, spiritual matters, and finding money to support the activities of the committee.

Our families today would argue that half a century later as we continue to meet on the fourth Sunday of each month for our subtribal meetings, we have those same concerns as our priority—attending church at the marae in the morning to meet our Christian obligations and in part our spiritual needs, wondering how we will meet the financial pressures of the day, planning for the secondary and postsecondary education of our children, and improving our health. The loss of most of the land around the marae remains a painful reality as our two neighbours grind up the surface of the road to the marae, knowing nothing of the history of the marae on their boundary. Over the years we have wondered how we might find opportunities to buy back some of the land that surrounds our ancestral home. It might be later in the 21st century before that happens and another generation will be our subtribe's leaders.

Do we dwell in the past, live in the present, or plan for the future? As Māori we do all of these things at the same time. I have been secretary of the marae committee since 1982, reflecting on the actions and advice of my Elders, dealing with current issues, and planning for our future. I will now give an overview of the activities of the marae and of the marae committee over this relatively short period.

Generation 2000

In 1975 a member of our subtribe named Whatarangi Winiata, who had been an academic in North America for 15 years, returned to Ngātokowaru and to New Zealand to settle at home permanently. He launched a tribal development program that was named Generation 2000. He wanted us to prepare for the 21st century and was clear that we should not just let things happen to us in a haphazard, even accidental way, but that we should take control of ourselves as a tribe and subtribe, set our goals, and aim for the stars. Our subtribe enveloped the development program Generation 2000 with considerable enthusiasm, as did Ngāti Raukawa, Ngāti Toa, and Te Atiawa, the confederation of three tribes located on the west coast of the North Island of Aotearoa. These three tribes have historical links and have been involved in cooperative ventures over time.

Generation 2000 was a further opportunity for a cooperative venture. The program had three streams—what Whatarangi called three missions. While the concept of missions has negative connotations for many Indigenous peoples because of the effects of the colonizing missions, it was reasoned at the time that not only would the tribal members require faith that missionaries possessed when they undertook missionary work, but we would also need a measure of "missionary zeal if the project is to succeed" (Winiata 1979: 69). Hence, the term *mission* was used to describe each stream.

The Education Mission included identifying 11 professions in which we thought we should be represented in greater numbers by the turn of the century. These were in accountancy, agriculture, architecture, dentistry, engineering, secondary school teaching, law, medicine, ministry, music, and veterinary science.

From this confederation of tribes five secondary school teachers were identified in 1975; the plan was to have 15 trained secondary school teachers by 1985 and 30 by 1990. Two medical doctors were identified as being from the confederation of tribes in 1975. The goal was to have 10 by 1990, 20 by 2000 (Winiata 1979: 72). Improved educational attainment was and is seen as a key to our future by the tribes and my subtribe. This education plan focused on the future.

A second stream was the Pākehā mission—a plan to educate non-Māori, Pākehā people about the culture, beliefs, and values of Māori people so that they would not only learn more positively about us, but they might also acknowledge our culture and identity, and our right to determine for ourselves our own future. It was proposed that we hold conferences and weekend seminars for Pākehā people on our marae to teach them about us. We would invite them into our marae world, which had remained a Māori world even after 200 years of intercultural contact.

The third stream was our own tribal mission, in which we would encourage our tribal members to return to ancestral and traditional homes to learn about ourselves, our history, and our traditional ways, and to make decisions about our future direction. During the mid-1970s many of our meeting houses and the surrounding marae and land were in a poor state of repair, having been neglected for a number of years. They were being used intermittently throughout the year, were regarded by many as dying institutions, and tended to be used for farewelling the dead. There were Elders who took the primary responsibility for maintaining the marae and buildings, but this often became a burden and the houses fell into disrepair. We had focused our energies on surviving in the Pākehā world; building our homes in the towns and suburbs, saving for mortgages and raising our children, only visiting the marae a few times during the year to meet our obligations to our Elders. The mission planned for our return to the marae to discuss its future and our future as Indigenous people. Today all 23 meeting houses in the confederation have been refurbished. Six have been rebuilt, one was opened in 1997, and many marae committees have rebuilt the dining rooms and other buildings associated with the complex.

As a marae committee we have been supporting Generation 2000 now for over 20 years. How have we done this? As a subtribe we have identified and encouraged our young people to be a part of the Education Mission. We hold seminars on our marae each year for the young people of the tribe to attend. These seminars may be for several days during school holidays or for a weekend. During this time genealogical links with one another are explored, educational aspirations discussed, and their educational needs identified. We have also invited young people to come to the marae to prepare for school examinations. Secondary schools in the region have cooperated by releasing examination candidates for a three- or four-day block, and as a tribe we have gathered strong and sympathetic school teachers to the marae to assist our students with examination techniques, confidence building, and goal setting, at the same time assuring them of our support. Each year our marae committee has strongly encouraged families to apply for scholarships for our children who attend secondary schools and postsecondary institutions. Though the amounts in terms of dollars received may be small, the children and families feel supported by the successful award of a scholarship, and it is hoped that in the future they may support others. We have also supported a total immersion Māori language week at the marae each year—a time for family and tribe to strengthen their skills in the Indigenous language.

The Pakeha Mission was a different challenge. In the late 1970s during the initial phases of the program, the Ngātokowaru Marae committee was one of the most active of the 23 marae committees of our region in terms of Pakeha Mission. We had completed and opened our new meeting house in March 1978—a larger, beautifully decorated house that could comfortably sleep 80 people and has over the years accommodated over a hundred visitors at a time. There has been a lot of interest from the Pākehā community in our tribal plan, and many groups have asked to bring their members to the marae to learn about the Indigenous people in their community. For four years after the opening of our house, we hosted groups at least once a month and at times more often. Schools wanted to bring their teachers for a marae experience for a weekend or their students for a day or up to a week, as did universities and colleges. Service clubs such as Rotary and Lions asked to bring their members. Television New Zealand arranged to bring their journalists to learn about the Māori people. Government agencies such as the Labor Department and the Education Department wanted their staff to experience such weekends. Church groups, community groups, foreign visitors, the young, and the old requested a weekend visit. Local Council members walked the banks of the Hokio Stream during visits and shook their heads at the levels of pollution from the lake and promised to help clean it up. Teachers undertook to provide greater help for Māori children in their schools.

We were inundated with requests, and we felt the strain. In some ways we were under a microscope, in a glass bowl. We sat at our monthly meetings, bombarded with requests and grappling with a process to deal with them. We had to prioritize requests and ask our families to spend their weekends at the marae hosting strangers. Some of these strangers were crass, insensitive, and patronizing; others were supportive and sensitive and went away genuinely grateful for an opportunity to know something about us, to learn about us in our own environment—our values, our hopes for the future, our aspirations and dreams. We sat on the veranda at dawn with some of our visitors watching the sun rise over the Tararua ranges and shared our worries about the future for our children. We hoped that they would all reflect upon their experience and their learning and respond to our people in more sensitive ways within the mainstream of society, particularly where they were in positions such as decision makers, employers, and teachers. We hoped that there would be mutual benefit that would extend into the future beyond a personally enjoyable weekend for an individual to a change in behavior or attitude in more meaningful ways. In some cases this has happened; in others we still wait for the benefits.

The marae committee continues to receive requests almost every month from groups that want to be invited to our marae for a weekend experience. The desire to have a challenging weekend reflecting on our history and debating the future still draws groups. Currently we have requests from a national museum group wanting to bring staff, from an Anglican church youth group, from a school wanting to bring 9- and 10-year-olds over two days, and from representatives of city councils wanting a conference venue. We consider these requests each month as well as receiving bookings from our own family who want to hold a wedding, a birthday, a meeting, a baptism of a child, or a family reunion.

The third stream or mission was a tribal mission in which we would offer opportunities for our own families to return to the marae and the meeting house to learn about ourselves. As a result of over 150 years of colonization, many family members now live as Pākehā people, only vaguely aware that they have what are called links to a marae and a tribe in the Horowhenua. Inevitably as we hosted groups from the other two streams, those of us who lived within sight of the Tararua ranges and could travel to the marae to assist with hosting the groups also learned about ourselves. We wanted to dedicate some weekends solely to ourselves so that we could concentrate on those things that were important to us as a subtribe. Relationships between families were examined, genealogies traced, customs and protocols explored so that we as a subtribe and groups of families grew stronger in the knowledge about ourselves. Many family members also learned the language and dedicated themselves to teaching their children their Indigenous language.

From this desire to teach the language, in the early 1980s a group of young parents gathered and decided that they wanted to return to the marae each day with their preschool children and operate their own preschool totally in the Māori language. The kohanga reo movement, an immersion preschool movement, was in its infancy in Aotearoa, and our young parents wanted to join the movement and dedicate themselves to reviving the language. They began in the marae garage, an iron-clad shed facing the same Tararua ranges and the rising sun. Each morning they arrived at 9 o'clock with their children and their packed lunches, and they offered their children a preschool opportunity immersed in the language that had been the only language spoken when our great-grandmother had settled and lived on that block of land 100 years earlier. Their days were spent near the site of the original house, which had been built of swamp weed, and which had housed the first children born there a century before. Granny Ema Hapai's great-grandchildren who had been born into a Pākehā-dominated world were being returned to their ancestral land to learn from their parents and family members in the language of our ancestors, our tupuna.

The Hokio stream provided a source of food, but nowhere near as abundant as in the pre-European days when the lake and stream were unpolluted and clean. Still the children learned about eeling and fishing, preparing food, and growing gardens. And, most importantly, they learned in the language of their great-grandmother.

By 1997 there were over 750 kohanga reo—immersion preschools—which were established by Māori and are determined and managed by Māori in Aotearoa. Some are small family preschools; others operate in similar ways to day care centers, opening for longer hours to provide child care service for working mothers. Kohanga reo are located in almost every community in New Zealand. They are supported by the families, the subtribes, and the tribes. They offer a Māori environment for Māori children to learn in the Māori language. They may well be responsible for the survival of the Māori language. A high level of commitment is required by families of the enrolled children because it is these families that manage the kohanga reo through parent committees.

At Ngātokowaru marae our kohanga reo began in the garage, and eventually in 1987 an old wooden house from the town was moved to the marae and placed on the rise beside the meeting house to be used as the kohanga reo. The community had raised the funds to renovate the house so that they would have a home dedicated to the purpose of offering a Māori preschool environment.

The house was renovated over the next year and formally opened in the autumn of 1988, 10 years after the new meeting house. In 1978 Ngātokowaru had been completed and opened at a formal traditional dawn ceremony. Because the kohanga reo was not a new building, it was decided by the marae committee chairman that a dawn ceremony was inappropriate and that we would invite family and tribal members to a dedication ceremony on a Sunday morning in May. There was great excitement among the children because they had a new home for their kohanga reo and among the parents because they had a home dedicated to the nurturing of their children. For grandparents it was exciting to know that their children's children would learn in the language that had been denied them in their education, and for the Elders and supporters of the marae and its people there was further evidence of flourishing activity and commitment by the younger generation. There have been struggles with keeping the kohanga reo at our marae active because it is located in a rural area that has no public transport and few of our families live within that area. Urban kohanga reo have continued to thrive and all are now part of a national organization.

Ngātokowaru marae and its people, the descendants of Pareraukawa, now face a critical time. Because of the Generation 2000 program, and also because of the growing strength of Māori people in society, we have over the past 20 years increased our knowledge about ourselves, and we are at a crossroads in needing a clear direction for our future as a people. We have hosted and continue to host hundreds of visitors to our marae, and we need to evaluate where we want our energies to go in the future. We have produced graduates in some of the 11 professions identified in the 1975 Generation 2000 Education Mission. Few of them live within our area, and we may aim to bring them back to spearhead a new education mission for our own hapū—subtribe. We are examining whether to continue with the same missions after the turn of the century, or whether we need a new burst of energy in another direction.

As a marae committee we continue to meet each month. The year 2000 marked our triennial election of officers. This group and committee have moved us into the new millennium and will serve Ngāti Pareraukawa until March 2003. The physical development of the marae has been extensive. Our buildings and assets now exceed half a million dollars. The grounds are well maintained; we now have tables and chairs and pots and stoves to prepare food for our visitors, and mattresses and linen for them to sleep on. However, the physical buildings are only a small part of the story.

We are still concerned that our human potential is not being realized. In many cases it is wasted. Many of our family are in jails, are unemployed, are in poor health; they suffer from alcoholism, drug addiction, family violence, asthma, obesity, diabetes, and smoking-related illnesses. Fay Selby-Law, who is a health professional, has asked the family to develop a health plan for the future. At a presentation to the marae committee in 1996, she challenged us to aim to have the best health in the world, to set goals in terms of our health as descendants of Pareraukawa. The marae committee has yet to respond to her challenges—perhaps afraid of facing our own weaknesses. While the Tainui people in the north have given notice that they aim to be smoke-free as a people by the year 2000, and many marae are now smoke-free, we sit in our meetings amid clouds of smoke and as yet are unable to take that step towards a smoke-free marae. Ironically, we have declared that the marae is to be drug-free, that illegal drugs are not to be brought to the marae, and we have a policy regarding limited use of alcohol on the marae, but we do not yet have a clear and visionary policy about our health.

As Māori we want to include within a health policy not only our physical health and the health of our families but also our spiritual and emotional health. We have a proposal, which has been tabled by Whatarangi Winiata and his son Huia, entitled "Ngāti Parerarukwa: A Case Study: Raising and Maintaining the health and wealth of the hapū." They have proposed a framework that we might use to evaluate our present status, to give us data to use in order to plan our future. We have a planning proposal currently being considered by our families. The challenge is to bring a good number of our people together and to find the balance between reflecting on the past and how things were done then and drawing us forward to seriously plan for a realistic future.

Conclusion

Much of the current energy in Māoridom is perceived to be going into researching historical grievances against the Crown—the partner to the Treaty of Waitangi signed in 1840 between Queen Victoria's representatives and the representatives of the Tribes of New Zealand. The New Zealand government was seen to reorder our priorities in 1995 when it announced that all historical claims had to be made and settled by 1999. While the Crown's proposal was unanimously rejected by Māoridom, many claimants moved into a frenzy of activity trying to register claims and find resources for researchers so that the claims could be settled. Within our own hapū we have our own Elders working in the area of Treaty claims as well as on many other fronts. They are often drained by the demands on their time and talents. Within this context, we are also asking for their leadership to assist in our own education, in extending our knowledge of our past, and developing a plan for the future. It feels as if we are asking our leaders and Elders to be superhuman. There is a sense of urgency to settle the past, deal with the present, and plan the future with limited financial resources and too few human resources with the necessary expertise to complete all that needs to be done.

In 1900 the Mayor of Auckland, our largest city in the north, arranged to have a monument erected on Maungakiekie, an extinct volcano now generally known as One Tree Hill. It was a memorial to the dying race—the Māori people. Our population at that time was at its lowest, having been reduced from an estimated 150,000 in 1800 to 43,000 in 1900. It was expected that we, like the volcano, would soon be extinct.

The Māori population now exceeds 500,000 and life expectancy nearly doubled in the 20th century (Durie 1994:63). There is little chance of us sharing the same fate as Maungakiekie and every reason for us to plan for the future. We have experienced a language revival, a revival at our marae, an increase in population, and an increase in life expectancy. Our children and grandchildren will again be bilingual, and the opportunity for them to grow up knowing who they are, where they come from, and where they are going is now theirs for the taking.

Our hapū is in better health than it was 100 years ago, our numbers are greater, and our life expectancy higher, our prospects for higher educational achievement have increased. We are far from extinction.

When the first rays of the sun glistened on the eastern horizon on January 1, 2000, our family sat quietly on the veranda at our ancestral home. The children moved softly; our mothers and grandmothers stared at the sun's rays, as their grandmother, Granny Ema Hapai, had done 100 years before from the same place. It was an awesome and moving experience. We were silently aware that none of us would be here to welcome in the New Year in 2100. We wondered whether our descendants will thank us for maintaining the marae, for leaving the legacy we have been left. As the sky slowly brightened and the light spread over our land, we peered into the half light across damp pastures, over the headstones in the cemetery, across the darkened lake to the deep blue mid-summer hills of Tararua, our mountain, grateful to those who have gone before us.

PART V
Culture and Language Survival

CHAPTER 12
FIGHTING THE WINDS OF CHANGE

By Bonnie Heavy-Runner

Bonnie Heavy-Runner (posthumous) was Director of the Department of Native American Studies at the University of Montana from 1991 until her passing away in 1997. She earned her bachelor's degree in social work in 1983 and her law degree in 1988. A highly respected educator, Bonnie was the driving force behind the creation of Montana's first Native American Studies major. In 1996 Bonnie received the Joann Youngbear Community Service Award for her contribution to the health, social, educational, spiritual, and cultural well-being of the local Indian community. In February 1997 she was presented with the Robert T. Pantzer Award, which recognizes an individual for making the University of Montana a more open and humane learning environment. Bonnie's dedication to her students and the Native American Studies Program made her passing away in November 1997 a great loss to her family, her daughter and son, the Blackfeet community, and many friends at the University of Montana.

By Darrell Robes Kipp

Darrell Robes Kipp is a grandson of Last Gun and Yellow Bird Woman. Last Gun was a survivor of the infamous 1870 Bakers Massacre on the Bear River in Montana. Darrell grew up in Blackfoot, Montana, and graduated from eighth grade in 1958 from a one-room school in Blackfoot. Subsequently he graduated from Browning High school in 1962, Eastern Montana College in 1966, Harvard University in 1975, and Vermont College. Darrell is one of the founders of the Piegan Institute founded in 1987, which researches, promotes, and preserves Native American languages. He is the Executive Director of Nizipuhwahsin (Original Language) Center. This center, which offers full day programming for children age 5 to 12, is nationally recognized as a successful and effective model for Native language immersion with a multigenerational approach. Nizipuhwahsin Center's mission is to use the Blackfeet language as the tool (not object) of instruction within a local context to produce fluent speakers of the Blackfeet language.

By Stephen Greymorning

Stephen Greymorning implemented the first language-immersion preschool classes on the Wind River Reservation in 1994. In 1995 he founded Hinono'eitiino'oowu' (Arapaho Language Lodge) and continues to serve as the Executive Director and founder of Hinono'eitiit Hoowu', the federally recognized nonprofit House of Arapaho Language.

SECTION ONE: A CULTURE IN CRISIS

By Bonnie Heavy-Runner

Introduction

To begin, acknowledgment is due my sisters Linda Warden, Iris Heavy-Runner, and Reno Cherette. I would also like to acknowledge Professor Greymorning, who approached me and asked if I would participate in a project that he was working on. He wanted to compile a book about Indigenous issues and it sounded like something that I would be interested in, so I thought about it for a while and told him that I would do it. A draft was finally turned in as a work in progress. The first thing I would comment on is that these are my memories and I believe that it is a privilege to have them shared. Probably some people who shared the same experience would have a different memory. But keep in mind that, as my memories, these are things that I see affecting the Blackfeet people as we have moved through a period of time.

The name of this chapter is "Fighting the Winds of Change: A Culture in Crisis." This has been written from a personal perspective and is intended to focus only on the Blackfeet nation. The issue of cultural crisis will touch all Indigenous peoples at some point. I will bring the reader through a period of time in which the Pekani (Blackfeet) people's way has been impacted through education, politics, and personal choice. I will use the Thunderpipe Ceremony as a point of reference.

The Good Old Days

I was born in 1951. My earliest memories of a sacred ceremony began when I was about six years old. As children we were accepted and included in any event. This meant that there would be a lot of us running around, playing, listening, crying, sleeping, and wallowing in an experience we did not understand. Our mothers would instruct us in a gentle but firm manner that we should behave and be respectful. This guidance led us to the doors of many homes in which sacred ceremonies were held. The host welcomed, fed, and tolerated everyone, even the children.

As a child I enjoyed watching the old people arrive. They were our dignitaries. At that time we treated them with ultimate respect, ever watchful of their dignity as spiritual ambassadors. I listened to my mother and relatives tell stories of each one as they arrived and were seated. It was obvious that there were clear boundaries within the ceremony for men and women.

The most remarkable aspect of this memory is that with the exception of the children, 85 percent of those present spoke the language. One could take all the knowledge and speaking ability of us as children, and it would not equal a fluent speaker, unless you were a child from Star School, Heart Butte, or Canada, where the Blackfoot language was used. The new education system had created an impact on our language in less than 30 years. The third generation's cultural voice was caught in our throat and we did not realize it at the time.

As children we did not need to be told that the ceremony was starting. You could sense it. A hush would travel around the room, out the door, and into your spirit. I remember feeling fearful at the power produced by prayer that was expressed in its purest form, Blackfeet style. As children we could not understand what the medicine people were saying, but because you were immersed in the experience you knew it was prayer. My memory is slightly foggy, but I do recall several men who were noted for their ability to dance. When they would stand up, we were hushed by grandmas, aunts, mothers, and cousins. No one looked at them or made a move. My heartbeat quickens even now at the thought of that first drumbeat signaling the beginning of a spiritual ballet.

Most of these ceremonies were held in small houses. There was standing room only, and so the overflow would hover outside the door. No one ever complained about the space.

Names are important in this first memory because they no longer exist except in our minds. When the first generation began to die, we started a painful shift of learning that included the second generation. I'll discuss this later. The men had names like Dan Bullplume, Charles Rebis, Charlie Horn, Fish Wolfrope, John Ground, James Whitecalf, Juniper Old Person, Bear Medicine, Old Chief, Morning Gun, Theodore Last Star. These men were viewed as holy. To call their names out loud now in mistake would summon energy that I am not prepared for. I do recognize that this energy is like a music, and it is very tempting, especially when you miss the good old days.

The men would arrive with their wives to take their designated places. The ceremony would not begin unless certain individuals were present. Waiting was an art and was incorporated into the culture through the value system known as patience. When the dancers began, we would tremble with fear because they were so powerful. I remember wanting to stare but being afraid that I would be singled out. It seemed that the first dancers would compete in a gentle sort of way for the audience's praise. Each dancer would carefully select an item from the holy bundle and prepare it for use. The preparation to dance was intense because of the prayer. We all prayed with the dancers so that nothing would drop on the floor. If something fell, it was a bad sign that required attention to prevent disaster. I didn't understand all of this at the time because of my age. As I grew older, the implications were obvious to me. Today the sight of something falling from the medicine pipe creates a spiritual anxiety that is comparable to mass hysteria without the radical expression.

Special people are designated to pick up the fallen item. The dancer then makes an announcement that includes asking for forgiveness, prayer for his family, and a vow to feed the pipe at some future date. I have seen the old men cry out, which is a rare expression among our people. The incident would be talked about for days if not for months. If fate dictated that the individual or family member suffered some illness or tragedy, the point of reference for answers would be the ceremony. This type of respect had its place in preserving the sacred nature of the ceremony and a way of living right. It also served to promote the event as a central aspect of Blackfeet cultural ways at that time.

The ceremony seemed to take a lot of time when we were small because of the dancers. Included in this was the ritual of being painted with the sacred paint from the bundles. I grew up being told not to wash my face until after sundown in honor of the Creator. As children we would line up to participate in this ritual. It seemed as though the old woman's hands were made of silk as she would slowly draw the sacred marks, praying with each stroke of her fingers. As we stood and turned, gentle hands would guide us back through the crowd. I remember feeling slightly embarrassed because everyone was watching. When we went outside, we would compare paint marks; it was a way of belonging to our people. Each part of the ceremony served to reinforce our identity. No one openly spoke of being Indian at that time. We were comfortable in our own way with who we were.

Food is viewed as a vehicle for spiritual expression in this ceremony. As small children it was novel to attend these events because of the food. Our parents knew this, and so we were carefully instructed about eating and praying. It was important to understand the protocol around food. An example is berry soup. This is a central aspect of our sacred ceremonies. Each summer women and children would go into the river areas and mountains to pick servisberries, chokecherries, and huckleberries for ceremonies. We never dreamed that canned fruit would someday be used for the soup in some of the ceremonies. The berry soup is carefully prepared by the cooks and is usually served warm. It is sweet and full of bitterroot or other roots. As children we would wait for this moment only to wait again. The ceremony required prayers of thanksgiving. This meant that you were instructed to take a single berry and hold it while you prayed. The problem with this is that often you had to wait until all of the soup was given out, which could take a long time to a child. It was a great relief when we were allowed to eat the soup.

My children participate in this waiting ritual today, and there are no questions asked. The important point to this berry story is that the offering was a dividing line for personal knowledge and responsibility. It also served to teach patience. The dividing line occurs at about three years old. Before this, children are allowed to make mistakes because they are children. Careful instructions are given about not eating the berry until the prayers are offered. I consider this sacred teaching. If a small child eats the berry or the soup, no one gets upset. By the time you are three, you are expected to know what to do. As children we would police each other about the ritual. The beauty of the extended family is that we become caretakers of communal spirituality, even as children. I see the ritual of berry soup continuing through today, and it still serves as the same teaching tool.

Each year the ceremony followed the same pattern and time frame. After the first thunderstorm announcements would go out about dances. All of the communication was word of mouth. As children we moved with the times. I don't recall thinking of the ceremony until the time arrived. As we grew, so did our knowledge base. Modeling is important because that is what Indian parents did for their children. I remember watching my mom and dad in the spring. When it would thunder, they would look at the sky and look at each other and some thoughts would pass between them that we could not hear. Almost always they would pass these signals about the meaning of the first thunder. An explanation of this exchange would be to understand it as a sign from the Creator that it was time to open the bundles. The thunder represented the call from nature.

As I grew, the questions about the ceremony increased. Today I find myself pausing during a rainstorm to listen to the thunder. If I hear it, I wonder if someone at home is planning a medicine pipe dance. I strain emotionally, yearning to be a part of the ceremony. Now my questions have new meaning because I am older and I have my children to raise in this way.

From the Sacred to the Profane

In this second part I want to make a transition in moving away from this cultural concept of the sacred. I don't know how old I was when Catholicism was introduced. I do remember being tall enough to see over the top of the teacher's desk. It was summer and school was out. We were told that some Catholic nuns were coming to hold classes for our first communion. I was typical for a seven- or eight-year-old, bored and curious. The nuns who came to Browning fascinated me with their habits. They were dressed in long brown robes with white veils. I thought they looked like penguins. We had classes in the old elementary school. The goal was to learn about the sacrament, memorize the prayers, and have fun doing arts and crafts. All of this moved you toward making your first communion. I didn't know what this meant at the time. During the course of the summer I found myself feeling sick at the thought of eating Jesus because the nuns told us that the host was his body. As children we shared numerous stories, none of which were very true about this act. In addition, I could not imagine drinking blood and felt very lucky when we didn't have to do this.

A week before the ceremony of first communion my mother bought me a special white dress with a veil. She said this represented purity, and I was very proud. I was excited until the nun teacher told me that I might not pass the class because I would not memorize the prayers. I could not understand this concept because I was used to seeing people pray from their hearts. Did they memorize the prayers they offered in ceremony? I asked myself.

The night before communion I was sitting in the basement of the rectory with one of the meanest nuns. She was old and very impatient. She told me over and over again that there wasn't much hope for me in heaven because I would not memorize the prayers. Finally, I decided to show her that I knew what to do. I passed her test and marched down the aisle the next day with my class. Because we were children, we followed the leader very well. We did not question authority. We believed the nuns when they taught us about God being everywhere and punishing our sins. Prior to this I did not know about sin. After this I remember hiding or helping friends hide when we would do something that we perceived as wrong, fearful that God would punish us.

We lived a half a block from the church. Each day I would make the sign of the cross in passing because it was God's house and I was afraid of being struck down. You can imagine the depth of my fear when a man died in front of the church from a heart attack. I didn't know why he died, and for the longest time I believed that he must have done something very wrong to make God that angry.

During this period of our being Christianized there was an absence of Blackfeet ceremonies. I began to question a wrathful God, feeling resentful that someone was always watching me. I could not accept that what I felt in my heart was not right. I listened with keen interest to stories about mean priests who would embarrass our tribal members when they went to confession. I could not understand their ability to represent God and their tendency to berate people in public. This is a violation of our value system, and the conflict for me was never settled. I have always wondered about the silence displayed by the victims of this dogma. Today I understand our cultural way of communicating, and it is sad that some people never got the chance to stand up for who they were, Pekani.

The priests and nuns were intolerant of our value system. They did not understand that it is wrong to chastise a person in public. They wielded their power so well that people would tremble in fear at the mention of a certain priest's name, Father Gillin. This man was a spiritual tyrant, and he was shameless in my eyes. I recall many instances of standing in line on a Saturday for confession. I would watch the adults go into the booth smiling and come out crying. This was always confusing. Finally, one day this man was yelling so loud at a woman that everyone could hear him. We all exchanged glances. Slowly people began to leave the church.

When I went into the booth, the fear of this man would confuse me. I would not know what to say. I would forget all the sins I had planned to talk about.

The end result was a child making up what she believed to be sins and a priest who did not know the difference and did not care. He would take great pride in assigning penance.

During my entire association with the Catholic Church, I never saw anything Indian. In fact some of the priests discouraged people from attending ceremonies. But today most churches in Indian communities have incorporated many Native aspects, including beadwork, pipes, sweet grass, drums, and songs. I personally resent this and feel that it is a form of exploitation of a person's need to feel welcome. This is a dichotomy that will never be reconciled because we have moved so far from our roots. Where is the happy medium? I ask myself. At this time there is none and so I made a personal choice to leave it all behind. Many have made the same decision and never returned.

I attended Chilocco Indian School in Oklahoma all four years of high school. I had never been away from home before, and I didn't know about identity and so it wasn't an issue because no one talked to us about it. Chilocco was a federal Indian boarding school established during the assimilation period. It was based on military philosophy and, when I first attended in 1966, not much had changed except that we didn't wear uniforms and march around. The focus was on academics, vocations, and activity. The only opportunity for cultural identity expression came in the spring during a cultural pageant. The school officials planned this for surrounding communities that were primarily white. It was my first exposure to dances and ceremonies from other tribes. I don't recall Blackfeet being chosen to represent anyone. I assumed it was because the school was in Oklahoma and they were in control. The point of relating this experience is that I went through four years of high school isolated from any Native cultural activity. The school was not bound to offer or promote cultural identity. As students we were oppressed and did not question it.

The closest city, Arkansas City, was in Kansas four miles away. There were many times that we were mistreated in this local city. No one stood up for us. No one saw; no one cared. We felt shamed because we were Indian. I actually came to accept this difference in treatment as being normal. This was the darkest part of my life as a cultural being. I didn't have any connection with my early foundation of ceremony; I had left the conditioning of the church behind and I was lost.

Our tribe holds sacred ceremonies in the fall, winter, and spring. When I returned for the summer, everyone had finished their vows and the focus was on the local powwow. I did not seek out spiritual connections because I was a teenager, more interested in the social scene. My center became my friends at that time.

Shifting the Cultural Paradigm

The ceremonies that we grew up with began to fade in the late 1950s because the first generation was dying and no one had taken their place. Alcohol played a significant role in crippling a desire to carry on the traditions. Some of the young men who should have been heir to a sacred bundle died before their parents from cirrhosis or accidents. It was at this point that people would talk about how alcohol was consuming our tribe. They were sad that even the sacred ceremonies could not keep someone sober. On more than one occasion key individuals would show up under the influence of alcohol, which was frowned upon. Slowly, ceremonies began to fade. Elders made the decision to transfer their rights to someone outside of the family. This is significant because some of the sacred bundles were actually sold to private collectors either by the owner or by a family member suffering from alcohol.

My grandmother, Grasswoman, made the choice when she was near 80 years old to seek out a couple that she felt would carry on the traditions of her pipe. Her old man died in 1951. She looked for a long time. When she made her choice, it was supported by her children out of respect. I didn't know at the time how the grandchildren felt. The transfer took place and was left alone for several years.

Browning was established by key families that still reside on the reservation. Businesses flourished when the agency was moved from Old Agency to Browning proper. The first trading post was started by Thadeus Scriber. It was called Browning Mercantile or Browning Merc or Scriber's depending on whom you talked to. Thadeus had two sons, Harold and Robert. Harold followed his father's lead and carried on with the store until his death in the mid-1980s. Robert was a teacher and taught music locally until he began his art business. Thadeus Scriber was accepted in the community. He extended credit to almost everyone he knew. Some tribal members suffered from extremes of poverty after the buffalo disappeared. The rations provided by the government were sparse and not enough to feed families. A family of four received a pound of meat each week. It is no wonder that historic photos showed Blackfeet women and children in slaughterhouse yards pulling entrails out of the sheds. It became a secondary food source that history portrayed as barbaric, but it kept us alive. Because of the poverty and the influx of traders, some members traded or sold whatever they possessed. It is unfortunate that this included sacred objects. Our oral historians relate how old people loaned articles to Scriber, and I want you to consider that word *loaning* as opposed to *selling* or *exchanging*, because in the Blackfeet way, that seemed to be the interpretation. The issue remains whether the traders returned the items or kept them when bills were paid.

In 1988 Thadeus Scriber's son Robert sold the collection that the family had amassed to the Provincial Museum in Edmonton, Alberta. Included in the collection were several sacred objects such as bundles and pipes. My grandfather Heavy-Runner's medicine pipe was in the collection and was valued at $125,000. The sale was and still is controversial because it marks a place in our history as Blackfeet people when our basic foundation slipped through our fingers for money. It also marks the passing of a system of belief that was based on goodwill and spiritual respect. When our medicine man lit the transfer pipe and handed it to the museum curator and he accepted it, we all wanted to believe that it would be the key to repossession of our sacred items. We were very wrong. The pipe meant nothing to the curator. As we moved down that hall to the room where the collection was displayed, my heart was in my throat. I cried as I saw the collection behind 12-foot walls of plexiglass. The sacred bundles were placed the highest out of reach. I was embarrassed to watch the Elders beg the curator to touch the bundles, to take care of them, they said. Finally, he relented and the bundles came down. I cried with the old women as they talked to the spirits and called them friend. The next 20 minutes were a blur.

A young member of our tribe made the personal decision to capture the pipe Blackfeet-style. When he picked up the last star pipe and called out, no one answered but the museum people and I wondered why. They wanted him to put it down and he refused. The room was sealed off with security, the Elders were taken by surprise; they didn't want any trouble, and they began to talk to the young man. I witnessed the struggle between generations. I could see at that point that he was committed and didn't care what would happen. Finally, out of respect, with tears in his eyes, he handed the pipe to the curator and walked out. When I left the building, I could feel a thousand spirits hovering around us. I saw the young man crying, angry and confused because their whole belief system had crumbled in less than an hour. It was a long trip home that day in the midst of a very powerful thunderstorm, which was very symbolic. It seemed that day we acquiesced to a system that would continue to be more powerful because of money and sovereignty.

Since 1988 change has continued among our people. The Elders continue to grow old and leave us. Ceremony is changing because there is a language gap. Some Elders talk of retiring their bundles because they don't feel secure in the transfer. Some of my generation are trying to fit in. They are taking classes in language and setting up apprenticeships with Elders to learn the way. It is encouraging when you see someone being groomed as a singer because most of the singers are also gone and they are critical to the ceremony. I see great hope when I attend a ceremony where there are over 200 people and there is still standing room only.

In the spring of 1997 I went to a pipe ceremony in Browning once again. I watched the young men help one of the Elders to his feet and stand in for him during the dance because he was too old and feeble to dance by himself. My heart felt good when I watched a young pipe holder pick up the sacred pipe and gracefully step out into the middle. His head was high, back straight, and eyes on the Creator as he gently moved around the room. Suddenly, I knew that hope is real for the Blackfeet people. We have a lot to learn, and this includes trusting each other as people to do the right things—our way.

SECTION TWO: A CULTURE IN RENAISSANCE

By Darrell Robes Kipp and Stephen Greymorning

In Section One of "Fighting the Winds of Change," Bonnie reflected on the crises that face Blackfeet culture. Much of that crisis came about during the 20th century. One area of crisis was to the Blackfoot language and came as a result of the boarding school experience. The impact that boarding schools had was not limited to the Blackfeet, since a primary goal for the vast majority of

Indian boarding schools throughout North American was to eradicate Indigenous peoples' languages. Boarding schools brought about a significant decline in the population of fluent language speakers throughout North America, and severely diminished the vitality of Indigenous North American languages and the continuity of languages being transmitted to younger generations. For the Blackfeet, as well as for other Indigenous peoples, language loss has created a language gap between Elders and youth that can ultimately impact ceremonies. Two reasons can be given for this. One reason is that certain phrases carry different meanings within ceremonies, and the other reason is that some phrases do not readily translate into English. For example, the phrase "ciinóh-woo" means "pour it," but within a certain ceremonial context, it will mean "quit dancing."[1] Because language and ceremonies are markers of culture, language loss further adds to the culture crisis.

At the end of Bonnie's article, she spoke of watching a young man pick up a ceremonial pipe and how his movement around the room with it made her realize that hope is real for the Blackfeet people. One Sunday evening in June 2002, I (Stephen Greymorning) had the opportunity to speak with Darrell Robes Kipp of the Blackfeet nation. We spoke casually about a number of things regarding Bonnie's article and the Blackfoot language. Darrell had this to say about "Fighting the Winds of Change" and the connection between language and culture.

> First of all the paper that was written by Bonnie, in my opinion, was an excellent recollection on her part and she really brought out the beauty and the purist elements that are present even today in the Thunder Pipe Ceremony. I also want to acknowledge that I felt what she wrote was important in that it was able to capture some of the very subtle and beautiful nuances of the Thunder Pipe Ceremony.
>
> As far as the connection between language and culture, the word *culture* is often used with Native peoples in reference to elements such as ceremonies and material culture, dancing, and singing. On some level I feel the word does not fully capture the spirit and determination of people when they are practicing the elements that have been important to their heritage for the past several hundred years. I was very impressed and moved by her ability to capture the experience of being in the Thunder Pipe Ceremony. For example, one of the things she writes about is when she had her face painted. Recently, they opened the Thunder Pipe at the sound of the first thunder. I was present at one of the openings and one of the things that both captured my imagination and the moment happened after the painting of the faces. A group of about eight or nine young women, dressed in long dresses with their hair braided and their shawls and moccasins still on, had had their faces painted and were sitting in a cluster on the floor near the front of the ceremony. They were very beautiful in how relaxed and very comfortable they were. The scene, in my mind, related to me the continuum of the various culture elements still very much present within many tribes. Although we may worry about the demise or weakening of cultures, we should be encouraged when we see that these ceremonies today are still holding true to the fashion of the tribe years after Bonnie attended. And, although the ongoing practice of tribal traditional ceremonies is often seen as an archaic residue of a past era, these ceremonies are in fact well attended in the modern day. There is the saying good things stay the same, and it applies to

tribal ceremonies today. An older friend shared with me the thrill of taking her young granddaughter this past summer (2002) to a long-standing tribal ceremony. She said it was special because she remembered her participation in the ceremony as a child, and more so, because her great-grandfather conducted the ritual many times in his lifetime. If we consider the continuum involved in her story, it becomes clear tribal people have not abandoned their ceremonies as popular fallacy may imply.

For Darrell, the stability of Blackfeet ceremonies rests upon their continued presence and practice through successive generations. When bringing language into the picture, it can be said that language stability, like ceremony, similarly rests upon a continued presence of application and use through succeeding generations. And, in spite of continued assault, with language-immersion efforts at work among the Blackfeet, its presence is bridging a gap between young and old and helping to keep the language viable.

> Despite being under a severe siege mentality in educational and social institutions to eradicate Native languages in favor of American English, there is no reason to believe tribal members do not still hold their language in high regard and continue to use it for their own benefit, or comfort. In addition, Native American educators have utilized their acquired knowledge about educational formats to come to a better understanding of the merits of revitalizing the tribal language in the Native American community and classrooms. A strong review of language-acquisition formats clearly supports the merit of inclusion of a tribal language into the learning environments of Native children. Today one of the great challenges to those educators knowledgeable of the merits of multiple language-acquisition formats is to persuade fellow teachers and an education cadre to at least investigate the basis of these successful teaching and learning methods.

As Darrell became more involved in studying the Blackfoot language, he was naturally drawn by his intuition and strict obligation as a speaker and advocate of the language to attend various ceremonies. While he has remained committed to this for about 10 years now, it has only been in the last five years that he has been aware of a change.

> For example, for many years, there was a lull within the older generations to transfer ceremonial rites to younger individuals in the tribe. Part of their concern was to not have the ceremony lose its purity of form and maybe a questioning of the responsibility levels of younger people. The younger individuals seeking to have these ceremonies transferred were subject to lengthy periods of participation in the ceremony before deemed ready to be handed over the important roles of ceremonial keepers. Today, almost all of the important long-standing ceremonial rites are conducted by middle-aged people. Again, according to the assimilation fallacy that these younger generations were too far removed from their heritage responsibilities to be interested in a serious participation in the ceremonial continuum proved to be untrue. Today, particularly through the auspices of federal repatriation legislation that allows for bundles and various religious artifacts to be returned to the tribe and put back into use, many more younger people are seeking the teachings that will enable them to obtain rights to conduct many of the original ceremonies.

What I have seen over the last five years are that those people who are knowledgeable and who possess the rights to transfer the cultural elements to younger people have been doing so in full force within the Blackfoot confederacy and particularly on the Blackfeet reservation. For example, this spring, at the sound of thunder, at least three Medicine Pipe ceremonies were held. The ceremonies were all conducted by young Pipe holders under the age of 50, who now are bona fide and accepted as keepers of these Bundles. These husband and wife teams have developed a respect from the communities to conduct these ceremonies. Because the older leaders of these ceremonies were strict in how they transferred these rights and rituals, it is safe to say that these ceremonies are being conducted exactly in the fashion that they were conducted throughout the history of the tribe, and this is extremely heartening.

The crucial importance handed down by the older generations is the responsibility of keeping the ceremonies intact as they were handed down to them from generations past. This is why my friend can feel thrilled at the aspect of her granddaughter being in a ceremony being conducted precisely as it was in her day, and in the days of her great-grandfather, and for that matter, his grandfather. This type of continuation is the legacy of the strength of tribal heritage and illustrative of what responsible homogeneous people can maintain regardless of the intensity of an unbridled assimilation campaign against their rituals and language. It also speaks to why a tribal language should be revitalized and used in a modern context: because it serves a purpose to a group of people long connected in body and mind to origin practices. It is obvious preservation of heritage elements can be done successfully in an assimilation society. Amongst the Blackfeet confederacy, which includes three tribes in Canada, there are at least a dozen long-standing ceremonies held each year conducted by a new generation of keepers. There have been three Beaver Bundle openings that I know of and also each summer at least three of the Medicine Lodges have been held. So we see amongst the Blackfeet confederacy ceremonies very much present and continuing to be carried on.

Not losing sight of the language issue, I again pressed Darrell for his thoughts on the relationship of language and ceremony.

I think the language-revitalization movement amongst the tribes, although not directly connected to tribal ceremonies per se, has gone hand-in-hand in supporting a better understanding of the rituals and ceremonies. And those people who have become involved with the various ceremonies realize the importance of the language always being present in the ceremonies. So now you can go to the ceremonies and often see very young children who are students in the language program attending the ceremonies. So I am confident that there are very strong elements to keep and maintain these rituals and ceremonies and that these elements tend to support each other even when they are not directly related.

This is reflected in the need to begin to utilize new words and images in describing contemporary Native American communities. Although there is a strong emphasis on the words and images of the past, an entirely new era has emerged in need of a much more sophisticated lexicon than what has been handed down and ingrained in contemporary usage. The fact is revitalization of tribal languages, as well as the many other updated heritage factors, requires new words and images to move it well beyond the confines of the restrictive days of the past.

There is no reason to doubt the articulate fluency of a young child in their tribal language and English at the same time, or insist young children cannot successfully think in more than one language. Insistence on monolingual students in the name of educational process is on inspection actually anti-intellectual since it places limitations on the capacity of the human brain. Further, in regards to Native American children, it insinuates only one social matrix is acceptable, and denigrates cross-cultural behavior and mores as unnecessary or divisive. In order to deflate notions of monolingual and mono-cultural superiority, I advocate a closer inspection of the definitions used on and too often by Native Americans themselves. For example, the fragmentation terminology of yesteryear has no place in today's emerging tribal populations. The use of terms such as "mixed breed," "half-breed," and even "full blood" is in this day and age archaic and defenseless. The use of the word "traditionalist" is wide spread in the lexicon of Native American descriptions, along with "elder," "medicine man," and other age-old definitions. Along with the pedigree or blood quantum-based inflammatory wordings, these words imply a primordial or primitive life way and mind view, and cannot convey the reality of Indian life today. Must everyone who respects their tribal beliefs and rituals be first a medicine man or woman? I say no more than all Christians must be priests or pastors in order to embrace their religion. The definition of traditionalist today seems to be those who speaks their tribal language and hold true to the past knowledge base with the implication that a refusal to embrace change is paramount to the term. In fact, children today in tribal language-immersion programs know their tribal language, have consummate knowledge of their tribe, as well as the greater English-speaking society, and would be better termed "modernists," than the archaic term "traditionalist."

Darrell's journey as a leader, pioneer, and advocate of the Blackfoot language came after years of absence from the reservation. After his return in 1980, he spent about five years getting settled and grounded back home before he began to get involved in the work of studying the Blackfoot language. Specifics of this time and what actually motivated him to get involved in the language revitalization movement were explained as follows.

One of the things that occurred to me when I returned was that the language was not a daily presence in the way I had remembered it in the late 50s and early 60s as a child and a young man. During the early 1980s, in discussions with other colleagues my age, one of the things that occurred to us was that we had a desire to learn more about the language. That led to the early elementary study of the Blackfoot language. This was difficult at the time because we did not know of much material. We were not aware that any material was readily available on the language. Also, there was still reluctance on the part of fluent speakers to teach or share the language, and this was a result of the conditioning reproaches they had as young children. But by 1985 at least 20 or 30 community people, along with myself, spent quite a bit of time investing and writing to libraries, archives and others, trying to recover Blackfoot dictionaries, grammars and other materials on the language. Probably by 1990 we had collected practically every written piece on the language available. In 1994 we began a serious effort to learn and teach the language. As a consequence, by 1995 we built a one-room school and a number of very young children were placed in it. We began to seriously consider teaching children to become fluent speakers, because by that point we had figured out that the mechanical apparatus and technology weren't going to do us any good. It wasn't going to do us any good to record language on CD-ROM or to write another linguistic study, although getting those things done are important, because at that juncture the fluent speakers who were still left were all over the age of 60, and their numbers were dwindling. We realized the real important issue was to teach very young children the language so they could become fluent speakers. One thing simply led to another; the desire to learn the language led us to research it and collect the materials. After a thorough collection of the materials was completed, we then believed we could study and learn to speak the language. This led us to a whole series of experimenting with different techniques of learning the language. We mimicked some of the standard language approaches utilized at universities and public schools, and ultimately settled on a technique that was defined and developed by Dr. James Asher called Total Physical Response (TPR). This was a real breakthrough for us because it allowed us to learn the language quickly. That led us to the notion that having learned the language we could not only teach it, but that it could be learned and taught in a relatively effective and efficient way. This led to the building of the first school and then the first school led to the second and ultimately the third. So all and all, just simply starting with the basic personal desire to know more about the language has developed into what we call the Nizipuhwahsin or a large-scale language program on this reservation for children.

For the Blackfeet, this large-scale language program moved through a number of stages, starting at one level with a particular methodology and then moving on to another level until it eventually reached an immersion methodology. The early days of Blackfoot language restoration primarily involved adults, especially adults who had a special interest or a strong personal desire to learn the language. During this early period adult instruction usually came in the form of learning words from word lists, learning grammatical structures, and using standard memorization techniques. For Darrell and his efforts to bring about the type of changes that would help keep the Blackfoot language alive and healthy, the break finally came when in 1993 he had the privilege of visiting a Hawaiian Punana Leo immersion school. Here he got to see immersion classroom techniques, and children literally staying in the tribal language all day.

> This really impressed us because it was an answer to something we had been thinking about, particularly those adults in the program who had children. They had been teaching their children at home in the same fashion they were being taught. Suddenly it was presented to us that we could go the complete route and simply begin to teach children much the way that any child is taught his or her first language at home. By 1995 we, along with a group of people from the community, decided that we wanted to have a small classroom where we could teach children. We kept on with the adult learning programs, but we added the one-room school. So in 1995 we built a small one-room school, located on four city lots. We teamed up a fluent speaker with a teacher trainer and had 20 children between the ages of two and three, because we understood

that by starting them as early as possible they had the best chance for success. I believe for the most part out of those 20 children a majority of them are still with us, and they are now in fourth, fifth, and sixth grades. Once we realized the success of the immersion program, then we stuck with it as the key to saving the language and have become strong advocates of that system. Although we don't denigrate other systems, we believe those tribes that have severe pressure to save their language, or have very limited number of fluent speakers left, should concentrate on developing immersion schools to try and increase the number of fluent-speaking children as much as possible. Then if they want to continue with other formats at the same time, that's fine and dandy. The key, however, is producing children as speakers; I can see no other alternative to saving or revitalizing a language without the aid of children. Still, after 20 years of toiling in this field, there are those occasions when I wonder if we will be all right.

Although my own entry into this field of language revitalization was only 10 years ago, I too have known those occasions as times that test one's soul. This is not made any easier by persistent questions that demand justification of the work. I asked Darrell to comment on this.

I am often asked why anyone would bother to revitalize a tribal language. All I can reply is that if one is a member of a tribe, and holds that dear, then as a responsible citizen of that tribe it is his job to hold the tribe together as much as he can possibly do. When enough do, then people will rejoice, as my friend did, when they bring a grandchild to a ceremony and relish in its purity, strength, and celebration. This is the result of the work of those responsible tribal members who understood the notion good things can stay the same.

By 1996 things were pretty much in full swing, and with each passing year Darrell had groups of children coming into the school and moving up through the grades. At this point in time he had approximately 60 children involved in Blackfoot language-immersion classes. One of the strong aspects of this is that between 1995 and the year 2000, some children had spent three to four successive years in this language-learning program. In 2001 there were 40 children in the immersion program, and they are expecting 40 students to begin the program in September 2002. The language revitalization work is yielding impressive results, and to this end Darrell had more impressive results to share.

Since 2000, and over the past two years, we have had five students complete the eighth grade. Two of these students probably represent the ideal situation, finishing the eighth grade with exceptional academic achievement, as well as being extraordinarily fluent in the Blackfoot language and also able to read and write in the language. The true goal of the school is to produce healthy Blackfeet children with choices that lead to parity.

With regard to "Fighting the Winds of Change," the latter part of the article depicted an event in which a young man helped an elder to his feet and stood in for him during one of the dances. For numerous Indigenous North American communities the future well-being of a tribe and its youth is of primary importance, a focus also very much a part of the Blackfeet immersion movement.

Having had over 60 children go through the immersion schools up to the eighth grade, Darrell related what these children represent to the Blackfeet people as far as the survival of Blackfeet culture and language.

I consider them of paramount importance, and I will give you an illustration. In every tribal community where I have been a visitor or have at some level taken part in a ceremony, almost all tribal ceremonies and gatherings begin with a prayer. It is very important to tribes to open almost any event, be it a powwow, funeral, an informal community gathering, or a formal tribal council meeting, with a prayer. So the whole spectrum of tribal activities is usually based on a prayer or an oratory in the language. What has happened in the Blackfeet tribe and other tribes is that the number of individuals who fill this role, who are respected within the community and who are viewed as holy people, have diminished greatly. Additionally the majority of them who can still do this are for the most part home bound and are not able to attend all the functions as they did when they were younger. So it is really a special occasion when one of these individuals is able to come to a naming ceremony or a wedding or any activity and deliver the blessing.

I had made a statement that I almost had to take back when I said that by the year 2005 fluent-speaking students from the Nizipuhwahsin School will begin to fulfill the role of those venerated older people. When I made that statement, people believed it to be a rather brash statement and thought that 2005 was too early. What has already begun to happen is that the students and children noted for their speaking ability in the school, all the way down to the very young children, have already been called upon by the tribal council to deliver the opening prayer at a variety of gatherings. Some of the older seventh- and eighth-grade students who are extremely good, fluent speakers and attend many tribal ceremonies such as the pipe ceremonies and the medicine lodge ceremonies and are well schooled and versed in tribal protocol, etiquette, and responsibilities have more and more been asked to get up and deliver these prayers. This has had a double impact in which the community is extremely impressed and moved by these children, and also by the children's mature way of delivering the prayers and delivering them correctly in fulfilling a role that previously was held only by older people. I believe that as the years go by and as these children become older, they will almost exclusively fulfill the role of delivering the tribal prayers in the language. I also believe that they will serve as the orators of the language as a result of the number of the fluent speakers in the older-age categories becoming fewer and fewer.

Now, when I've been at Pipe Dances and other ceremonies, I recognize that at least half of the children present are also members of the immersion-school program. So when Bonnie indicated a culture in crisis, I think that she would be moved and happy to hear that today the culture is not so much in crisis as it is in a state of evolving, and that some of the obstacles of the past have been removed. She would also be pleased to know of the positive community involvement that is taking place. For the community these signs are a strong indication that the continuation of cultural elements that so many people have worried about will not disappear. It is a never-ending battle, though, as it is not something that is ever guaranteed. Nevertheless, I am seeing a renaissance and revitalization of culture and language beginning to move through the community. I feel that with support and continued efforts language immersion will do a great deal to enhance this cultural involvement in a manner that will move it away from a culture in crisis toward a cultural renaissance.

NOTE

1. For a more in-depth discussion of how language shapes perception and reality, see Benjamin Whorf, *Language, Thought and Reality* (New York: MIT Press, 1956); also refer back to Chapter 1, "Culture and Language: Political Realities to Keep Trickster at Bay," in this volume.

CHAPTER 13

REFLECTIONS AND FEELINGS DERIVING FROM A PULAKAUMAKA WITHIN MY HEART

By Kauanoe Kamanā

Kauanoe Kamanā is a founder and the current president of the nonprofit Hawaiian language revitalization organization ʻAha Pūnana Leo. She is also a faculty member of Ka Haka ʻUla O Keʻelikōlani College of Hawaiian Language at the University of Hawaiʻi, for which she serves as director of its Hawaiian medium laboratory school program. Besides providing direction for the laboratory school program at Nāwahīokalaniʻōpuʻu School, Kauanoe is currently teaching third, fourth, and fifth graders in its new charter school component. After having taught the original Pūnana Leo children in preschool and intermittently throughout their middle and high school years, she finds that teaching these young children now brings her work full circle, a satisfying endeavor.

SECTION I: ENGLISH TRANSLATED TEXT

The Kalihi area of Honolulu on Oʻahu is where I was born Kauanoe Kamanā, daughter of Paul Kiaʻipō Kamanā and Ella Kauanoe Kaʻai. I was raised in Honolulu and the Island of Molokaʻi, where my mother was born and which is also the site of the Hawaiian Homestead Lands (similar to Indian Reservations) where the majority of my parents' generation of relatives as well as my own generation of relatives were raised and nurtured with aloha. It is from my own family that I derive my worldview of loyalty to the concepts of love for God and the spiritual aspects of life, love for the family and geneological connections, and love for knowledge and learning. They are the source of my personality, my culture, my fears, and the lack of fear that I have today. My heart holds their lessons firmly as a pulakaumaka, a constant all-powerful vision, within my mind. This pulakaumaka has set the course of what I have done every day of my life.

So if I am asked why I became involved in the revitalization of our Indigenous language here in Hawaiʻi, the answer is very clear. It is my responsibility, a joyful burden that must be carried, and because there are so very few who are seeking out the beautiful goal of a restored, living Hawaiian language in its own homeland, I have no choice. The same holds true for others born and raised throughout our Hawaiian Islands.

In 1971 I heard about a Hawaiian language program on KCCN Radio in Honolulu broadcast on Sunday evenings. I saw my father listening to this program, but this fact did not register as important. However, later it interested me how my father would laugh at what they were discussing on the radio. I did not understand much of what was being discussed. Because my father enjoyed the program so much and the fond memories that it brought back to him of his childhood with his parents, I seem to have internalized that aloha during those evenings in our little urban apartment. And although my mother had already passed on, we had the opportunity to sit and enjoy daily living along with playing Hawaiian music together. I then realized in my heart that Hawaiian culture and language were something important for me to have for the future. Therefore, when I heard of the Hawaiian language program at the university, I applied and was accepted.

While I was at the University of Hawaiʻi at Mānoa on Oʻahu, I was majoring in Hawaiian Studies and I graduated with a BA in 1975. After that, I continued seeking an MA in Linguistics and graduated with that degree in 1978. At that time there were not many people seeking a degree in Hawaiian language and culture. I was one of the first majors in the field of Hawaiian studies. When people asked me about my major, they were often shocked that I could seek such a form of education. "What good is such a major? You can't earn a living in that!" But I did not listen to their criticism of what I was doing at that time. I am not exactly sure, but I think that when I heard that sort of criticism, it became clear in my heart that what I was doing was right.

I found learning about the Hawaiian language very interesting because I was not raised speaking it. When I was a child, Hawaiian was only used between the generation that was our parents, aunts, and uncles and our generation of siblings and cousins when we were being scolded or for joking and plays on words. When I went to the university, I realized the value and beauty of that language knowledge for a family, and that is when I began to increase my skills in the Hawaiian language. I took the four years of language courses available at that time, and I also took other courses relating to Hawaiʻi and Polynesia. That is how I began my education about our Hawaiian language. I had no idea or premonition at all at the time regarding the physical and emotional experiences that lay before me.

At that time there were perhaps 2,000 native speakers living, and these native speakers were invited to go to KCCN Radio and appear on a program with Larry Kimura and Pila Wilson and talk about their personal histories. They spoke of their birth and childhood, the way they lived, traditional stories, famous people, sites of cultural importance, and things of that nature. Many topics were discussed, and the audience at home also telephoned to introduce themselves and talk with each other. Everyone participated in singing and seeking out the genealogical and other relationships that connect us, a behavior that is so familiar to us and one that gives us an internal sense of satisfaction that what is being done is being done in a Hawaiian manner. That way of interacting is something Hawaiian that has continued until the present time. The guests were so happy and so filled with aloha for the earlier days of their lives. However, at the same time everyone was aware that the number of native speakers was rapidly diminishing and that most of them at that time were over 70 years old. So it was at that time that we Hawaiian language teachers began to look for a new way for our language to grow. There was much fear of the outcome of not being alert for an answer regarding the slipping away of our Native speakers and the reduction of the uniquely Hawaiian voice to the point of silence. This loss of our people's language represented the flickering end of the fire that kept the mauli, the life force, of our people alive. We had to find a way to stoke that fire of life. We had to concentrate on finding a new way for the language to survive.

In 1976 my companion in our work, William (Pila) Wilson, and I were married, and we decided that we would involve ourselves in this work as a team seeking out a way to have the language live in Hawaiʻi where we had both been born. We also determined that our children, when they were born, would be raised in a totally Hawaiian-speaking home as was then only occurring within the tiny and remote community of Niʻihau. Our son Hulilauākea was born in 1981, and our daughter Keliʻihoalani in 1983. Today Hulilauākea is 19 years old and Keliʻihoalani is 17, and they have both been raised in our beloved land and language until today. It was the strength of this love for our land that provided direction until it became a pulakaumaka that resulted in the Hawaiian language becoming the living language of our home.

Love of the land is very strong, and all of us involved in learning Hawaiian who were connected to Larry Kimura's radio program felt the love of the land urging us to revitalize its Indigenous language. In 1983 we formed the ʻAha Pūnana Leo, a tax-free organization taking on the responsibility of the arduous task of revitalizing the language by establishing a program for children between the ages of two and a half and four for Hawaiian-speaking families and those who wished to become Hawaiian-speaking. That was the sole pulakaumaka that brought us into this effort. We did not know anything about early childhood education but had heard about the concept from our Māori friend from New Zealand, Tāmati Reedy, a fellow graduate student of ours at the University of Hawaiʻi at Mānoa. According to him, New Zealand and Hawaiʻi were experiencing the same problem, and it was important that babies and grandparents be brought together and to have them talk to each other. When we heard his words, we decided to seek a means to remove the fearful fate of complete disappearance, and we became steadfast and worked together to refuse to have the language lost and to seek out the skill necessary to establish new preschools to be called Pūnana Leo. The deep-rooted sense of responsibility was planted among those with the Pūnana Leo schools with the vision statement: E Ola Ka ʻŌlelo Hawaiʻi ("The Hawaiian Language Shall Live").

Just as we had experienced before, there were very many people who doubted the value of this new activity of ours. "What good would such schools be? What about English? The children will not be able to go on to the university. They will not be able to earn any money to support their families!" These people believed that we were actually abusing the children and their families. However, there were some families who craved for the hope of having their children educated through the indigenous language of the land. They understood how this program was different, and that there were no other schools like this anywhere in Hawaiʻi. Over the years, we came to realize that such schools were nonexistent, not only in Hawaiʻi, but in the entire United States.

Those children were the first involved in this new approach to education. Those first families have been followed by others, but no others have had to experience what the first families did. We enrolled entirely on faith, working and shouldering responsibilities together. When there were legal barriers, we sought out a means to change the law and we broke down those barriers. When we did not know how to teach early education, we sought knowledge from the most expensive private schools here in Hawaiʻi so that we would have information out of which we selected what was best for the children. If we did not know something, we immediately sought out the answers needed to move the program forward. This became a totally internalized way of doing things among the pioneering families in the program. This was the way in which the work succeeded, and we did not allow the path to a living language to be entangled or blocked by anything. We knew that the answers were with us. We knew that we had the responsibility to seek out what we needed.

Taking responsibility for the life of our language, taking responsibility for the life of our Hawaiian culture, taking responsibility for the survival of a grounded Hawaiian identity—this was the shouldering of the ancient heritage of our people by new generations. The normal situation was that these were not things that were much considered. They were things that people just knew

without effort. But for the Hawaiian, it was important to once again establish
the foundation that had fallen into disrepair and have our house stand once
again to embrace the life of our people. There are times when our emotions
are torn and we spend much time brooding over the history of the Hawaiian
people, but the way to solve the situation is in seeking to establish a new house
to assure survival, including the features of a living Hawaiian identity through
spirituality; in speaking the Hawaiian language; in our customs, protocol, and
ways of acting; and in caring for our traditional knowledge. Ma ka hana ka 'ike
(it is through action that knowledge is acquired) is a famous saying among the
Hawaiians. It becomes a fact when one becomes involved with one's own
hands.

Today, there are 11 Pūnana Leo schools here in Hawai'i and about 2,000 students learning through the Hawaiian language from preschool, elementary
school, intermediate school, to high school. These students, together with those
learning Hawaiian in English medium schools and colleges, increase the numbers to approximately 5,000; therefore, the establishment of these educational
facilities is the result of the steadfastness of the families and the support of the
general public for the survival of the Hawaiian language and culture. These
schools were established because of the hard work of people who believed that
the program could be successful. Although there were many people who were
opposed to Hawaiians among them, the initial small activities were slowly built
to provide the important little footholds by which we would leave the pain and
sorrow of having relinquished our power to others, and by which we would
steer for our vision and refuse to be pulled into the realm of clouds and confusion. That is how those footholds were emphasized until we are now approaching Nōla'ela'e, a land of clarity.

Today, many parents have gone to the university to seek out teaching
degrees and have returned to our schools to teach in the Pūnana Leo and Kula
Kaiapuni Hawai'i, which are the Hawaiian medium schools that serve students
after the preschool stage. Because there is a requirement of physically assisting
in the Pūnana Leo schools, they begin to take on tasks such as delivering snacks
or cutting grass or cleaning the school. It is through such work that their aloha
grows for the program and those caring for the children. One cannot feel this
until one becomes actively involved personally and interacts with the people of
the school. Once a system is established for including the participation of people in such activities, they become familiar with the types of relationships that
serve the interest of the children. If the parents and teachers do not clearly
understand this, the lessons of knowledge needed for the survival of the language and living identity both in the school and the home will not grow.

It is an arduous task to continually focus on the vision because people are
accustomed to the general Anglo-American (haole) culture that has encircled
the globe. They have become deaf to noise, blind to the glare of light, numb to
the deliciousness of what they have before them, strangers to the sweet scent
of the land, uncertain and confused in touching the skin of human relationships
with their fellow Hawaiian people. Language revitalization is by no means an

easy task for this generation accustomed to the slang of the haole people. This is something that has affected the Hawaiian people for a number of generations.

How does one turn around those features that have become ingrained in the youth as well as adults? Although we are content with daily things within that culture, there are times when we become very upset with haole customs and procedures that are in conflict with those of our Hawaiian people. We may not realize it and then become involved in some circumstances that create unease and even repugnance within our hearts.

It is at such times that a person realizes whether he or she has a living Hawaiian identity life force or a non-Hawaiian one. People know very little and think very little about the living Hawaiian life force. To some people, this is not something important. If they lose the living Hawaiian life force, it is not important. For others, the thought creates great anger in them and they begin to vent their anger on other races that have come to Hawai'i. For others, they simply continue to carry out the normal activities of living as Hawaiian families, without becoming emotionally entangled. We are all people.

The proverb is I ka 'ōlelo nō ke ola; I ka 'ōlelo nō ka make, "Language is the source of life and language is the source of death"; but just speaking the Hawaiian language is not the full vision. Revitalizing our Hawaiian mauli, our Hawaiian life force, through the Hawaiian language is our full vision. Our language will not be true if it does not relate to all aspects of our mauli and verifies the healthy state of our mauli every day and everywhere. It is not verified simply by shallow acts and showy pretensions. Therefore, as we live through this period of widespread craziness and destructive tumultuousness among people in various lands, and the entrance of these same features here into our own land of Hawai'i, what will become of our children? What can we do for them?

We must return to our Hawaiian knowledge base, because each person has the responsibility of evaluating and repairing his connection and lack of connection to the Hawaiian knowledge base. That is how I became involved in seeking to revitalize our language through this approach of establishing schools. But I, like every other person, have within me my own geneology that will serve my own children and the new generation. We must seek the answer within our own hearts, the resting place of our feelings and lessons and the inheritance that has come to us from the distant past. We must expand our thinking and ability to analyze to serve our people. Our familiarity and knowledge of the features of our own ways is the base from which we must come to know our fellow human beings.

My family never told me "You are a Hawaiian so you must do this or do that." Many things were explained to me without words. But what they believed and wanted was very clear to me. I have never been in doubt regarding my Hawaiian identity nor my responsibility of carrying out the duties that need to be done. Love of God, love of family, and love of knowledge and education are features of the worldview of my family, and that is how I have come to be able to perceive what is real and what is not in all activities. At this point in my life in this world, I have no conflicts or frustrations over what has been mine to experience. While I may wonder and marvel at what those of the future may experience, we must continue to maintain that which is real; that is we must continue in our work until our final days.

I feel the same about our two children. They have been raised with aloha by their own relatives and the relatives that are theirs through their schooling from the time they were babies at the Pūnana Leo preschool until the present. Now they are in the bloom of their youth with their fellow young Indigenous-language-speaking descendants of our land. These young people are all Hawaiian-speaking people, people with a living Hawaiian mauli, a living Hawaiian life force. This is the new generation that stands upon the foundation of the Hawaiian worldview. They began to bear that foundation as their responsibility on the day they were born, and they continue to carry that joyfully shouldered burden until today.

This is truly an inheritance that we carry. It is not a choice. Each must know his own mana or spiritual power. Each must seek the knowledge to benefit us all. Each must share and show assistance to others. Each must have appreciation for the talents that are the Hawaiians' and must work to revive our culture. Each must have a heart at peace with itself. And each must honor our ancestors in what he or she does every day.

It is truly an honor to participate in the revitalization of our language. I am pleased with the many blessings that have been experienced in these 17 years since the beginning of the 'Aha Pūnana Leo, and I am truly proud of the many children speaking Hawaiian throughout Hawai'i today. To be able to make the technological world a Hawaiian world is also a point of pride. To make the business world Hawaiian is another point of pride. To bring back the world of schooling as something Hawaiian is another point of pride. To make all the different worlds that we live in Hawaiian worlds again—that is the point of pride that is needed to bring life back to our mauli, our life force. And reestablishing life in our mauli, our core life force—that is the beloved pulakaumaka, the burning vision, that I carry with me.

SECTION II: HAWAIIAN TEXT

He Hali'a, He Aloha Na Ka Pulakaumaka Mai

Ma Kalihi ma Honolulu ma O'ahu i hānau 'ia ai wau 'o Kauanoe Kamanā, ke kaikamahine na Paul Kia'ipō Kamanā lāua 'o Ella Kauanoe Ka'ai. Hānai 'ia ma Honolulu me Moloka'i ka 'āina hānau o ko'u makuahine a kahi ho'i o nā 'apana 'āina ho'opulapula i hānai a pūlama aloha 'ia ai ka nui o ko ko'u hanauna mau mākua me ko'u hanauna pono'ī nō. No ko'u 'ohana ko'u kuana'ike ao he kūpa'a ma luna o ke aloha akua, ke aloha 'ohana me ke aloha na'auao. No lākou ko'u 'ano, ko'u mo'omeheu, ko'u mau maka'u a maka'u 'ole o kēia lā. Mau nō ia mau ha'awina a pa'a ma ko'u na'au, he pulakaumaka e kia ai ka'u hana o kēlā lā kēia lā.

No laila, ke nīnau 'ia mai au no ke kumu i komo ai wau ma ka papahana ho'ōla 'ōlelo 'ōiwi o Hawai'i nei, he ahuwale ka hā'ina—'o ko'u kuleana ia, he luhi e pono e ʻauamo ʻia a ʻoiai he nui ka nele o ke kanaka e ʻimi ana i ia nani o ka ʻōlelo ola o ka ʻōlelo Hawaiʻi ma ko mākou ʻāina ponoʻī nō, ʻaʻole ia he mea e nūnē iho ai. Pono me kēlā ka noʻonoʻo me ka hana a ka poʻe ʻē aʻe i hānau ʻia a hānai ʻia ma Hawaiʻi nei a puni.

Ma ka makahiki 1971, ua lohe wau no kēia polokalamu ʻōlelo Hawaiʻi ma ka lēkiō ma KCCN ma Honolulu a i nā ahiahi Lāpule, ʻike wau i koʻu pāpā e hoʻolohe ana i ia papahana. ʻAʻole naʻe wau i manaʻo he mea nui ia akā ma hope, ʻano hoihoi wau i ka ʻakaʻaka ʻana o koʻu pāpā i kā lākou e walaʻau ana ma ka lēkiō. ʻAʻole naʻe wau i maopopo nui i ka mea e walaʻau ʻia ana. Ma muli o ia hauʻoli o koʻu pāpā me kona haliʻa aloha i ka wā i hala , kohu mea ua ili ia aloha ma luna oʻu ma ia mau ahiahi ma ko māua wahi keʻena hale a ʻoiai ua hala mua koʻu māmā, ua loaʻa ko māua wā e noho pū ai a e oʻonanea ai ma ka hoʻokani pila me nā hana maʻamau ʻē aʻe o ka hale. Ua ʻike maila wau ma koʻu naʻau ʻo ka moʻomeheu Hawaiʻi me ka ʻōlelo Hawaiʻi kekahi māhele hana e pono ai wau no kēia mua aku. No laila, ua lohe wau no ka papahana ʻōlelo ma ke kulanui. Ua noi a komo akula i ka papahana.

ʻOiai wau ma ke kulanui ma Mānoa, Oʻahu he mēkia Haʻawina Hawaiʻi kaʻu a ua loaʻa mai nei ke kekelē B.A. ma ka makahiki 1975. Ma hope, ua hoʻomau au ma ka ʻimi M.A. ma ke kālaiʻōlelo a loaʻa mai nei ke kekelē M.A. ma ka makahiki 1978. Ma ia wā ʻaʻole nō i nui loa ka poʻe e ʻimi ana i kēkelē ma ka ʻōlelo me ka moʻomeheu Hawaiʻi, ʻaʻole hoʻi i hoʻokumu ʻia ka māhele moʻomeheu me ka ʻōlelo Hawaiʻi a hiki i ka makahiki 1972. Ke nīele ʻia wau no kaʻu mēkia ʻo ka ʻōlelo wale maila nō ia o ke kāhāhā i ia kiʻina hoʻonaʻauao. "I mea aha lā ia ʻano mēkia? ʻAʻohe kālā ma laila!" ʻAʻole loa wau i puni i kā lākou ʻōlelo ʻimihana i kaʻu hana ma ia wā. ʻAʻole maopopo loa iaʻu akā ma ia ʻano ʻōlelo wau i ʻike ai ma koʻu naʻau he pololei kaʻu hana. Ua nui koʻu hoihoi i ka noke i ka hoʻonui i ka naʻauao no kaʻu ʻōlelo Hawaiʻi no ka mea ʻaʻole wau i hānai piha ʻia ma loko o ka ʻōlelo Hawaiʻi. I koʻu wā kamaliʻi, ma ka nuku me ka pāʻani ʻōlelo wale nō i lohe ʻia ai ka ʻōlelo Hawaiʻi ma waena o mākou nā hoahānau me ko ka hanauna makua. I ka hele ʻana aku i ke kulanui, ua ʻike ihola wau i ka waiwai me ka nani o ia ʻike ma waena o ka ʻohana. Ma muli o kēlā, ua noke wau i ka hoʻonui i koʻu mākau ʻōlelo Hawaiʻi. Ua komo wau i nā papa ʻōlelo i loaʻa ma ia wā, he ʻehā makahiki a ua komo pū wau i nā papa ʻē aʻe i pili iā Hawaiʻi me Polenesia. Pēlā wau i hoʻomaka ai i ka ʻimi naʻauao no ka ʻōlelo Hawaiʻi ma ke kulanui. ʻAʻole loa wau i manaʻo a wānana iki i ia wā i nā haʻawina o ka ʻili a me ka naʻau e waiho ana i mua oʻu.

Ma ia wā, ua loaʻa ma kahi o ka 3,000 poʻe mānaleo e ola ana a ua kono ʻia kēia poʻe mānaleo e hele i KCCN a kau ma ka lēkiō me Larry Kimura me Pila Wilson a kamaʻilio a walaʻau no ko lākou mau moʻolelo, no ka hānau a hānai ʻia ʻana, no ke ʻano o ka noho ʻana, na kāʻao, ka poʻe kaulana, no nā pana ʻāina a pēlā wale aku. Nui loa nā kumuhana i hāpai ʻia a ke lohe ʻia ma ke ākea komo pū ka lehulehu e hoʻolohe ana ma ka hale a ʻo ke kelepona koke akula nō ia a hoʻolauna a walaʻau kekahi me kekahi. Komo ka poʻe a pau i ka hīmeni me ka ʻimi aʻe i ia ʻano pili kamaʻāina e ulu ai ka ʻoluʻolu o ka naʻau, he Hawaiʻi nō hoʻi ke ʻano. Mau nō kēlā ʻano o ka Hawaiʻi a hiki loa mai i kēia lā. Nui ka hauʻoli a he aloha maoli nō ka lohe i ka ʻōlelo haliʻa i ko lākou mau lā i hala loa aku nei. Eia nō naʻe, ma ia wā nō, ua ahuwale ke emi wikiwiki ʻana o ka nui o nā mānaleo, ʻoiai ua piha i ka hapanui o lākou he 70 a ʻoi makahiki ma ia wā. No laila, ma ia mau makahiki mākou i hoʻomaka ai i ka ʻimi i ala hou e ulu ai ka ʻōlelo, he haʻawina maoli ia na ka naʻau. Nui ka hopohopo a me ka makaʻu i ka hopena nalohia o ka ʻōlelo a ma muli nō hoʻi o ka makaʻala ʻole ʻia. E mio ana nā mānaleo i ka hala a e emi ana a hāmau loa ka leo Hawaiʻi, ka napenape o ia ahi e pumehana ai ka mauli. ʻO ke kahukahu wale nō ka hana e pono ai. Ke kia ma luna o nā hana e ulu hou ai ka ʻōlelo i loaʻa ma ia wā, a ke hoʻokumu i nā hana kikoʻī e hoʻolako ʻia ai ka ʻōlelo no kēia au hou, e pakele ana ka ʻōlelo i ia hopena ʻo ka nalohia. ʻO kēia ko mākou manaʻo.

Ma ka makahiki 1976, ua hoʻoholo māua ʻo kaʻu kāne ʻo William "Pila" Wilson e komo piha ma kēia hana ma ke ʻano he kime e ʻimi ana i ala e ulu ai ke ola o ka ʻōlelo ma Hawaiʻi nei ko māua ʻāina hānau. Ua holo pū ko māua manaʻo ē i ka wā e hānau mai ai kā māua mau keiki, e hānai ʻia i loko o ka ʻōlelo Hawaiʻi wale nō, he mea i loaʻa i ia manawa i loko wale nō o ke kaiaulu ʻohana Niʻihau ma ka mokupuni ʻo Niʻihau. Hānau ʻia kā māua keiki kāne ʻo Hulilauākea i ka makahiki 1981 a ʻo kā māua kaikamahine ʻo Keliʻihoalani i ka makahiki 1983. I kēia lā, ua piha he 19 makahiki iā Hulilauākea a he 17 iā Keliʻihoalani a no loko mai nō o ke aloha ʻōlelo me ke aloha ʻāina i hānai ʻia ai lāua ʻelua a hiki mai i kēia lā. No ka ikaika o kēia aloha ʻāina i hoʻokele a lilo i pulakaumaka i lilo ai ʻo ka ʻōlelo Hawaiʻi ka ʻōlelo ola o ko mākou hale.

Ma ka makahiki 1983, ua hoʻokumu mākou, nā hoa aʻo ʻōlelo Hawaiʻi i ka ʻAha Pūnana Leo, he hui ʻauhau ʻole e ʻauamo ana i ka luhi o ka hoʻōla ʻōlelo ma ke kūkulu i papahana no nā kamaliʻi ma waena o ka 2.5 me ka 4 makahiki no nā ʻohana ʻōlelo Hawaiʻi a me nā ʻohana e makemake ana e ʻolelo Hawaiʻi. No ia pulakaumaka hoʻokahi i komo ai mākou a pau ma kēia hana. ʻAʻole mākou i maopopo iki no ke aʻo kamaliʻi akā ua lohe mākou ma o ko mākou hoa Maori no Aotearoa ʻo Tāmati Reedy, he haumānā M.A. ma ke kulanui ma Mānoa. Wahi āna, ua like nō ka pilikia ma Aotearoa me ko Hawaiʻi nei a he pono e hoʻohui ʻia nā pēpē me nā tūtū a e hoʻowalaʻau iā lākou. Ma ia ʻōlelo i hoʻoholo ai mākou i ka ʻimi i ala e ʻoki ai i ia hopena weliweli o ka nalohia, ua kūpaʻa a alu like i ka hōʻole i ka nalowale loa o ka ʻōlelo. Ua hoʻohiki i ka huli a loaʻa ka mākau e pono ai nā kula kamaliʻi hou ʻo ka Pūnana Leo. Ua kanu, hoʻoulu a paʻa ka mole ʻike kuleana o ko ke kula Pūnana Leo ma ka nuʻukia: "E Ola ka ʻŌlelo Hawaiʻi". Paʻa loa kēia a hiki i kēia lā.

E like nō me ka mea i ʻike mua ʻia, ua nui a lehulehu ka poʻe kānalua i ka waiwai o kēia hana. "I mea aha lā kēia ʻano kula?" Pehea ka ʻōlelo Pelekānia? ʻAʻole ana e hiki i nā keiki ke hele i ke kulanui. ʻAʻohe hana e loaʻa ai ke kālā e pono ai ka ʻohana!" Ua manaʻo lākou he hana ʻino kēia hana i nā keiki me nā ʻohana. Eia nō naʻe, ua loaʻa nā ʻohana i hoʻohihi i ke kupaianaha o ka hoʻonaʻauao ʻia ʻana o kā lākou poʻe kamaliʻi ma loko o ka ʻōlelo Hawaiʻi wale nō, ka ʻōiwi o ka ʻāina. I loko nō o ka maopopo o nā ʻohana no ka ʻokoʻa loa o kēia papahana, me ka loaʻa ʻole hoʻi o kēia ʻano kula a puni ʻo Hawaiʻi nei, ua ʻike pū ihola lākou ma ka holo ʻana o nā makahiki, ʻakahi a ʻike ʻia kēia ʻano kula ma ʻAmelika Hui Pū ʻIa a puni. ʻAʻole ia he mea hou ma Hawaiʻi wale nō.

'O kēlā mau keiki ka makamua o kekahi mana'o hou no ka 'imi na'aua'o 'ana. A hiki loa mai i kēia wā, 'a'ole loa'a kēia kūlana i nā 'ohana 'ē a'e i hahai mai i ka papahana. No ia mau 'ohana mua wale nō kēia ha'awina. Ua komo nā 'ohana ma ka hilina'i wale nō, ma ka hana me ka 'auamo like nō. Inā ālai ana ke kānāwai,'o ka 'imi wale nō ia i ka hana e ho'oponopono ai i ia kānāwai a wāwahi loa 'ia ia 'āke'ake'a. Inā 'a'ole mākou i maopopo no ke a'o 'ana i nā ha'awina kula kamali'i, 'o ka 'imi wale nō ia i ka 'ike ma waena o nā kula kaulana a kū'ono'ono loa o Hawai'i nei a loa'a ka 'ikepili e wae 'ia ai nā mea pono no nā kamali'i. Inā 'a'ole i maopopo, 'o ka 'eleu wale 'ana akula nō ia o ka 'imi i hā'ina e pono ai ka holomua o ka papahana. Ua ma'a a kuluma kēia ma ka na'au o ia mau 'ohana mua i komo i ka papahana. 'O kēia ke ki'ina i puka aku ai ka hana a hiki loa mai i kēia lā, 'a'ole e 'ae 'ia ka ho'ohihia a ho'oke'ake'a 'ia o ke ala e pono ai ka 'ōlelo Hawai'i ola. Aia ma waena o mākou ka hā'ina. No mākou ia kuleana 'o ka 'imi.

'O ka 'auamo i ke ola o kā mākou 'ōlelo, ka 'auamo i ke ola o ka mo'omeheu Hawai'i, ka 'auamo i ke ola o ka mauli Hawai'i he mau luhi kēia o ka ho'oilina kahiko o ka lāhui i ili ma luna o mākou a e ili hou ana ma luna o nā hanauna hou. 'O ka ma'amau, 'a'ole ia mau mea he mea e no'ono'o nui 'ia. He maopopo wale. Eia nō na'e i kēia au hou e holo nei, he pono ka ho'opa'a hou 'ia o ka paepae i helele'i ai ka ikaika o ka 'ōlelo. He mea nui ka ho'ohana mau 'ia o ka 'ōlelo, ke kūkā 'ia 'ana o ka 'ōlelo me ka mauli. He mea nui ka hō'oia hou 'ana ma ke po'o. 'A'ole ma ka na'au wale nō. Pēlā e pa'a hou ai ke kahua ola o ka mauli Hawai'i. I kekahi manawa he hukihuki a nalunalu ka na'au i ka mō'aukala o ka po'e Hawai'i akā ma ke kūkulu hou wale 'ana nō e ola ai a ma luna o nā hi'ohi'ona o ka mauli Hawai'i ma ka pili 'uhane, ma ka 'ōlelo i ka 'ōlelo Hawai'i, ma nā loina me ka lawena a ma ka mālama 'ana i ka 'ike ku'una e pono ai. "Ma ka hana ka 'ike" he 'ōlelo laha ma waena o ka Hawai'i. Lilo ho'i he 'oia'i'o ke hana maoli 'ia.

I kēia lā, ua hua mai ka hana a loa'a he 11 kula Pūnana Leo ma Hawai'i nei a he 2,000 haumāna e kula 'ia nei ma o ka 'ōlelo Hawai'i ma nā kula kamali'i, nā kula ha'aha'a, nā kula waena me nā kula ki'eki'e. Ma kahi o ka 5,000 ka nui ke ho'ohui 'ia me nā haumāna e a'o nei i ka 'ōlelo ma nā kula 'ōlelo Pelekānia. No laila, 'o ka loa'a o kēia mau wahi ho'ona'auao ka hua o ke kūpa'a o nā 'ohana a me nā kāko'o o ka lehulehu i ke ola o ka mo'omeheu Hawai'i. Ua loa'a mai nei kēia mau kula ma muli o ka hana nui o ka po'e i piliwi a hilina'i i ka pono o ka ho'ōla 'ōlelo. 'Oiai ua loa'a ka po'e Hawai'i a Hawai'i 'ole i kāko'o 'ole i kēia papahana, ua kūkulu mālie 'ia nō ma nā hana 'u'uku i pono ai ia mau ke'ehina li'ili'i mua a i kēia lā ua loa'a ka hua e hō'ole ai i ka 'oia'i'o o ka lu'ulu'u a kaumaha o ka nalowale loa o ka 'ōlelo. 'A'ole hiki ke ho'oku'u na ha'i e hopohopo a e ho'oponopono. E ho'ohana 'ānō i ko kākou mana e kia ai i ka nu'ukia. E hō'ole mau i ka na'aupō me ke kūpono 'ole. E kālele i nā ke'ehina hana e kokoke a'e ai i Nōla'ela'e.

I kēia lā, he nui nā mākua i ho'i i ke kulanui a i 'imi i kēkelē a'o a ho'i akula i ke kula e a'o ai ma ka Pūnana Leo me nā kula kaiapuni Hawai'i, nā kula 'ōlelo Hawai'i ma hope o ka pae kula kamali'i. 'Oiai ua loa'a ke koina kōkua no nā mākua o ke kula, hoʻomaka lākou ma ka lawe i kahi meaʻai māmā a i ʻole paha he ʻoki mauʻu a hoʻomaʻemaʻe i ke kula. Ma ia ʻano hana e ulu ai ka pili me ke aloha i ka papahana, ka poʻe e mālama nei i nā keiki a me nā ʻohana ʻē aʻe. ʻAʻole hiki ke ʻike i kēia a hana maoli ʻia nō ma ka lima a e launa pū me ko ke kula. Ke paʻa ka ʻōnaehana e maʻa ana ka poʻe a pau. Inā ʻaʻole mōakāka i nā mākua me nā kumu, ʻaʻohe ana ulu o ka papahana e pono ai ka ʻōlelo me ka mauli ma ke kula me ka hale.

He hana nui ke kia mau ma luna o ka nuʻukia no ka nui o ka maʻa o ka poʻe i ka moʻomeheu haole ʻAmelika i laha a puni ke ao. Ua hele a kuli i ka hanakuli, makapō i ka māʻamaʻama o nā kukui, ʻaʻole ʻono i ka meaʻai i loaʻa, malihini i ka honi i nā ʻala o ka ʻāina a kuhihewa a kānalua ka ʻili i ka launa kanaka. ʻAʻole loa ka hoʻōla ʻōlelo he hana malani a oki loa i ka maʻa i ka ʻōlelo me ka palaualea a ka haole. Ua ili ma lunao nā hanauna Hawaiʻi no ka manawa lōʻihi.

Pehea e hoʻohuli ai i ia mau hiʻohiʻona i maʻa a kuluma i kēia poʻe ʻōpio a me nā mākua pū kekahi? ʻOiai ua ʻoluʻolu i ka nui o nā hana maʻamau o kēlā lā kēia lā, he loaʻa nō ka wā e ukiuki ai ka naʻau i nā loina o ka haole me nā hiʻohiʻona kūʻēʻē i ko ka Hawaiʻi. ʻAʻole naʻe maopopo a komo nō hoʻi i loko o kekahi pōʻaiapili e ulu ai ke ʻano ʻē a hoʻopailua o ka naʻau. Ma ia wā e ʻike ai ke kanaka no kona kahua mauli Hawaiʻi a Hawaiʻi ʻole paha. Nui ka ʻike ʻole a me ka noʻonoʻo ʻole o ka poʻe no ke kahua mauli Hawaiʻi. I kekahi poʻe, ʻaʻole kēia he mea nui. Ke nalowale ka mauli Hawaiʻi, ʻaʻole ia he mea nui. No kekahi poʻe, he mea hoʻohuhū wale nō a ʻo ka ʻimihana wale nō ia o ka hana i nā lāhui ʻē i hiki mai i Hawaiʻi nei. No kekahi, he hoʻomau wale aku i nā hana maʻamau o ka pili ʻohana Hawaiʻi, ʻaʻole hihia nui o ka naʻau. He kanaka wale nō kākou.

ʻŌlelo ʻia, "I ka ʻōlelo nō ke ola; I ka ʻōlelo nō ka make", eia nō naʻe ʻaʻole ʻo ka ʻōlelo Hawaiʻi wale ʻana nō ka nuʻukia. ʻO ka hoʻōla hou i ka mauli Hawaiʻi ma o ka ʻōlelo Hawaiʻi ka nuʻukia piha. ʻAʻohe ana e ʻoiaʻiʻo ka ʻōlelo inā ʻaʻole ia pili i nā ʻaoʻao o ka mauli e hōʻoiaʻiʻo ai i ke ola o ka mauli i nā lā a pau ma nā wahi a pau. ʻAʻole ma ke ʻano he hoʻokohukohu wale nō. No laila, ʻoiai kākou i loko o kēia wā laha o ka pupule a hoʻohaunaele o ke kanaka ma nā ʻāina like ʻole, a ua hōʻea mai nei hoʻi ia ʻano i Hawaiʻi nei, he aha ana lā ka hopena no nā keiki? He aha kā kākou e hana ai no lākou?

E hoʻi hou i ke kahua ʻike Hawaiʻi no ka mea aia i kēlā me kēia kanaka ke kuleana o ka loiloi a me ka hoʻoponopono i kona pili a pili ʻole i ke kahua ʻike Hawaiʻi. Pēlā wau i hoʻoholo ai no kēia hana o ka hoʻōla ʻōlelo ma loko o ke kiʻina aʻo kula. Eia nō naʻe aia i loko oʻu e like hoʻi me nā kānaka ʻē aʻe a pau, ka mana o koʻu moʻokūʻauhau ʻo ka mana hoʻi e pono ai kaʻu mau keiki a me ka hanauna hou. E ʻimi a loaʻa ka hāʻina ma ko kākou naʻau ponoʻī iho nō, ka waihona o ko kākou mau haʻawina me ka hoʻoilina i ili mai ma luna o kākou mai o kikilo mai. E hoʻākea i ka noʻonoʻo me ke kālailai e pono ai ka lāhui. ʻO ko kākou kamaʻāina a maopopo i nā hiʻohiʻona o ko kākou ʻano iho, ʻo ia ke kahua kuanaʻike e pili aku ai i ko kākou hoakanaka.

ʻAʻole i haʻi mai koʻu ʻohana iaʻu, "He Hawaiʻi ʻoe, a no laila e hana ʻoe me kēia a hana me kēlā". Nui nā mea i wehewehe waha ʻole ʻia mai akā ua ahuwale ko lākou manaʻo iaʻu me ko lākou makemake noʻu. ʻAʻole nō i kānalua iki no koʻu ʻano he Hawaiʻi me koʻu kuleana i ka ʻauamo i ka luhi e pono ai. ʻO ke aloha akua, ke aloha ʻohana me ke aloha naʻauao nā hiʻohiʻona o ke kuanaʻike ao o ka ʻohana, pēlā e maopopo ai ka ʻoiaʻiʻo no nā hana a pau. I kēia wā ma ka noho honua ʻana, ʻaʻohe e hukihuki a uluhua i nā haʻawina e ili mai ana ma luna o kākou. ʻOiai he haʻohaʻo paha i ko ka wā e hiki mai ana, ʻo kā kākou wale nō ka ʻoiaʻiʻo, ʻo ka noke i ka hana a hiki i ko kākou lā hope.

Pēlā nō me nā keiki ʻelua a māua i hānai aloha ʻia e ka ʻohana ponoʻī me ka ʻohana hoʻi o ke kula, mai ko lāua wā pēpē ma ka Pūnana Leo a hiki loa mai i kēia lā, ia wā nani o lāua me ko lāua mau hoa, nā mamo ʻōlelo ʻōiwi o ko mākou ʻāina. He mau kānaka ʻōlelo Hawaiʻi lākou a pau, he mau kānaka o ka mauli ola Hawaiʻi. ʻO kēia ka hanauna hou, e kū nei ma luna o ke kahua kuanaʻike ao Hawaiʻi. Ua hoʻomaka lākou i ka ʻauamo i ia kuleana ma ka lā i hānau ʻia ai lākou he mau pēpē a mau ka ʻauamo i kēia luhi o ka lāhui a hiki loa mai i kēia lā.

He hoʻoilina maoli kēia e hāpai ʻia nei. ʻAʻole ia he koho. E maopopo kēlā me kēia no kona mana ponoʻī nō. E ʻimi kēlā me kēia i ka naʻauao e pono ai a e hoʻokaʻaʻike a e hōʻike i ke kōkua. E mahalo kēlā me kēia i ke kālena o ka Hawaiʻi a hoʻōla i ka moʻomeheu. E maha ka naʻau o kēlā me kēia a e hoʻohanohano i ko kākou mau kūpuna ma kāna hana i nā lā a pau.

He hanohano ke komo i kēia hana o ka hoʻōla ʻōlelo. Hauʻoli wau i ka nui o ka pōmaikaʻi i ʻike ʻia ma kēia mau makahiki he 17 mai ka hoʻomaka ʻana o ka ʻAha Pūnana Leo a he haʻaheo maoli ka loaʻa o nā keiki he nui e ʻōlelo Hawaiʻi ana mai ʻō a ʻō o Hawaiʻi nei i kēia manawa. ʻO ka hoʻolilo ʻana i ka honua ʻenehana he honua Hawaiʻi, ʻo ia kekahi haʻaheo. ʻO ka hoʻolilo ʻana i ka honua pāʻoihana he Hawaiʻi, ʻo ia kekahi haʻaheo. ʻO ka hoʻihoʻi ʻana mai o ka honua kula he Hawaiʻi, ʻo ia kekahi haʻaheo. ʻO ka hoʻolilo hou ʻia ʻana o nā honua like ʻole a pau he Hawaiʻi, ʻo ia ka haʻaheo e pono ai ka mauli ola kuʻu pulakaumaka aloha.

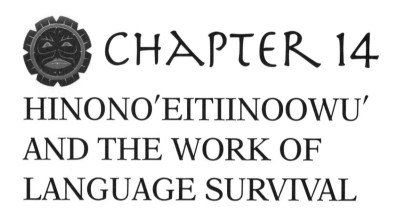

CHAPTER 14

HINONO'EITIINOOWU' AND THE WORK OF LANGUAGE SURVIVAL

By Hiitoo3oobetit Neniiche'ooke'

Hiitoo3oobetit Neniice'ooke' is an Associate Professor in the Departments of Native American Studies and Anthropology at the University of Montana. From 1988 to 1992, he taught at the University of Alberta while completing his doctoral dissertation. After receiving a Doctorate from the University of Oklahoma (1992), he served as Director of the Arapaho Language and Culture Project for the Wyoming Indian Schools. While maintaining academic interests in Native sovereignty issues, he continues his work in developing strategies toward Native language restoration. In this capacity he continues to serve as the Executive Director of Hinono'eitiit Hoowu' (Arapaho Language Lodge) in Wyoming. His publications include *Running the Gauntlet of an Indigenous Language Program* (1999); *The Colonization of Indigenous North America* (1999); *The Imperialism of Cultural Appropriation* (1997); *In the Absence of Justice;* and *Aboriginal Case Law in an Ethnocentric Court* (1997).

Introduction

The Northern Arapaho of the Wind River Indian Reservation in Wyoming have long known the work needed to survive in times of crisis. During the mid-1800s, when United States government officials worked to place tribes on reservations, Arapaho leaders dedicated a quarter of a century to diplomatic resistance, negotiation, and survival—at times in a harsh and hostile environment. Their efforts eventually secured for them a place in Wyoming.[1] Their ability to assess and negotiate new conditions also proved to be an important factor in keeping religious practices and ceremonies viable when threatened by government efforts to eradicate Indigenous belief systems. Time after time, though beset by crisis, the Northern Arapaho have commandeered their way through and have prevailed. Having entered the 21st century, they, along with the majority of other Indigenous North Americans, now face perhaps their biggest challenge, that of turning the tide of language loss. If measures to pass Native languages on to younger generations do not prove successful, it may take only 15 to 20 years before as much as 80 to 85 percent of all Native languages now spoken in North America will be extinct.[2] Under the weight of this reality the Northern Arapaho again find themselves working to secure their future; this time, however, it is for the survival of their language, which ultimately stands as a marker of their culture and identity.

Language Loss and Acts of Resistance

One of the primary influences of the Boarding School era was to lead Indigenous North American peoples to believe that their languages would be a hindrance to their children if they were to become valued "American" citizens. This resulted in an almost complete acceptance of Arapaho people not speaking Arapaho to their children and of English becoming the standard language of communication. This led to a steady decline of Arapaho as a spoken language. Based on an article written by James J. Bauman, Arapaho can be viewed as a language in serious decline.[3] While this reflects a bleak situation for the Arapaho language, it should also be explained that Bauman's categories do not neatly fit all Indigenous contemporary language situations. Bauman's article lists six markers under declining language and six under obsolescent language. The situation for Arapaho, however, is that it does not fit the declining category, because it meets three of the criteria, but does not conform to the other three criteria. It also does not fit the obsolescent category because it meets two of the criteria but not the other two. In part this is because, contrary to the category, the language still adapts to new situations, and, as a result of Arapaho language revitalization efforts, children are beginning to learn the language in the home and there is a growing literacy rate in the language.[4] Thus, when trying to fit the Arapaho language to Bauman's categories, it falls somewhere between the two.

The Northern Arapaho have been grappling with the issues of language survival and maintenance since the middle of the 1970s. It was during this period that steps were initially taken toward preserving the language. In an effort to address the decline of language speakers, members of the Arapaho community first took action in 1976, when a number of language and culture programs for youth and adults were introduced within the school system. While some of these efforts took the form of summer language camps, with the explicit goal of instructors' speaking only Arapaho to participants, the outcome fell way short of the intended objective of creating Arapaho language competency among school aged children. Sustained efforts ultimately resulted in language classes being successfully integrated into the school system from kindergarten to grade 12. In spite of this, by 1984 it was observed that the language classes had little to no impact on slowing the rate of language loss. This was most likely because language-preservation work during this period placed a major emphasis on teaching vocabulary, and although numerous audio- and videocassette recordings of older fluent speakers were also created, they were archived and rarely found their way into any practical use.

After six years, when it was again noted that little change had occurred, strategies were explored on how best to intensify efforts to revitalize the language. This led to a myriad of experts and workshops being held in an attempt to slow the tide of language loss. It wasn't until 1992, after observing that the language was still being lost, that what appeared to be a radically new approach was taken at bringing a new vitality to the language. While continuing with adult and youth language classes through the school system, the community endorsed a language-restoration method that sought to develop new Arapaho speakers among three- to five-year-old children through a process of language immersion. The objective behind this was to create a learning environment within which only Arapaho would be spoken. The following represents a time line of program initiatives and activities from 1993 to 2001.

Immersion Initiatives and Activities Timeline

September 1993: Half-day kindergarten immersion class established in the Wyoming Indian public elementary school. Immersion class is presently operating.

January 1994: Pilot preschool-immersion class runs eight hours a week from January to May.

February 1994: Test voice dub samples for the adaptation of *Bambi* in Arapaho.

June 1994: Final edits completed on *Bambi* movie in the Arapaho language.

September 1994: Nine-month-long Arapaho-language-immersion preschool class implemented.

November 1994: The adaptation of *Bambi* in the Arapaho language premiered by Disney Studios in Lander, Wyoming.

September 1995: First full-day language-immersion preschool class established at Ethete.

September 1996:   Second full-day immersion preschool class opened at Lower Arapaho.

March 16, 1998:   Pilot project, Mother/Toddler language class, implemented at Ethete, Wyoming.

June 1998:   Funds raised to send language-teaching staff to a language conference in Hawaii to give a presentation on Arapaho immersion schools. While there staff visited Hawaiian immersion schools as a part of teaching training.

August 1998:   Language-immersion class at lower Arapaho closes due to funding loss.

September 1998:   Federally recognized nonprofit organization, Hinono'eitiit Hoowu' (Arapaho Language Lodge), established to help generate funding opportunities for language-immersion program.

October 1998:   Stipend implemented into Mother/Toddler language class as a motivation for increased parental involvement.

September 1998:   Master-Apprentice language-mentoring class implemented.

January 1999:   Mother/Toddler language class ends as a result of low participation.

January 2000:   Tribal Council assumes funding responsibilities of immersion class.

May 2000:   First adult-language apprentice achieves a beginning conversational level and program deemed a success.

September 2000:   Program development of an intensive language-immersion curriculum begins.

September 2001:   Implementation of immersion curriculum.

An Overview of the State and Health of the Arapaho Language

The *Atlas of World Languages* listed that there were 1,500 Arapaho speakers out of a population of 5,000 in 1994.[5] In an Internet article, current to 2002, researcher James Estes listed the number of Arapaho speakers, including 20 to 30 speakers of Southern Arapaho in Oklahoma, at approximately 1,038.[6] By all appearances these figures seem to reflect what one might expect. However, upon a closer look, one will discover some problems with these figures. The figures from the *World Atlas of Languages* have a copyright date of 1994, and it is probably safe to assume that the *World Atlas* is the compiler of the data and that the data were collected sometime between 1990 and 1994. Figures from Estes, on the other hand, were adapted from B. Grimes's 1996 figures, which came from 1990 census material, which Estes reports as unchanged in 2002. If these figures are taken at face value, then the figure from Estes reflects that there were originally fewer speakers at 1,038 in 1990 than the *World Atlas* figure of 1,500 speakers in 1994, and this simply is not the case. Before beginning my position at the University of Montana in 1995, I was living on the Wind River Reservation and believed the number of speakers to be less than 1,000 at that time. According to the Arapaho Office of Tribal Statistics, by the end of 1997, there were approximately 5,000 enrolled Arapaho living on the Wind River Reservation. The following chart represents figures of Arapaho-language-speaking abilities for Arapaho people living on the Wind River Reservation for the year 2000.[7]

	AGE GROUPINGS				
Speaking Ability	3–5	6–9	10–54	55–64	65+
None	250	350	1,575	120	30
Limited vocabulary	100	60	1,210	150	55
Extended vocabulary	80	100	60	100	140
Fluency			5	350	450

On the basis of language assessments charted above, it is estimated that some 1,575 people possess a limited Arapaho vocabulary (defined as 20 to 40 words and phrases), while some 2,325 possess no real speaking ability. Though many of the people between these two groups can comprehend a fair amount of what is said in Arapaho, English is the only language spoken. Of the remaining 1,285 people, about 805 can claim true fluency in Arapaho, and of this figure all with the exception of about five are over the age of 50. Obviously my figures differ from those reported by the *World Atlas of Languages* and Estes. The reason for these differences can be attributed to biased responses, a point that Michael Krauss states occurs with some speakers' denying their own language-speaking ability and others' overestimating their language-speaking ability.[8] On the basis of this observation, it is easy to accept that some people who fall within the extended vocabulary group have probably reported themselves as fluent speakers.[9]

Language Levels and the Rate of loss

When looking at levels of fluency, the youngest fluent speakers among the Northern Arapaho fall between the ages of 51 and 54 with only five self-identified speakers. While there is a marked jump in the number of fluent speakers between this group and the next, ages 55 to 64, because the people in these two groups use Arapaho only within a limited range of everyday experiences, a significant amount of vocabulary has been forgotten and is no longer in use. For instance, although many of the people in this age group can easily converse in Arapaho, many can no longer name things like body parts, animals, or other elements that surround them. They thus possess a diminished level of fluency. The 65-year-and-older group represents the strongest fluent Arapaho speakers. Within this group, there are approximately 350 fluent speakers. While the combined number of fluent speakers may seem encouraging, because Arapaho speakers can spend as much as 90 percent of their day speaking English, a lot of words are no longer present in their working vocabulary.

Occasions where Arapaho is primarily spoken are at ceremonies, funerals, and powwows. In addition to these places Arapaho may be used to varying degrees within many households, depending on who is speaking and being spoken to. Arapaho is also spoken by language instructors in the schools, and to a limited degree by those children currently being taught Arapaho in the language-immersion class. With regard to the Arapaho immersion classes, a special comment should be made about children between the ages of three and four. As a result of the Arapaho-language-immersion program, which has operated from 1994 to present, approximately 80 children in this age bracket now demonstrate a language use that has not been seen in children in the past 40 to 50 years. Another impact that these language classes have had has been to increase the amount of Arapaho being spoken within the homes of children participating in the immersion project.

Because more than 450 fluent speakers are over the age of 65, it is estimated that if steps are not taken to fortify the number of speakers, in another 10 years almost half the number of Arapaho fluent speakers will have passed away. The Arapaho language is thus at a critical point, and it is crucial that language-restoration efforts slow and eventually reverse the rate of language loss. It was with this realization that in December 1992 I accepted a two-and-a-half-year contract to direct a culture and language project in the Wyoming Indian School system at Ethete.

Program Inhibitors and Language Restoration Efforts

One of the most significant inhibitors that face language instructors' efforts to teach the Arapaho language in the Wyoming Indian public school system is that almost all language classes meet an average of 15 minutes per day. Over the course of a 180-day calendar school year this equals only 45 hours of language instruction. In June 1993, the Indian Elementary school principal agreed to allow an immersion kindergarten class to start up in September. The immersion class met from 9 to 11:30 A.M., allowing for 2.5 hours of Arapaho-language instruction per day. Having the children move as a group from the immersion kindergarten class straight to lunch, however, increased this time from 2.5 to 3 hours. Over the course of a 180-day school year this meant that the children in this class could receive as much as 540 hours of Arapaho-language instruction during the course of a school year. With the kindergarten immersion class in place there was a new expectation that children could potentially achieve an age-appropriate level of fluency by the end of the school year. For the children outside of this immersion class, about the best the other Arapaho-language classes could hope for was to function as a language-maintenance program, provided that the children who attended those classes had already achieved a speaking ability. Since this was not the case, then logically it made sense to me to try and get children fluent before they entered kindergarten. If this could be achieved, then the language program within the school system could function to maintain and perhaps even expand on the children's Arapaho-language skills. With this realization, the goal then became to create an Arapaho-language-immersion preschool.

The Work of Language Restoration: Continuing the Journey

Starting up an immersion class for preschool children was a major commitment that meant interviewing, hiring, and managing staff; locating a place to hold the class; developing a language curriculum; and purchasing materials and various supplies for the class. Of course all of this meant funding had to be raised to sustain the project for more than a few months. Once these crucial steps had been worked out, the actual first step taken was completing an application for funding from the Wyoming Council for the Humanities. Through a number of discussions it was decided that the best approach for funding was to create a pilot language-immersion preschool class that would operate from January to May 1994. By implementing the project in this way, I was relatively confident that I could obtain additional funding from the same funding agencies for the implementation of an immersion class that could operate over the course of an entire school year. The pilot immersion project operated Mondays to Thursdays, two hours a day. The budget requested for the project covered rent, supplies, second-hand furniture, and an honorarium for the two Arapaho-language instructors. Once funding for the pilot project was secured, the next task was to work out an interview process to get the right people hired for the class.

As my focus was turned to the interview process, I came to realize that fluent Arapaho speakers generally were not speaking Arapaho to children. At first I was puzzled by this, but soon I realized that fluent speakers would not talk to anyone in Arapaho if they believed the person lacked the ability to speak back in Arapaho. Although I explained that children would never learn to speak Arapaho if they were never spoken to in Arapaho, it seemed to have little impact. On occasion my encouragement generated some attempts to informally speak to children, but when no response was returned, speakers tended to think the exercise was silly. From these early observations I realized that whoever was hired as language instructors would have to be committed to carrying out the directives and philosophy of the immersion project. This meant that Arapaho was to be the only language spoken to the children in the classroom.

Interviews were set up to ascertain whether those being interviewed were comfortable working with children and could competently work in an immersion environment. The first 30 minutes of the interview entailed explaining how the actual interview would be conducted, and then learning what the individual knew and thought about teaching Arapaho through an immersion technique. The interviews were videotaped and set up so that each candidate would spend about 30 to 40 minutes in an actual immersion setting with children. Each candidate was handed an outline detailing the activities that needed to be covered, plus the amount of time that should be spent on each activity. All prospective candidates were told that they absolutely were not to speak English to the children. Thus, it was interesting to see that when actually faced with having to speak Arapaho to children, some of the best speakers could not get beyond their barrier of feeling it made little sense to speak to children if they could not understand and answer back. This resulted in some individuals not saying much of anything to the children and mostly speaking to me. As the children became familiar with the routine, when they encountered speakers going silent, they would actually cue (in Arapaho) the person being interviewed of the activity they were supposed to be moving on to. In one example when the person being interviewed fell silent for quite a while, the children kept saying "niibeet hiinikotiinoo" ("I want to play"), which was the next activity they were supposed to have been doing. On another occasion when children were supposed to have been told that they were going to eat, the children started repeating "heesneenoo" ("I'm hungry") because the person being interviewed fell into silence. Even though the children were saying this in Arapaho, it wasn't until I said "Woweetni' nooxowotii" ("you can feed them now") that anything happened.

After all of the interviews were conducted, the videotapes were reviewed and a list was made that consisted of pluses and minuses, representing strengths and weaknesses of how each individual handled each activity. These pluses and minuses were next added up on each individual, and the candidates with the best scores were hired. Although there were some objections to the interview process, because it was clear that everyone interviewed was a fluent speaker, the process held on the grounds that what was determined was how well an individual could work with children in the language.

Walking through the Doors of an Immersion Classroom

The first Arapaho-language-immersion preschool class met for two hours each day, four days a week, from January to May 1994. There were six children in this first class and a language teaching staff of two. The class originally started out in a cafeteria that was used by the Headstart program. Officially, although the Headstart program was the sponsor of the immersion class, it soon became clear that there was little tolerance for another program invading their classroom space. After two months the situation had become so stressful that we decided we needed to move the class to another location. We soon located a new classroom, and although it was cramped for space, staff and children took little time to settle in and see the new site as our own.

The pilot project ended May 1994. After assessing the results it was obvious that two hours a day and four days a week were not enough time to have any lasting impact on the children's ability to converse in Arapaho. Though the class did not produce any new speakers, it did have the effect of producing children with an appreciable Arapaho vocabulary. The children's newfound Arapaho verbal skills impressed family members enough for parents to inquire if the class could extend into the summer. A grant proposal was written for a summer program to operate three days a week for three hours each day on a $2,000 budget. Unfortunately, none of the agencies approached funded the project. In desperation I turned to the parents and instructors themselves. I explained to the instructors that if they would work the summer program at half the hourly income they had received from the pilot project, I believed that the parents would agree to make up the rest of their salaries.

On the majority of reservations in the United States unemployment rates are over 75 percent. On the Wind River Reservation the average unemployment rate is about 78 percent, and during the summer months the unemployment rate will exceed this. It was within this harsh reality that parents made a commitment to pay a summer tuition for their children to attend the language-immersion class.

The summer project ran nine hours a week, from June to July, on a $500 budget. Each parent paid a $20 tuition fee, and the instructors agreed to work for $5 an hour. This level of commitment to the project probably represented one of the most significant acts of support ever given to a program on the reservation. Before the summer had ended, the Wyoming Council for the Humanities agreed to fund the project from September 1994 to May 1995, allowing the project to increase its hours from 8 to 15 a week and increase the teaching staff to three. I was still very much aware that the project needed at least 30 hours a week in order to have any hope of developing speakers, but at least with this increase the language project was moving in the right direction.

With the classroom doors open I scheduled regular visits to observe the project's progress. Each time I visited the class, however, I was surprised to hear instructors speaking English. I soon came to realize that although the instructors knew the project's goals, they still lacked a firm commitment to the methods of immersion. I constantly tried to convince the instructors of how essential it was not to speak English to the children. From the instructors' perspective it was rationalized that the children were speaking Arapaho as a result of instruction being given in English and Arapaho when they spoke to the children. By April 1995 it was apparent that the goal of producing new speakers among the children was not going to be achieved. This realization made me press even harder for a full-day program.

In September 1995 the Arapaho-language-immersion class was extended to 30 hours a week and, as a result of grants awarded by the Wyoming Council for the Humanities and the Lannan Foundation, the project entered its third year. The enrollment for the 1995–96 year averaged about 12 children. A salaried director/curriculum developer position was also added to help tighten up on the administrative duties. Though this new position left me fairly confident that we might see a new generation of Arapaho speakers by the end of the program year in May, by December I became disheartened when the Arapaho instructors were discovered to be still using English in the classroom. I again spoke to them about the importance of maintaining an Arapaho-only language classroom. When I departed, it was with the hope that with language instruction having been extended to 30 hours a week, it might make the difference in achieving the program's goal. When the end of the program year arrived, although participating children demonstrated an impressive speaking ability in Arapaho, they still had not attained a conversational level.

Intensifying and Diversifying

In December of 1995 I was in my office at the University of Montana when I received a phone call from within the chambers of the Arapaho Business Council. The call was a request to write a grant to the Administration for Native Americans (ANA) for federal funding for a second language-immersion class that would operate in the Lower Arapaho district on the reservation. I had unsuccessfully written this grant two other times. With this attempt, however, I was determined to write a grant that could not be refused. In all, I wrote three grants, one to the Wyoming Council for the Humanities, one to the Lannan foundation, and one to ANA in such a way that they were all integrated. The Wyoming Council's grant paid three instructors for the morning hours of instruction at the Ethete immersion project. Funding from the Lannan Foundation paid the same three language instructors' salaries for their afternoon hours, plus the Director's salary. The Director's position was written into the ANA grant so that he was responsible for both the Ethete project and the ANA project, which also had three salaried language instructors. Writing the ANA grant this way enabled me to show a 50 percent cash match and also allowed me to keep the total amount requested below half of the $125,000 maximum amount allowable per project year. All three grant applications were awarded to fund two immersion classes.

By this point, even though the instructors had participated in a few teacher-training workshops, it became clear that having a program run six hours a day would not necessarily produce fluency, especially when the instructors' teaching and immersion techniques were not strong enough. What the instructors needed was specific training on the principles and methods of second-language acquisition through immersion. If fluent-speaking children were going to come out of the program, then an immersion specialist had to be hired to train and guide the instructors on a daily basis. In 1996 I found such a specialist during a trip to Hawaii and negotiated a three-month contract with Pueo Pata, a young California Indian who was living in Hawaii and had become a fluent Hawaiian speaker as a volunteer in the Hawaiian immersion preschool. By the end of this three-month period the language instructors had completely committed to using only Arapaho with the children in the language classes. In spite of this, by the end of the project year, May 1997, the children still had not become conversant in Arapaho. It was back to the drawing board. I decided to travel to New Zealand to look at one of the most successful Indigenous language-revitalization programs. Before leaving I wrote a grant to implement a mother-toddler language project. The project's goal was to provide young parents with the language necessary to care for their child or children in Arapaho. With this added aspect of the project it was also hoped that adult speakers might be generated who eventually could replace current language instructors when they decided to stop teaching. The time spent among the Maori of New Zealand was truly inspirational.

Maori language and cultural revival efforts had begun in the 1970s as a result of Whatarangi Winata, a Maori man who had been impressed by First Nations people of British Columbia while earning his Doctoral degree and living in the province. When he returned to New Zealand in 1975, he called many Maori together to devise a plan called Generation 2000.[10] During the course of the years leading up to 2000, the Maori had established over 700 preschools, some 596 K–12 language schools, seven colleges, and two universities. All of these schools taught through the medium of the Maori language, and all were under the control and exclusive management of the Maori. Education was not the only area targeted during this period. Maori people were groomed for positions in medicine, media, law, and government, where they now hold 12 seats in New Zealand's government. Through my discussions with many of the leaders in this movement, I was continually asked, "Where is the heart of your people?" This was also a question that had been asked of me while in Hawaii. When I returned in December 1997, this became an area I began to see as an essential aspect to the success of any language-revitalization or -maintenance effort.

When the project year concluded, the immersion classes had produced some of the strongest speakers yet. Children were able to express themselves in Arapaho for periods of 30 to 40 minutes without using English. With these successes I decided to raise funds to get language instructors from both immersion classes over to Hawaii so they could observe firsthand the work of very successful programs.

In June 1998 four of the immersion staff traveled to Hawaii, and over a four-week period traveled to Punana Leo immersion schools on the islands of Hilo, Maui, and Oahu, where they also took part in a week-long language teacher-training workshop. When everything looked to be heading in a direction that would finally result in the immersion project's first speakers, disaster struck.

In 1999 two of the project's major granting agents withdrew funding that amounted to $90,000. As a result of this the immersion class in the area of Lower Arapaho was lost, and the project in the area of Ethete was in serious jeopardy of having to discontinue. A General Council meeting was scheduled for April, and we were able to get the immersion project on the agenda. At the meeting some 300 to 400 community members were present. The meeting closed with the immersion staff's speaking of the project's plight and a plea for support. Right up to the final minutes of the meeting, parent after parent of children from present and past immersion classes poured out their hearts, giving testimony of the strength of the project.

In September 1999 the immersion project entered its sixth year with a grant of $13,500. Not wanting to lose any instructors, we dropped the class down to five hours a day. In addition to this the program moved to include an adult language Mentor-Apprentice class that met two hours a day in intensive language-learning sessions. Of the three language instructors, one was kept as a primary instructor for the preschool class and the two other instructors were switched between the immersion preschool class and the adult Mentor-Apprentice class every other month. While classes continued under this format, meetings were held with the tribal council until, on January 5, 2000, with enough money for only one more payroll, the Council's heart embraced the language-immersion class and picked up 80 percent of costs to keep the immersion-class doors at Ethete open. For the first time since its inception the project did not have to face the threat of ending because of grants not being awarded.

In the spring of 2000, after several years of observing and hearing about some of the needs of various people working with their languages in their communities, I began working on a curriculum specifically tailored for the implementation of language immersion. Although the curriculum is still being developed, we decided in September (2000) to begin putting into use the first 12 weeks of it. By the end of the summer of 2001, 30 weeks of curriculum had been roughly developed and the first 12 weeks had been field tested and revised. By the start of the September 2001 immersion-school term, the immersion curriculum was implemented in earnest, and by the end of the immersion class year (May 2002), we were all very impressed with the level of speaking skills observed among the children.

As the Arapaho Language Immersion Program grows, it continues to draw inspiration and guidance from Hawaiian and Maori language-immersion programs. When I was in New Zealand, the Maori spoke to me of one of their immersion principles, which they refer to as "language from the breast." Children who can barely walk are continually surrounded by Maori language, culture, caring, and love, as it traditionally was in our own languages and cultures, and so it should continue to be. As we look back, around, and ahead, we have seen struggles, frustrations, and successes, and although with the work of language immersion come challenges and setbacks, if our languages are to survive, then it is a necessary work.

If I had but one image to end with to illustrate the commitment needed to embrace the work of language revitalization and maintenance, then it would be something that happened to me in June 1994. There was a scheduled weeklong language-training workshop at the Wyoming Indian High School. When I arrived and started to walk into the building, I paused to look out over an area, several hundred yards below the high school, where an Arapaho summer ceremonial is held. As I stood up on that rise, visualizing how the land would be transformed by the encampment when the ceremony was in progress, I was startled as in my mind I saw an image of a huge wall of water moving toward the ceremonial grounds. For me that wall of water symbolized the worst of development and technology: that which would destroy language, culture, and all of what those before us had fought so hard to protect for future generations. It was frightening, and I remember standing there, seeing that wall of water and thinking, "I will hold you back." But when I defiantly said the words, the power of that approaching force made me think how foolish and small I was and I dropped to one knee and wept. As I knelt there, something came over me that I can only express as the Spirit of the Dog Soldiers. These were the warriors who would lash themselves to a wooden stake or arrow driven into the earth and from that spot they would meet the enemy, fighting for the safety and well-being of their people and, in essence, their culture. Touched by this presence I symbolically tied the leather thong around my leg, stood up, and, with a determined conviction, quietly said, "I *will* hold you back."

We can succeed in our efforts to pass healthy and viable languages on to successive generations. But to succeed we must remain unconditionally anchored to our heritage languages (and those languages only), with the unwavering commitment of a Dog Soldier, for the future well-being of our cultures, our communities, and our children.

NOTES

1. For more details about Arapaho-white political interaction, see Loretta Fowler, *Arapahoe Politics, 1851–1978: Symbols in Crisis of Authority* (Lincoln, Nebraska: 1982).

2. For more on the issue of language loss at a global level, see Jared Diamond, ed., "Speaking with a Single Tongue," in *Discover* (Chicago, 1993), pp. 78–85, and "Saving Dying Languages" in *Scientific American* 287, no. 2 (2002), pp. 78–85.

3. See James J. Bauman, *A Guide to the Issues in Indian Language Retention* (Washington, DC, 1980).

4. The primary contributing factor for this is due to children going home from immersion classes and using Arapaho in their homes. This in turn has proven to be a motivating factor with grandparents using Arapaho with their grandchildren.

5. Christopher Mosley and R. C. Asher eds., *Atlas of the World Languages* (New York: Routledge, 1994).

6. James Estes, *How Many Indigenous American Languages Are Spoken in the United States? By How Many Speakers?* at http://www.ncbe.gwu.edu/askncbe/faqs/20natlang.htm (2002).

7. Figures were extrapolated from 2000 census figures, Shoshone and Arapaho vital statistic figures, Wyoming Indian School figures, and general survey questions.

8. M. Krauss, "The Condition of Native North American Languages: The Need for Realistic Assessment and Action," in *International Journal of the Sociology of Language 132* (Mouton De Gruyter, 1998), pp. 9–21.

9. The extended vocabulary group represents speakers who possess basic conversational abilities but who are not able to fluently express themselves through the Arapaho language.

10. I first learned this information through personal discussions with Whatarangi in 1997. For more information on the topic of Generation 2000, see Rachael Selby's article, *Tararua Is My Mountain* in this volume.

SUGGESTED READINGS, VIDEOS, AND WEBSITES

READINGS

Alfred, T.
1999   *Peace, Power, Righteousness: An Indigenous Manifesto.* Toronto: Oxford University Press.
1995   *Heeding the Voices of Our Ancestors: Kahnawake Mohawk Politics and the Rise of Indigenous Nationalism.* Toronto: Oxford University Press.

Asch, M., ed.
1997   *Aboriginal Treaty Rights in Canada: Essays on Law, Equality, and Respect for Difference.* Vancouver: University of British Columbia Press.

Barsh, R. L., and J. Y. Henderson.
1980   *The Road: Indian Tribes and Political Liberty.* Berkeley: University of California Press.

Bartelson, J.
1995   *A Genealogy of Sovereignty.* Cambridge: Cambridge University Press.

Biersteker, J., and C. Weber, eds.
1996   *State Sovereignty as a Social Construct.* Cambridge: Cambridge University Press.

Bricker, Victoria.
1981   *The Indian Christ, the Indian King.* University of Texas Press.

Bunzel, Ruth.
1981   *Chichicastenango.* Guatemala: Seminario de Integración Social de Guatemala.

Cancian, Frank.
1969   *Economics and Prestige in a Maya Community: The Religious Cargo System in Zinacantan.* Stanford: Stanford University Press.

Casaverde, Juvenal.
1976   *Jacaltec Social and Political Structure.* Ann Arbor: University Microfilms International.

Clark, B.
1990   *Indigenous Liberty, Crown Sovereignty: The Existing Aboriginal Right of Self-Government in Canada.* Montreal: McGill-Queen's University Press.

Colby, Benjamin N., and Lore M. Colby.
1981   *The Daykeeper: The Life and Discourse of an Ixil Diviner.* Cambridge: Harvard University Press.

Cornell, S.
1988   *The Return of the Native: American Indian Political Resurgence*. New York: Oxford
         University Press.

Cox de Collins, Anne.
1980   *Colonial Jacaltenango, Guatemala: The Formation of a Corporate Community*.
         Ann Arbor: University Microfilms International.

Cutzal Mijango, Salvador.
1990   "Creo en un Dios Pobre," *Noticias Aliadas*. Octubre 4, Mexico, D.F.

Deloria, V., Jr.
1970   *We Talk, You Listen*. New York: Macmillan.
1988   *Custer Died for Your Sins: An Indian Manifesto*. Norman: University of Okla-
         homa Press.

Deloria, V., Jr., and C. M. Lytle.
1983   *American Indians, American Justice*. Austin: University of Texas Press.

Durie, M.
1994   *Whaiora: Māori Health Development*. Auckland: Oxford University Press.

Falla, Ricardo.
1992   *Masacres de la Selva: Ixcan Guatemala (1975–1982)*. Editorial Universitaria,
         Coleccion 500 Anos, vol. 1, Universidad de San Carlos de Guatemala.

Farriss, Nancy.
1984   *Maya Society under Colonial Rule: The Collective Enterprise of Survival*. Princeton
         University Press.

Fleras A., and J. L. Elliott.
1992   *The "Nations Within": Aboriginal-State Relations in Canada, the United States, and
         New Zealand*. Toronto: Oxford University Press.

Foucault, M.
1980   *Power/Knowledge: Selected Interviews and Other Writings, 1972–1977*. C. Gordon,
         ed. and trans. New York: Pantheon Books.
1997   *The Politics of Truth*. S. Lotringer, ed. New York: Semiotext(e).

Gossen, Gary H.
1984   *Chamulas in the World of the Sun: Time and Space in a Maya Oral Tradition*.
         Prospect Heights: Waveland Press, Inc.

La Farge, Oliver, and Douglas Byers.
1931   *The Year Bearer's People*. The Tulane University of Louisiana. Middle American
         Research Series, Publication No. 3.

Laughlin, Robert M.
1988   *The People of the Bat: Maya Tales and Dreams from Zinacantan*. Washington, DC:
         Smithsonian Institution Press.

Lovell, George.
1985   *Conquest and Survival in Colonial Guatemala: A Historical Geography of the Cuchumatan Highlands, 1500–1821.* Kingston and Montreal: McGill-Queen's University Press.

Lyons, O., et. al.
1992   *Exiled in the Land of the Free: Democracy, Indian Nations, and the U.S. Constitution.* Santa Fe: Clear Light Publishers.

Makemson, Maud W.
1951   *The Book of the Jaguar Priest: A Translation of the Book of Chilam Balam of Tizimin.* New York: Henry Schuman.

Manz, Beatriz.
1988   *Refugees of a Hidden War: The Aftermath of Counterinsurgency in Guatemala.* Albany: State University of New York Press.

Matthiessen, Peter.
1991   *In the Spirit of Crazy Horse.* New York: Viking Press.

Matul Morales, Daniel E.
1989   "Estamos Vivos: Reafirmación de la Cultura Maya." *Nueva Sociedad,* 99, Caracas, Venezuela.

Menchu, Rigoberta.
1984   An interview in *When the Mountains Tremble.* Directed by Pamela Yates and Tom Sigel. New York: Skylight Pictures.

Montejo, Victor D.
1984   *El Q'anil: The Man of Lightning.* Carrboro: Signal Books.
1990   "The Elders Dreamed of Fire: Religion and Repression in the Guatemalan Highlands." Challenge 1, no. 3, Epica, Washington, DC.
1991   *The Bird Who Cleans the World and Other Maya Fables.* Willimantic: Curbstone Press.
1993   "Tying Up the Bundle and the Katuns of Dishonor: Maya Worldview and Politics." *American Indian Culture and Research Journal* 17, 1: pp. 103–114.

Montejo, Victor, and Q'anil Akab'.
1992   Brevìsima Relación Testimonial de la Continua Destrucción del Mayab' (Guatemala). Providence College, Providence: Guatemalan Scholars Network.

Patton, P., ed.
2000   *Political Theory and Indigenous Rights.* Cambridge: Cambridge University Press.

Perera, Victor.
1982   Los Ultimos Señores de Palenque: Los Lacandones Herederos de los Mayas. Editorial Argos Vergara, España.

Recinos, Adrián.
1983   *Popol Vuh: The Sacred Book of the Ancient Quiche Maya.* Norman: University of Oklahoma Press.

Redfield, Robert, and Alfonso Villa Rojas.
1964   *Chan Kom: A Maya Village.* Chicago and London: University of Chicago Press.

Rotman, L. I.
1996   *Parallel Paths: Fiduciary Doctrine and the Crown-Indigenous Relationship in Canada.* Toronto: University of Toronto Press.

Royal Commission on Aboriginal Peoples (Canada).
1996   Report, 5 vols. Ottawa: Canada Communication Group.

Salazar, Tetzaguic, and Manuel de Jesus.
1992   "La Comunidad maya y los ancianos." Rutzijol, Seleccion Quincenal de Noticias Acerca del Pueblo Maya, Centro Maya Saqb'e, Chimaltenango, Guatemala.

Sandoval, Franco.
1992   "Los Ancianos: Leccion del Popol Vuh." Rutzijol, Seleccion Quincenal de Noticias Acerca del Pueblo Maya, Centro Maya Saqb'e, Chimaltenango, Guatemala.

Spinner, J.
1992   *The Boundaries of Citizenship: Race, Ethnicity, and Nationality in the Liberal State.* Baltimore: John Hopkins University Press.

Tully, J.
1992   *Strange Multiplicity: Constitutionalism in an Age of Diversity.* Cambridge: Cambridge University Press.

Vogt, Evon Z.
1969   *Zinacantan: A Maya Community in the Highland of Chiapas.* Cambridge: The Belknap Press of Harvard University Press.

Wilkinson, C. F.
1987   *American Indians, Time, and the Law: Indigenous Societies in a Modern Constitutional Democracy.* New Haven: Yale University Press.

Winiata, H., and Winiata, W.
1996   *Ngāti Pareraukawa: A Case Study: Raising and Maintaining the Health and Wealth of the Hapū.* Otaki.

Winiata, W.
1979   "Generation 2000: An Experiment in Tribal Development" in *He Mātāpuna: Some Māori Perspectives.* Wellington: New Zealand Planning Council.

Wolf, Eric.
1957   "Closed Corporate Peasant Communities in Mesoamerica and Central Java." *Southwestern Journal of Anthropology* 13, no. 1: pp.1–18.

VIDEOS

White Shamens and Plastic Medicine Men. Bozeman, Montana: Montana Public Television, 1995.

Incident at Oglala. Distributed by Live Home Video. Carolco Home Video: Van Nuys, CA, 1992.

Broken Rainbow. Los Angeles, Calif.: Direct Cinema, Ltd., 1987.

Naturally Native. Mahantucket Pequot Tribal Nation and Red Horse Native Productions, 1997.

Once Were Warrior. New Line Home Video, 1995.

Dead Heart. New York : Fox Lorber Home Video, 1998.

WEBSITES

Department of the Interior, Bureau of Indian Affairs:
http://www.doi.gov/bureau-indian-affairs.html

Gathering Place, First Nations Canadian News:
http://www.gatheringplacefirstnationscanews.com

House of Aboriginality Macquarie University, Sydney, Australia, website on issues of cultural appropriation and integrity in the merchandising of aboriginal cultural symbols and images: http://www.mq.edu.au/house_of_aboriginality

Indigenous Peoples of Western Papua New Guinea struggle for freedom:
http://www.eco-action.org/opm

National Congress on American Indians: http://www.ncai.org

Stabilizing Indigenous Languages: http://www.ncela.gwu.edu/miscpubs/stabilize/

Teaching Indigenous Languages: http://www.jan.ucc.nau.edu/~jar/TIL_Contents.html

University of Northern Colorado's Fighting Whites website delivers a message about ethnic stereotyping: http://www.fightingwhites.org

U.S. Senate Committee on Indian Affairs: http://www.senate.gov/~scia

CREDITS

TEXT

Chapter 1

Stephen Greymorning: "Language and Culture Political Realities to Keep Trickster at Bay." A shorter and earlier version of this article appeared in Corrigan & McCaskill eds. *The Canadian Journal of Native Studies,* volume 20, number 1, Manitoba press, Manitoba, Canada.

Chapter 2

By permission of Peter Irniq

Chapter 3

By permission of Larissa Behrendt

Chapter 4

By permission of Henrietta Mann

Chapter 5

Ward Churchill. Excerpts from "A Question of Identity." From *Many Americas: Critical Perspectives on Race, Racism, and Ethnicity* by Gregory Campbell. Copyright © 2001 by Kendall/Hunt Publishing Company. Used with permission.

Chapter 6

By permission of Moana Jackson

Chapter 7

Taiaike Alfred. From "From Freedom to Soveriegnty." In Deloria and Sallisbury, eds., *Blackwell Companion to American History.* Blackwell Publishing, 2001. Reprinted by permission Blackwell Publishing.

Chapter 8

By permission of Sharon Venne

Chapter 9

By permission of Arleen Adams

Chapter 10

By permission of Victor Montejo

Chapter 11

By permission of Rachael Selby

Chapter 12

Section I: By permission of Aislinn Combes

Section II: By permission of Darrell Robes Kipp

Chapter 13

By permission of Kauanoe Kamanā

PHOTO

About the Editor

Gail Jacob

Chapter 7

Troy Hunter

MAP

Front Matter

Amber Greymorning